MATTERING PRESS

Mattering Press is an academic-led Open Access publisher that operates on a not-for-profit basis as a UK registered charity. It is committed to developing new publishing models that can widen the constituency of academic knowledge and provide authors with significant levels of support and feedback. All books are available to download for free or to purchase as hard copies. More at matteringpress.org.

The Press's work has been supported by: Centre for Invention and Social Process (Goldsmiths, University of London), European Association for the Study of Science and Technology, Hybrid Publishing Lab, infostreams, Institute for Social Futures (Lancaster University), Open Humanities Press, and Tetragon.

MAKING THIS BOOK

Mattering Press is keen to render more visible the unseen processes that go into the production of books. We would like to thank Joe Deville, who acted as the Press's coordinating editor for this book, the reviewer Manuel Tironi, Jenn Tomomitsu for the copy-editing, Tetragon for the production and typesetting, Sarah Terry for the proofreading, and Ed Akerboom at infostreams for formatting the html version of this book.

COVER

Browsing books, on- or offline, entails comparison, of covers amongst other things. Designing covers too entails comparison, of typefaces, for example. Typographic judgments of aesthetic, use, and conceptual value are settled by comparing different typefaces that, to the trained eye, mark particular histories of craft, production, and thought. Books on graphic design, such as Josef Müller-Brockmann's great Grid Systems, establish 'good' typography by reference to a canon of classic, Latin typefaces, some of which you can compare, in practice, on this cover. Another tool of comparison, the Mango Maturity and Ripeness Guide, developed by the mango quality research team at the University of Florida and the University of California-Davis (available at www.mango.org), provides this cover with a colour scheme and its users with a means to establish if a mango is 'ripe' for consumption.

Mattering Press thanks Łukasz Dziedzic for Lato, our incomparable cover typeface. It remains one of the best free typefaces available and is released by his foundry tyPoland under the free, libre and open source Open Font License.

Cover art by Julien McHardy.

PRACTISING COMPARISON

Logics, Relations, Collaborations

EDITED BY
JOE DEVILLE,
MICHAEL GUGGENHEIM,
ZUZANA HRDLIČKOVÁ

MATTERING PRESS

First edition published by Mattering Press, Manchester.

Copyright © Joe Deville, Michael Guggenheim, and Zuzana Hrdličková, chapters by respective authors, 2016.

Cover art © Julien McHardy, 2016.

Freely available online at www.matteringpress.org/books/practising-comparison

This is an open access book, and the text and cover art are licensed under a Creative Commons By Attribution Non-Commercial Share Alike license. Under this license, authors allow anyone to download, reuse, reprint, modify, distribute, and/or copy their work so long as the material is not used for commercial purposes and the authors and source are cited and resulting derivative works are licensed under the same or similar license. No permission is required from the authors or the publisher. Statutory fair use and other rights are in no way affected by the above.

Read more about the license at creativecommons.org/licenses/by-nc-sa/4.0/

ISBN: 978-0-9931449-4-3 (pbk)
ISBN: 978-0-9931449-5-0 (ebk)

Mattering Press has made every effort to contact copyright holders and will be glad to rectify, in future editions, any errors or omissions brought to our notice.

CONTENTS

List of Figures   7
Contributors   9
Acknowledgements   15

1 · Introduction: The Practices and Infrastructures of Comparison
    Joe Deville, Michael Guggenheim, Zuzana Hrdličková   17

SECTION ONE: LOGICS

2 · Comparative Research: Beyond Linear-causal Explanation
    Monika Krause   45

3 · Cross Comparison: Comparisons across Architectural Displays of Colonial Power
    Alice Santiago Faria   68

SECTION TWO: COLLABORATIONS

4 · Same, Same but Different: Provoking Relations, Assembling the Comparator
    Joe Deville, Michael Guggenheim, Zuzana Hrdličková   99

5 · Pulling Oneself Out of the Traps of Comparison: An Auto-ethnography of a European Project
    Madeleine Akrich and Vololona Rabeharisoa   130

6 · Frame Against the Grain: Asymmetries, Interference, and the Politics of EU Comparison
    Tereza Stöckelová   166

SECTION THREE: RELATIONS

7 · Lateral Comparisons
    Christopher Gad and Casper Bruun Jensen   189

8 · Comparative Tinkering with Care Moves
    Peter A. Lutz   220

9 · Comparing Comparisons: On Rankings and Accounting in Hospitals and Universities
    Sarah de Rijcke, Iris Wallenburg, Paul Wouters, Roland Bal   251

10 · Steve Jobs, Terrorists, Gentlemen, and Punks: Tracing Strange Comparisons of Biohackers
    Morgan Meyer   281

11 · Afterword: Spaces of Comparison
    Jennifer Robinson   306

LIST OF FIGURES

ILLUSTRATIONS

FIG. 1.1 Relative frequency of the terms 'comparative sociology' or 'comparative anthropology' in books scanned by Google 1950–2008   19

FIG. 3.1 Triumphal Arches (comparing by building type), J.N.L. Durand, 1799   73

FIG. 3.2 Neolithic gravestone vs. Corbusier's Ronchamp tower, S. Giedion, 1968   77

FIG. 3.3 General Post Office, Calcutta, designed by W. Granville, 1864–1868   82

FIG. 3.4 Central Post Office, Panjim, Goa, designed by PWD, 1893   82

FIG. 3.5 Synchronised Timeline (establishment period shown in darker grey)   83

FIG. 3.6 Cathedral, Old Goa (sixteenth century)   85

FIG. 3.7 Victoria Terminus, Bombay (nineteenth century)   85

FIG. 4.1 A comparator chip   100

FIG. 4.2 The assembled comparator   108

TABLES

TABLE 5.1 Degree of stabilisation of issues vs. POs' alignment to the biomedical world   138

CONTRIBUTORS

MADELEINE AKRICH is a professor at the Centre de sociologie de l'innovation (Mines ParisTech). After being devoted to the sociology of technology for several years, her work has centred on medicine: firstly, on a comparative study of obstetrical practices between France and the Netherlands, and secondly, on internet discussion groups that focus on health problems. More recently, with Vololona Rabeharisoa, she has coordinated a European project on the engagement of patient organisations with knowledge and the transformative effects it has on their form of activism (see the recent special issue of *Biosocieties* on 'Evidence-Based Activism', 2014).

ROLAND BAL is Professor of Healthcare Governance at Erasmus University Rotterdam. His research interests include science-policy-practice relations and governance infrastructures in healthcare. More recently, he has researched the creation of public accountabilities in healthcare, studying the ways in which public service organisations 'organise for transparency'. He currently works with the Netherlands healthcare inspectorate in research projects on regulation and supervision. Roland's focus is on ethnographic, interventionist research methods. Recent publications have appeared in, amongst other journals, *Social Science & Medicine*; *Science, Technology, & Human Values*; *International Journal of Medical Informatics*; and *Public Administration*.

JOE DEVILLE is a lecturer at Lancaster University, based jointly in the Departments of Organisation, Work & Technology and Sociology, and is a co-director of the Centre for Mobilities Research. He completed his PhD at Goldsmiths in 2011 and published his first book, *Lived Economies of Default*, with Routledge in early 2015. He has written widely on issues of credit, debt, and disaster preparedness in journals including *Sociological Review*; *Journal of Cultural Economy*; and

Consumption Markets and Culture. He is also an editor for Mattering Press and *Journal of Cultural Economy*.

CHRISTOPHER GAD is Associate Professor at the IT-University of Copenhagen in the research group Technologies in Practice. His former and present research areas and interests include Science and Technology Studies, (post-)Actor-Network Theory, lateral thinking, ontological multiplicity and complexity, promises, aspirations and challenges related to information technologies, digitalisation and computational thinking in theory and practice, ethnographic, virtual, micro-sociological, mixed, and non-foundationalist approaches, democracy, elections and disability, bureaucracy and organisational theory, fisheries inspection, and surveillance.

MICHAEL GUGGENHEIM is a reader at Goldsmiths, University of London and a director of the Centre for Invention and Social Process (CSISP). He has published widely on social theory, disasters, buildings and inventive methods. Most recently he co-edited *Disasters and Politics* (Sociological Review Monograph series, Wiley-Blackwell, 2014) and published 'The Media of Sociology: Tight and Loose Translations' in the *British Journal of Sociology*. He is an editor of the journal *Demonstrations: Journal for Experiments in Social Studies of Technology*.

ALICE SANTIAGO FARIA is currently a research fellow at CHAM (FCSH, Universidade NOVA de Lisboa e Universidade dos Açores), and at the Centro Interuniversitário de História das Ciências e da Tecnologia (CIUHCT, Universidade NOVA de Lisboa and Universidade de Lisboa). She graduated in Architecture from Coimbra University (1997) and holds a PhD in Art History (Université de Paris I, 2011). Her research focuses on colonial public works in the Portuguese Empire during the long nineteenth century. She participated in the volume 'Asia' in *Portuguese Heritage around the World: Architecture and Urbanism* (Fundação Calouste Gulbenkian, 2010).

ZUZANA HRDLIČKOVÁ is a social anthropologist interested in gender, conflict, and disaster within and outside academic settings. She completed her

PhD – which analysed the impact of war in Sri Lanka on women – at Charles University in Prague in 2009. Between 2011 and 2015, she worked as a post-doctoral Research Associate at Goldsmiths, University of London, looking at disasters and their management in India. She has published numerous academic papers on these topics and she has co-edited special volumes, most recently 'Living with Disasters: Perspectives on the (Re) Production of Knowledge' in *Nature and Culture*. She is interested in bridging the space between academia and applied work.

CASPER BRUUN JENSEN is Senior Researcher at the Department of Anthropology, Osaka University. He is the author of *Ontologies for Developing Things* (Sense, 2010) and *Monitoring Movements in Development Aid* (with Brit Ross Winthereik; MIT, 2013) and the editor with Kjetil Rödje of *Deleuzian Intersections: Science, Technology, Anthropology* (Berghahn, 2009). His present work focuses on environmental infrastructures in South-east Asia.

MONIKA KRAUSE is a senior lecturer in sociology at Goldsmiths, University of London. Her research addresses comparative questions about specialised practices as well as issues in sociological theory. She is the author of *The Good Project: Humanitarian Relief NGOs and the Fragmentation of Reason* (Chicago University Press, 2015), which won the BSA's 2015 Philip Abrams Memorial Prize for a first book in sociology. An edited volume exploring the uses of the concept of field for global analysis (*Fielding Transnationalism*, with Julian Go) is forthcoming in 2016 as a Sociological Review Monograph (Wiley-Blackwell).

PETER LUTZ has published on the topics of human-nonhuman relations in home care for older people, as well as user participation for the design of new technologies. He draws inspiration from Science and Technology Studies and anthropology. His current interests include the use of participatory research in 'social sustainability' initiatives. He is presently based at Uppsala University.

MORGAN MEYER is a lecturer in sociology at AgroParisTech and a research affiliate at the Laboratoire Interdisciplinaire Sciences Innovations Sociétés (LISIS).

He holds a PhD in sociology (University of Sheffield) and has been a postdoc at the Centre for the Sociology of Innovation at Mines ParisTech. His current research focuses on two themes: the emergence, governance, and debates on new forms of biology (synthetic biology, do-it-yourself biology), and the spaces and practices of 'knowledge brokering' and the boundaries of science. He has recently edited a special issue of *Sociological Research Online* on 'epistemic communities' (with Susan Molyneux-Hodgson) and a special issue of *Science and Public Policy* on 'intermediaries' (with Matthew Kearnes).

VOLOLONA RABEHARISOA is a professor of sociology at the Centre de sociologie de l'innovation, Mines ParisTech. She is interested in the increasing involvement of civil society organisations in scientific and technical activities. She is investigating the engagement of patients' organisations with biomedical research, the governance of health, and the development of drugs and therapeutic strategies, notably in the area of rare diseases. Beyond the biomedical domain, she explores the emergence of new public issues around genomics. She is currently participating in a research project on forensics, looking at the uses of DNA fingerprints in crime investigations and criminal justice in France.

SARAH DE RIJCKE is Senior Researcher at the Centre for Science and Technology Studies (CWTS), Leiden University. De Rijcke leads a research group at CWTS that examines interactions between research assessment and practices of knowledge production. This research programme is situated at the intersection of Science and Technology Studies and the sociology and anthropology of science. The group is partner in national and international consortia that study new forms of research governance, policies for scientific excellence, and research integrity. Recent projects have focused on the interactions between performance metrics and epistemic decision-making processes in different disciplines.

JENNIFER ROBINSON is Professor of Human Geography at University College London. Her book, *Ordinary Cities* (Routledge, 2006) developed a postcolonial critique of urban studies. She is preparing a new book on Comparative Urbanism, to propose methodological foundations for a more global urban studies. Earlier empirical research explored the history of apartheid cities and the politics of post-apartheid city-visioning. Current empirical projects focus on transnational aspects of Johannesburg and London's policymaking processes and the politics of large-scale urban developments.

TEREZA STÖCKELOVÁ is a researcher at the Institute of Sociology of the Czech Academy of Sciences, Assistant Professor at the Department of General Anthropology, Charles University, and Editor-in-Chief of the English edition of *Sociologický časopis / Czech Sociological Review*. Her work is situated in between sociology, social anthropology, and science and technology studies, and draws upon actor network theory and related material semiotic methodologies. She has investigated academic practices in the context of current policy changes, science and society relations, and environmental controversies, and more recently has started an ethnography of the interfaces between biomedical and alternative therapeutic practices in the Czech Republic. She is a regular contributor to Czech public media and believes social sciences have to make sense beyond academia.

IRIS WALLENBURG is Assistant Professor of Healthcare Governance at Erasmus University Rotterdam. Her research interests are situated at the intersection of work on professionalism, organisations, and institutional theory, using ethnographic research methods. Recent projects have been on task reallocation in healthcare in Europe, performance measurement, professional behaviour, and 'place-making' as a way of perceiving healthcare practices.

PAUL WOUTERS is Director of the Centre for Science and Technology Studies at Leiden University and Professor of Scientometrics at Leiden University. He is Chair of the Dutch national graduate school, Science, Technology and Modern Culture. He has published on the history of the Science Citation Index, on scientometrics and on the way the criteria of scientific quality have been changed by citation analysis. With Anne Beaulieu, Andrea Scharnhorst, and Sally Wyatt, he co-edited *Virtual Knowledge: Experimenting in the Humanities and Social Sciences* (MIT Press, 2013).

ACKNOWLEDGEMENTS

The editors would like to express their gratitude to the range of individuals and institutions that made this book possible. Many thanks to Manuel Tironi for providing such a constructive review of an earlier draft of the text, to Jennifer Tomomitsu for the precise copy editing, to Endre Dányi, Noortje Marres, and Michaela Spencer for their comments on our own contributions to the book, and to all the authors in the collection for making our job so straightforward and enjoyable. We would like to thank all the participants at the 'Apples and Oranges' conference, which took place at Goldsmiths in September 2012, that began many of the conversations that this book continues. We are also grateful to the European Research Council for the funding which has made this book possible, as part of the Organising Disaster project (project number 263731). Finally, many thanks to the Goldsmiths Sociology department and the Centre for Invention and Social Process for their various forms of support.

INTRODUCTION: THE PRACTICES AND INFRASTRUCTURES OF COMPARISON

Joe Deville, Michael Guggenheim, Zuzana Hrdličková

TWO COMPARISONS

LET US PRODUCE A COMPARISON.

The first entity in this comparison comprises the opening lines from Reinhard Bendix's relatively early attempt to justify the comparative method within sociological research:

> Like the concepts of other disciplines, sociological concepts should be universally applicable. The concept 'division of labor', for instance, refers to the fact that the labor performed in a collectivity is specialized; the concept is universal because we know of no collectivity without such specialization. Where reference is made to a principle of the division of labor over time – irrespective of the particular individuals performing the labor and of the way labor is subdivided (whether by sex, age, skill or whatever) – we arrive at one meaning of the term 'social organization'. We know of no society that lacks such a principle; furthermore, we can compare and contrast the social organization of two societies by showing how their division of labor differs (Bendix 1963: 532).

The second is an extract from a chapter published just over twenty years later in the influential *Writing Culture* (1986a) collection, edited by James Clifford and George E. Marcus. This collection is often seen as capturing a major shift that was occurring within anthropology at the time. This approach highlighted the inevitable partiality of ethnographic truth and the way in which ethnographic accounts needed to be seen as irredeemably textual, rhetorical productions, through which cultures become 'invented' and not represented (see Clifford 1986). In this section the author, Stephen Tyler, takes on what he identifies as a dominant mode of ethnographic prose, rooted in 'easy realism of natural history', born out of an urge to 'conform to the canons of scientific rhetoric'. Its problem, he writes, is

> a failure of the whole visualist ideology of referential discourse, with its rhetoric of 'describing', 'comparing', 'classifying', and 'generalizing' and its presumption of representational signification. In ethnography there are no 'things' there to be the objects of a description, the original appearances that the language of description 're-presents' as indexical objects for comparison, classification, and generalization; there is rather a discourse, and that too, no thing (Tyler 1986: 130–31).

This comparison provides just a glimpse into the way in which the authority of comparison itself has changed and been challenged over the course of the relatively recent history of sociology and anthropology. It locates comparison against two radically different positions: what we might call methodological positivism, in Bendix's case, and methodological relativism in Tyler's (see Steinmetz 2004). The comparison, thus, highlights two ends of comparative (and anti-comparative) epistemology.

Let us produce another comparison (Fig. 1.1).

The chart uses Google's database of scanned books, narrowed down to include only those that refer to either sociology or anthropology, and looks at the changes in how often comparison is referred to in these books. The chart suggests that in both disciplines interest in comparison has increased since the beginning of the 1950s, and then peaked in anthropology in around 1960, and

FIG. 1.1 Relative frequency of the terms 'comparative sociology' or 'comparative anthropology' in books scanned by Google 1950–2008[1]

in sociology roughly a decade later to decline and later stabilise on a much lower level.[2] Both disciplines experience a similar rise and fall of interest in comparison.

One way we can use these comparisons is to bring them together: we can see that the first two statements map onto the historic rise and fall of comparison in the social sciences, with Bendix's enthusiasm appearing at a time when comparison was a hot topic and Tyler's radical critique coming at a point when comparison was on the way out.

In this volume we propose to re-engage the debates about comparison by learning from the close observation of (social) scientific practice. Rather than considering the problems of comparison as those of epistemology – for instance, whether we are for (Radhakrishnan 2013) or against (Friedman 2013) comparison, or whether certain forms of comparison are ethical and legitimate (Longxi 2013) – we start by treating comparisons as objects of analysis and which we and the other authors in this collection see as involving a range of actors (human and non-human), practices, and tools. To take the above two comparisons as a comparative example, one involves us, the authors, selecting and juxtaposing two texts, while the other involves a tool that draws on a database of millions of scanned books. As we will discuss, many comparisons are at least as complex and collaborative as the latter, involving hybrid combinations of teams, funders, fieldtrips, and different media which in turn are wrapped up in distinct cultures, histories, and power relations.

EPISTEMOLOGICAL INFRASTRUCTURES

Our attention is therefore on the situated practice of comparison – an approach that if not rendering the various epistemological debates around comparison irrelevant, then at least cutting them down to size. That is to say, the epistemological challenges to comparison that have arisen over the course of the latter half of the twentieth century become understood as just one part of the changing infrastructures of comparison, infrastructures that have at various points and in various different ways, rendered certain forms of comparison more or less credible.

Given that the challenges to comparison have been well documented and are touched on in a number of contributions to this volume, we will not dwell on them for too long in this introduction. The story, however, goes something like this. For a long time, comparison was seen as a crucial tool for identifying the universal forces that shaped social groupings, allowing analysts like Bendix to make the leap from the empirical to the conceptual and from the particular to the general. From the start this was itself guided by a contrast between the practices of social and natural sciences. For the social sciences, the attractions of the comparisons being produced by the natural sciences were manifold. First and foremost, scientists had proved themselves expert at using comparison to detect patterns of similarity and difference. Comparison also underpinned ideals of scientific rigour. Without it, neither principles of experimental replication, nor hypothesis testing, nor tests of statistical significance, would function. Within the social sciences, therefore, the hope was that by transferring a comparative method, its researchers might be able to emulate their natural scientific cousins and divide the world into fixed properties. This would allow them to identify not the natural laws of life, but its social laws.

However, a series of developments threatened this ambition, some of the effects of which we could try to tentatively map onto the above graph. The most major of these developments seemed, at first at least, to pertain to one discipline more than any other: anthropology. Anthropology seemed particularly wanting in the context of the major geopolitical shifts of the time. The 1960s and 1970s saw significant questions raised about its potential complicity with the European colonial project, whose damaging effects were becoming increasingly hard to ignore (see Gingrich and Fox 2002: 2). Comparison had moved from being an epistemological practice to being a political one. Seen from the perspective of this volume, this was not only a conceptual shift, but one in which the infrastructure of comparison had become newly problematic. Comparison was seen as an extension of colonialism, in which the infrastructure of colonialism served as a carrier for an epistemic project of subjecting other forms of life. The emergent issue centred on the fact that the people who embarked on the doing of comparison did so by means which were seen as compromising the very epistemological basis of their work.

The 1980s saw what might have seemed as narrow disciplinary-specific concerns flood into a number of other areas within the social sciences. First, the kinds of issues that had been raised within anthropology were shown to be as relevant to other disciplines. This became connected to a further set of attacks. A series of intellectual challenges, including Nietzschean perspectivism, poststructuralist deconstruction, postcolonial and feminist critiques, and research within science and technology studies (STS), shook many of the pillars upon which social science had been resting (see Dickens and Fontana 1994; Keane 2005). These threatened to destabilise the claim of the methods and writing practices of social research to be able to truthfully represent social life. They also threatened the idea, captured in the extract by Bendix above, that analytical concepts could be simply 'extracted' from empirical settings and made to circulate independently. In part this was because of the argument that different settings, different encounters between researcher and researched, possessed an inherent incommensurability (see Jensen 2011; Steinmetz 2004; Strathern 1988); in other words, they simply *could not* be compared in a meaningful way. And in part this was because of a suspicion of the very plausibility of concepts that could be 'transcendent'. Attention also turned towards researchers themselves. A range of work revealed research practice as always situated and never innocent from the values and biases of the researcher (see Haraway 1989; Harding 1986). Rather than the ships and practices of the colonials, the heads and bodies of researchers became the focus for the critique of comparison. Such conclusions also threatened the standard against which social science had previously measured itself: the natural sciences. As STS researchers showed, biases could readily be found here too (Latour 1988). Some of this critique is inflected in both *Writing Culture* (Clifford and Marcus 1986b) and Tyler's extract above.

Here, then, we can observe a shift from what we might call the colonial critique. In the colonial critique it was the global infrastructures of colonialism that were seen as fundamental obstacles to forms of meaningful comparison. The reflexive and epistemological critique, by contrast, while recognising key aspects of this argument, shifts attention from global practices and power relations to the individual. It is a critique that looks at comparisons as problematic effects of writing, which are seen to do violence to the uniqueness of the circumstances of the research subjects.

As we move closer to the present, we see that many if not all of these questions have lost little of their relevance.[3] While many social scientists may have rowed back from more strident anti-realist stances that characterised some of the postmodernist academic discourse in the 1980s and into the 1990s, there is little sense of a desire to return to the kind of methodological positivism that preceded these challenges. Feminist and postcolonial research and STS, meanwhile, in their moves towards a more constructivist understanding of the composition of the social and material world, continue to challenge the assumed neutrality of research and its claims towards objectivity.

With the increased normalisation of constructivism, however, we can find one further important but often quite implicitly articulated recent reappraisal of the status of comparison. While the postmodernist critique of comparison was that meaningful comparison is impossible because of the damage done to the entities under comparison, the constructivist critique adopts the seemingly opposite point of view: comparison, it is argued, is ubiquitous, as can be seen in the often cited words of Evans Pritchard that 'there is only one method […] the comparative method. And that [method] is impossible' (used as an epigraph in both Peacock (2002) and Jensen (2011)). Comparison thus becomes meaningless, but for quite different reasons: what becomes challenged is the idea that social science could deploy a comparative practice that is distinct from the comparative practices inherent to the world. As with the reflexivist critique, this view also tends to suggest that comparison is a purely epistemic practice. From such a point of view, there is indeed nothing special about comparison. As we will proceed to outline, however, what such a view ignores are the particularities and the practices through which social science does comparison.

Given these continuing epistemological concerns about comparison, the changes in academic practice that our chart at the start of this chapter indicated should not be surprising. Within many academic departments, the challenges documented above have markedly improved the status and authority of non-comparative, small scale, case-study oriented, qualitative and ethnographic research. New seemingly non-comparative methods have also taken hold: Actor-Network Theory (ANT), for instance, and the more loose assembly of research practices which it has influenced, has exhibited a suspicion of the imposition of transcendent categories into the research situation (see Law and Hassard 1999; Latour 2005). As Bruno Latour famously put it, 'nothing is, by itself, either reducible or irreducible to anything else' (1988: 158). This principle is at the heart of ANT, in which the researcher does not assume an a priori separation between social and material in the conduct of research. The researcher's main job in this situation is to identify the breaks that allow the production of continuity (e.g. the continuity of scientific practice), rather than introducing these breaks him or herself by leaping to a different comparative setting (see Latour 2013: 33).

COMPARATIVE OPENINGS?

There are, then, a considerable number of actors exerting a potentially strong pull against the use of comparative approaches. Despite this, and against the odds perhaps, we may be seeing the door to comparative social scientific practice opening a little wider than it has done for some time. A number of books and journal collections have begun to reinvestigate questions of comparison. These have taken on important unresolved questions of epistemology – for instance, examining whether poles as seemingly opposed as comparison and relativism can, in fact, be placed into productive dialogue (see Jensen (2011) and others in the *Comparative Relativisim* Special Issue). They have also begun, with some overlaps with the concerns of this book, to unpick some of the challenges that face those interested in developing different, potentially more productive and potentially more reflexive forms of comparative practice. This includes asking how comparison might become 'thicker' (Scheffer and Niewöhner 2010), more relational (Ward 2010; Cook and Ward 2012), and/or more modest, postcolonial and attentive to modalities of difference (McFarlane and Robinson 2012; Robinson 2011; and others in the Comparative Urbanism Special Issue).

There has been a very visible push by funders for researchers to adopt comparative methods (see in this volume, Akrich and Rabeharisoa, Deville et al., Stöckelová). For instance, the stated rationale accompanying the regulatory foundation for the EU's funding programme for the 2014 to 2020 period (known as Horizon 2020) points to the need for comparison given the increasing 'complexity' of the challenges facing Europe. These are challenges that 'go beyond national borders and thus call for more complex comparative analyses to develop a base upon which national and European policies can be better understood' (European Union 2013: 162).

There is another actor that has the potential to pull comparison in a different direction, and that is STS. This might be surprising, given that it is one of the subdisciplines that has both opened up the contingencies of knowledge production, while also developing what seems to be a non-comparative methodology. However, STS appears to be offering important practical pointers towards what the development of a new, less hamstrung comparative practice might look like.

First, STS is doing comparison. Bruno Latour's recent major work, *An Enquiry into Modes of Existence*, quite explicitly puts comparison to work. Its ambition is to examine the productivity of putting, side by side, 15 different 'modes' through which existence is produced. Latour talks about comparison as a 'test', the criteria for which are implied in the following questions (if the answers to each are negative, then comparison can be considered to have failed its test):

> Do we gain in quality by crossing several ontological templates in order to evaluate, little by little, what is distinctive about each one? And, an even more daunting subtest: do we gain in verisimilitude by treating all the modes at once in such a move of envelopment? (Latour 2013: 478)

We are back, then, to questions of similarity and difference. And to the ability of comparison to *make a difference*. What's more, 'irreduction' is revealed in the book not as the principle that should underpin *all* investigations of social life, but rather a particular way (albeit a crucially important one in the history of STS) to follow one of the fifteen 'modes': the 'network' mode. By virtue of its capacity to differentiate, comparison inevitably engages in activities of reduction. However, this should not be seen as necessarily problematic: reduction is productive not of 'less' in any simple way but rather difference (see Robinson, this volume). As such, it is an operation as indispensible to analysis as it is to life (see Bryant 2013; Halewood 2011).[4] In Latour's recent book, the role of comparison can be seen as assisting us in distinguishing between (productive) reductions.

The fact that – whether for pragmatic or intellectual reasons – comparative research is being done by STS researchers offers an opportunity. Here we have a body of researchers trained in the very art of detecting how scientific techniques and technologies affect the production of knowledge, using a method which has been so often criticised for how it does just that. Undertaking an analysis of their own research (as many in this book have done) and not just the research practices of others, may help us determine *in practice* what the dangers and opportunities of comparison actually are for social science (see Deville et al.; Stöckelová; and Akrich & Rabharisoa in this volume).

This leads to the second point. And that is that STS is, or at least it could be, well placed to hesitate, to slow down and recognise the power and potential of its own comparative practices before making assumptions about comparison. Many critics of comparative practice make rapid leaps between 'comparison', 'classification', 'generalisation', and the production of knowledge understood as 'scientific' and/or 'objective'. This obscures the translations and mediations that need to occur for each of these terms to have the power to define the other. Webb Keane has opened up some of these moves by demonstrating how in some social scientific settings the suspicion of comparison can be traced back to a very particular ethical project constructed in direct opposition to what he calls a 'hypostasized version of science' (Keane 2005: 85). This is important. As Stengers reminds us, '[e]xperimental sciences are not objective because they would rely on measurement alone. In their case, objectivity is not the name for a method but for an achievement' (Stengers 2011: 50). It is a very *particular* type of achievement to tie comparison to the production of the very *particular* kinds of knowledge that scientific methodologies seek to produce. It is perfectly possible for comparison to be directed towards quite different ends.

THE USES OF COMPARISON

To help us understand exactly how and why comparison is neither inherently innocent nor guilty of the various charges that have been levelled against it, we seek in this volume to accomplish two goals. Some of the articles focus on either one of these twin aspects, some on both. First, we seek to analyse how comparison is done, and second, we seek more productive ways of doing comparison, in part by challenging conventional comparative practices. To accomplish these goals it is important to accept the two points made above: first, that comparison indeed is a particular *research practice*, rather than merely a ubiquitous cognitive operation; second, that comparison as a research practice is necessarily *reductive*, and this is not in itself problematic.

Rather than dwelling on the epistemological concerns outlined above, then, it makes sense to look in more detail into the different uses of comparison and to begin to be able to ask critical questions about where and in what ways we practise comparison and with what ambitions in mind. We maintain here, as do the authors in this collection in various ways, that comparison can and should have uses that move far away from how it has been understood previously. We also maintain that focusing on the uses of comparison can help to free us from many of the attendant epistemological worries (see also Krause on this issue).

Thus rather than insisting on the problems associated with previous comparative research, and making an exception for non-comparative qualitative research in the mistaken assumption that it is automatically less reductionist, we insist that research is in itself a risky and necessarily reductive practice. This means that we should therefore ask where and when we want to reduce and with what goals in mind.[5]

Competition, for instance, is a particularly radical and often harmful form of comparison, as for example when it puts entities into a contest without having a theory of what guides the outcomes (for example, in the case of measuring academic productivity (see de Rijcke et al.)). Or there is comparison as critique (see Krause): it shares with competition the idea that we can use another object to assess the object in front of us; to understand what is good or bad about this object, or if we need another object that is different from, and better or worse than, whatever we are interested in. A number of writers have also noted how comparison may be pedagogic and creative: it allows the person or entity doing the comparison to learn from having objects, arguments, statements, and empirical phenomena contrasted with each other and, as a result of this contrast, for each to potentially emerge more clearly defined than before (see Schmidt 2008: 339; Stengers 2011: 62).

COMPARISON AS CREATIVITY

With this starting point established, it now becomes possible to compare different ways in which entities are constructed through comparison. The focus can thus move from criticising the construction of categories per se and the brutality with which objects are forced into categories through comparison, to analysing various forms of category creation. The construction of entities, and the reduction of the world in accordance with such entities, becomes visible as a process that is difficult, certainly, but also adventurous and creative. Throughout this volume, we can observe a number of such strategies. They all confidently establish categories, yet do so in a reflective and sometimes playful way.

The first strategy is to undermine the seeming self-evidence of the categories being used in a particular comparative undertaking, as can be seen in the articles by Akrich and Rabeharisoa, and Deville et al. In both studies, the self-evident category appears to be the state, yet in each case the authors dismantle the idea of a state as either homogeneous or consistent in different settings; instead the category of the state divides into various subsets, containing a varied and unpredictable selection of entities. In both, then, it turns out that states are above all convenient starting places for research, for the simple reason that they provide distinct legal and organisational contexts in which the research objects (patient groups and disaster management) operate.

A second version compares comparisons between social scientists and the field (see, to varying degrees, Akrich and Rabeharisoa, Deville et al., Gad and Jensen, Lutz, and Meyer). The idea here is based on the ubiquity of comparison in a context distinct from social science. This is a reflexive move which follows many other forms of constructive reflexivity in the social sciences. For example, Boltanksi and Thévenot's theory of justification is built on the observation that critique is not only in the hands of social scientists but also part of lay discourse, and that critical theory thus needs to turn into a theory of how critique is practised (Boltanski and Thévenot 1991). The reflexive comparisons in this volume similarly start with the observation of pre-existing comparisons in the field and use these to rethink the comparative practices of social science. The conclusions that stem from such a rethinking differ, however: some authors argue that social science should follow the comparisons in the field (Gad and Jensen, Lutz), while others maintain that there is something distinct about an explicitly directed social scientific approach to comparison (Akrich and Rabeharisoa, Deville et al., Meyer).

A third version creates different entities by turning towards asymmetrical comparison. Comparative asymmetries often follow from the need to discover the *tertium comparationis*. While normally the *tertium comparationis* is assumed to dictate the category of objects being compared (a state being compared with other states, etc.), it may help to embrace forms of analysis that shift across multiple comparative registers, with no desire to produce cleanly balanced comparisons. Categories of object might be compared with each other, with then further comparisons brought into play by shifting across different planes – across not just space but also time, for instance (see the discussion of Faria's chapter below).

THE COMPARATOR AND THE PRACTISING OF COMPARISON

To claim that comparison is always grounded in infrastructure forces us to analyse the relationship between such infrastructures and the practices of comparison. This volume is thus also concerned with the 'nitty-gritty' or the practical level of comparative practices as they are deployed across various social scientific comparative projects, the often unseen and unremarked dimensions of comparison upon which research practice nonetheless utterly depends. Akrich and Rabeharisoa, Deville et al., and Stöckelová each conduct types of auto-ethnography to show the diverse ways in which comparisons can be done. These contributions clearly show that comparative research hinges on a multiplicity of factors ranging from a particular zeitgeist (or research fashion), to the project structure and proposals made to funders, to the inner workings of the entity conducting the comparison. The latter is an entity we call the 'comparator' (Deville et al., this volume).

Let us take, first, the influence of funders. The priorities laid down for researchers by funding agencies influence the choice of the field to be studied and the planning and conduct of the individual steps of the project. The project has to *make sense* to the funders in order to be able to come into existence. And here is the paradox: some funders, particularly the EU under the various Framework Programmes, now prefer projects that have an element of international collaboration looking at the same topic. Therefore numerous academic teams based in multiple countries come together and 'do' comparisons. Very often, these comparisons are between nations (or more loosely, between practices situated in different places), but the sheer scale of EU funds often renders projects comparative on other axes as well. The availability of large-scale funding thus spurs a new kind of comparison which very often does not have its main purpose grounded in research problems. At least as often, such comparisons are driven by the political need of the EU to make sense of the EU as a 'union' of cultural practices and their internal differences. They are also driven by the fact that for large-scale research projects in the social sciences, 'comparison' is a convenient way of distributing and accounting for work. And finally, it is a way of making sense of individual subprojects of large-scale projects and claiming some kind of unifying theme of the work. It is unclear and has been barely analysed how such new forms of comparison relate to older formats. And, while earlier comparative practices, particularly in anthropology, tried to make sense of the 'periphery', the new EU funding regime looks at comparison to understand differences within the centre or to understand the relationship of centre and periphery.[6] This has also brought a new form of relationship between centre and periphery: this new model of comparative research does not centralise comparative practice, but rather assigns each field site its own usually 'local' research team. In other words, we can observe a move from an anthropological comparative strategy, in which researchers are strangers, to a sociological one (see Stöckelová).

Second, comparative work hinges on the set-up and running of the *comparator* – the human and non-human entity that jointly produces comparison (see Deville et al.). Humans combine their sensory and organisational apparatuses with those of tools and machines. Comparators are unique too, and vary between each project. They are assembled in part in accordance with the funding proposal, which details the number of their human and nonhuman parts and outlines modality of their work, while their shape and specific formatting also changes as the projects progress.

It seems that the *im/balance between humans and nonhumans* within a comparator profoundly impacts the modus operandi of work and its results. This is most tangible when comparing (again!) the work of single human researchers to that undertaken by teams. The advantage of comparators including a *single person* is that much of the comparator is located in one person, and thus many of its decisions do not need to be made explicit during the research process. One person's own intuition and preferences shape what is being researched and what lines of enquiry are being pursued. It is only when the comparator runs into problems, or when comparative research practice needs to be explained (as in academic texts), that the underlying assumptions of the comparator are made explicit.

Comparators that contain several persons face different kinds of opportunities and challenges. Most importantly, collaborative work tends to depend on making things explicit, and specifying and homogenising the comparator in far more detail. Therefore, assembling the comparator is a crucial element of comparison. Teams also choose different strategies for *calibrating* their comparators – allowing people, technologies, and other actors to adjust to each other and achieve 'compatible' ways of seeing and digesting data. This can include reading seminars, workshops, joint fieldwork, and so on. The scalar challenges of cross-national comparative projects, particularly favoured by large funding bodies, also increase the difficulties of making a comparator work (see Akrich and Rabeharisoa; Lutz; and Stöckelová, this volume). So too do the non-human parts of a comparator. All researchers also rely on a range of infrastructural tools to enable the conduct of their research. Luhmann was lost without his filing cabinet; ethnographic researchers would be lost without their notebook. Although tending to focus more on the natural sciences, STS has shown us repeatedly how such socio-material infrastructure can shape the conduct and outcomes of research. The fields themselves (and their various actors) also become part of the comparator and influence and shift our notion of comparison. This volume is full of accounts of how people and objects in the field change the course of comparative practice. And finally, the objects under examination possess different qualities to the researcher that make them comparable in different ways (see Faria, this volume).

If we think of the ways in which comparison is used, together with the various elements involved in practically doing comparison – beginning with the role of research funders, the internal set-up of the comparator and finally the role of the field itself – we can immediately see that the question of what is at stake when practising comparison cannot, and could never have been, whether comparison is good or bad, or whether it should be avoided. The question is rather *which* comparisons and which comparative infrastructures we want to implicate ourselves in, what we seek to understand with them, how we set up our comparator, and how we want it to relate to the field. There is no single, correct procedure for doing comparison, no correct answer to the question of what a good comparison is or should be. What the contributions to this book can do instead is to highlight some of their comparative decisions and selections, and some of the problems and conflicts that contributed towards comparisons being performed as they were.

OVERVIEW OF THE BOOK

The book is divided into three sections. The first, *Logics*, deals with how scholars of different disciplines conceive the rules of doing comparison. It offers an analysis of different objections and/or challenges to these rules, including situations where assumptions about comparison become a barrier to comparison itself.

When we speak about practising comparison, it is too easily forgotten that how we do comparison is guided to a great extent by books on method, methodological fashions, and previous comparative examples. A struggle common to all the contributions to the book is the very restricted ideas of comparison that exist amongst the imagery, methods, texts, and implicit rules of various disciplines.

The first two chapters take issue with such rules and constraints in very different ways. Monika Krause, in 'Comparative Research: Beyond Linear-causal Explanation', sets out to liberate comparison from its theory. She raises a charge: that comparative practice has suffered from an overly restrictive idea of comparison, one based on forms of 'like with like comparisons' drawn from ideas about linear causal explanation, with yet deeper roots in the randomised control trial. Measured against such standards, most comparisons of the social sciences fall short. Yet Krause maintains that social scientific comparison very often has quite different aims and that these should be conceived of according to different conceptual terms. She suggests that social scientific comparison instead often aims at better description, concept development, and critique, while providing explanations distinct from those of other disciplines. Such goals, then, imply the use of different kinds of comparison, ranging from what she calls 'like with unlike comparisons', to 'asymmetrical comparisons', to 'hypothetical comparisons', or to 'undigested comparisons'.

Alice Santiago Faria takes a different route, trying to find a new logic of comparison from within a particular case. In her chapter, 'Cross Comparison: Comparisons across Architectural Displays of Colonial Power', she begins by analysing the logic of comparison in architectural history and theory. This logic, she maintains, is focused on comparing either buildings from the same building type, the same epoch, or the same style (typical 'like with like comparisons', in Krause's parlance). Yet, drawing on her research on colonial architecture in Goa (India), she shows that focusing on the categories that guide architectural history does not illuminate the logic of colonial architecture. According to Faria, colonial architecture can be characterised as the display of power through the most prominent building type of a given epoch. This leads her to compare a Goan cathedral from the sixteenth century with a British-Indian train station from the nineteenth century. These buildings are radically different in terms of the traditional logic of architectural history: they come from different times, are built in different styles, and are different building types. Yet this apparent incommensurability comes to provide the very basis for a set of novel comparative movements.

The second section, titled *Collaborations*, deals with the various organisational, interactional, and political problems arising within collaborative research projects which are often strongly promoted by political donor entities, such as the EU. Project teams admit that collaboration can be laborious, as it brings unexpected challenges and twists when the imagined research ideas come to life and deal with incongruent realities of the field and diverse research practices across different academic traditions. It appears that the way the comparator (i.e. the entity that carries out the comparative work) is assembled and put to work determines what is and is not studied and put into mutual relation. In other words, collaborations shape the object of comparison just as the object shapes collaborations. This process involves endless adjustments or processes of calibration, through negotiations where hierarchies, personal relations, politics, and pragmatism co-produce the final end product – the outcome of research

33

projects. Comparison is thus often not a singular act but a continual collaborative process undertaken throughout projects, from their inception as proposals to the process of analysis and writing.

In their chapter, 'Same, Same but Different: Provoking Relations, Assembling the Comparator', Deville, Guggenheim, and Hrdličková give a new meaning to the term comparator, as has already been described. Their chapter calls for more attention to be paid to the contingent practices in which the comparator becomes assembled, fed, and calibrated, as it determines how objects of study are approached, and continually interacted with. Such mutual interaction can provoke further comparisons and realign the comparator. Their auto-ethnographic narrative, about carrying out a seemingly conventional comparison of disaster preparedness practices across three countries (the UK, Switzerland, and India), tells how various unanticipated factors, such as varied levels of access, absences or presences of certain phenomena, made the comparator devise coping strategies and realign the whole outlook of the project. This leads to some interesting findings which would not have come to light had the conventional rules of comparing 'like with like' been strictly applied.

Madeleine Akrich and Vololona Rabeharisoa in 'Pulling Oneself Out of the Traps of Comparison: An Autoethnography of a European Project' recount the proceedings of their EU-funded project looking at patient organisations dealing with four different health conditions in four European countries. They concede that pragmatism was a guiding principle for the duration of the project. In the application stage, their research proposal was a strategic compromise between their intellectual interest in knowledge practices and the funder's demands for an international/comparative/collaborative dimension. They thus deployed categories, narratives, and forms of reasoning which were not necessarily close to their interests, but that were crucial for obtaining the funding. Their comparative work thus did not result in typologies, as their research proposal might have suggested, but rather in multi-sited observations. Along the way they were producing and constantly calibrating comparators that would allow them to grasp singularities and commonalities, achieving a kind of common interpretive framework through sets of tools, instructions, and open discussions.

Reflecting on two of her research projects in the late 2000s – following women in science in five EU countries and the introduction of excellence frameworks in academia in the Czech Republic – Tereza Stöckelová's chapter 'Frame Against the Grain: Asymmetries, Interference, and the Politics of EU Comparison' raises the important issue of the conventions and forms of politics that permeate contemporary comparative practices in the social sciences in Europe (and, likely, elsewhere). Drawing on her own experience, she finds that research designs often correspond and speak to the (pre)existing political realities, infrastructures, and imaginations that are defined by funders, invoking unhelpful categories and comparative practices; further, that this imagination is reinforced through the multiple, recurring executions of projects reproducing these specific frames, units, and asymmetries. In making a case for a more critical form of collaborative comparison, she argues for social scientists and funders to go against the grain and to commit to creating investigative frictions by not allowing prevailing notions to dominate.

The third section is *Relations*. As we have alluded to above, comparison inevitably involves the forging of new connections between objects, persons, and many other entities besides (e.g. concepts, discourses, feelings, places, cities, states, and so on and so forth). The contributions to this section each in their various ways explore the consequences of this comparative relationality. In particular, they examine the forms of relation within which researchers become implicated in and through the particularities of fieldwork, with an attention to how comparative practice becomes shaped by the objects of comparison, including by the sometimes explicit, sometimes more implicit, comparisons that these objects perform.

Christopher Gad and Casper Bruun Jensen's paper on 'Lateral Comparisons' shifts authority for the production of comparison away from the social scientist to the field itself. Given that the field is densely populated with comparison, something a number of other contributors also note, they invite social scientists to allow themselves to travel on a journey with this existing and multifarious comparative endeavour in order to begin a process of 'inventing around' these practices. In outlining how this might be achieved, they focus on the comparisons that take place in and around a particular site: a Danish fishery inspection vessel. This involves paying attention to comparative relations that are put into play by both humans – notably the crew and fishing fleet inspectors – and a variety of non-humans, ranging from navigational aids to technologies that bring ships into direct comparative relation through monitoring activities. Practising comparison as a social scientist, then, is an act somewhere between a letting-go and a more active effort to resist the imposition of a layer of comparison on top of, and beyond, the various other, and often powerful, comparisons that are to be found once s/he starts looking.

This theme is taken up by Peter Lutz in 'Comparative Tinkering with Care Moves'. Like Gad and Bruun Jensen, Lutz draws attention to the significance of comparative relations that already exist in the sites we study. In his case, this is senior home care and its movements and acts of transformation. A key point of difference between the two papers (one inevitably emerging from comparison!) is that Lutz also examines how such 'found comparisons', as one could call them, might (or might not) enter into productive relation with what might seem to be the more arbitrary comparisons that a social scientist might want to perform (and indeed 'impose'). For Lutz, this is the attempt to bring together two sites that are spatially disconnected and organisationally and culturally quite distinct – senior home care in Sweden and the United States. Through a process that at once is reflexive about his own previous practice as a social scientist and takes the relations of comparison within field settings seriously, Lutz comes to advocate a process of comparative 'tinkering'. This involves recognising the relational composition of comparison in-between the researcher and the researched and the ongoing adjustments that are required, as well as frictions that emerge, in the construction (and recognition) of comparison. One consequence of the tinkered comparison, he suggests, is to disturb some of the more conventional, standardised categories of comparison that are often rolled out uncritically within the social sciences.

In the next chapter, by Sarah de Rijcke, Iris Wallenburg, Paul Wouters, and Roland Bal ('Comparing Comparisons: On Rankings and Accounting in Hospitals and Universities'), it becomes quite clear just what is at stake when some of these conventional categories of comparison begin to become deployed against the outputs of workers, including academic workers. Many readers of this book will already be experiencing the effects on their everyday practices of the increasing metricisation of academic outputs and, as a direct consequence, the rise of the comparative and competitive ranking of universities. By comparing ranking systems within Dutch universities to those used within hospitals, the paper examines just how such systems come into being, some of their performative effects, as well as, in a final 'jump' with parallels to Lutz's approach, reflecting on how this particular comparative technology sits against their own comparative practice. This helps reveal how uncomfortable it can be to at once be situated as an object of comparison and an analyst of this objectification, as well as the centrality of commensuration to all comparative practices. As the authors suggest, such acts of commensuration can come into tension with a researcher's desire (one common to STS researchers) to attend to empirical phenomena symmetrically.

Morgan Meyer, in the book's final empirical chapter ('Steve Jobs, Terrorists, Gentlemen, and Punks: Tracing the Strange Comparisons of Biohackers'), further pursues the tack of reflexively analysing his own comparative practices against those of his respondents, here 'biohackers'. These are individuals, inspired by the ethics of hacking and open source, who seek to mess with biology in a wide variety of ways. Including in his own previous work, Meyer finds that, in trying to pin down just what biohacking is and what it aims to achieve, it is something of a trope to place its practices into comparative relation, whether it be to terrorists, Steve Jobs, or seventeenth-century gentleman amateurs (or to many others besides). The task Meyer takes on is to uncover exactly what these various comparisons do to biohacking and biohackers. What he uncovers are a series of frames that shape how 'we', as scholars, and 'they', as practitioners, understand those 'yet-to-be-named transformative individuals working in biology', as Meyer at points calls them (given that the very term biohacking operates in a particular comparative register). Comparison is shown to be a deeply value-laden operation, one routinely involved in the construction of social identities. At the same time, Meyer suggests that such problematics of comparison cannot simply be solved by better, denser, 'thicker' description. Instead, comparativists – if that's what we (whether we like it or not) are – should be content to leave comparison as they find it, to allow it to exist in all its multiplicity and muddle.

The book ends with an Afterword by Jennifer Robinson, titled 'Spaces of Comparison and Conceptualisation'. In it, she responds to some of the questions the essays raise. In navigating her way through these contributions, Robinson is drawn to asking after the spatialities of comparison, as part of an ambition to forge a revitalised comparative imagination. On the one hand, she argues, comparison is often thought/imagined/done in such a way as to reduce the spatial contingencies composition of that which is being compared (the case, the local, the city, the global, for instance). On the other, attending to spatial specificity (indeed, singularity) and to the way that such specificity can, in both theory and practice, enter into relation with an effectively infinite range of other entities, opens the door to comparative multiplicity. Here determining the 'shared' and 'different' registers of life and experience demands not a comparative universalism, but an approach to comparison that is modest and open to revision.

This suggests that practising comparison involves not a definitive fixing of the qualities of the world but a 'holding steady' just long enough for questions of difference and similarity to come into view. This requires considerable work to bring logics, collaborations, and relations together with comparative infrastructures, field sites, research teams, objects, and technologies, as well as the power dynamics that inevitably cross-cut them. Analysing exactly what is at stake in this endeavour is what we hope this volume will begin to achieve.

NOTES

1   Using Google Ngram viewer. Percentage obtained by dividing total occurrence of terms (case insensitive) by the corresponding total occurrence of either the terms sociology/sociological or anthropology/anthropological (in order to control for an overall increase or decrease in the latter). 2008 is the most recently available data. A smoothing of 3 applied, using Ngram's smoothing function. See original analysis at http://tinyurl.com/orgo9cs.
2   A similar analysis with IBISS, a database with journal articles, returns similar curves of ascendancy and fall, but with peaks for both disciplines roughly a decade later. Given the critiques around the authoritative production of knowledge we explore below, we are particularly keen to point out that we see these more as rough indicators of tendencies

more than any definitive representation of trends. Far more work would need to be done to establish these tendencies firmly and authoritatively.

3 Concerns about comparison are of course not distributed evenly. Some countries' anthropological and sociological traditions move forwards to a greater or less degree unconcerned by such attacks. George Steinmetz, for instance, argues that much US sociology 'still seems to be operating according to a basically positivist framework, perhaps even a crypto-positivist one' (Steinmetz 2005: 276). Beyond sociology and anthropology, the extent to which these challenges have been taken seriously within the social sciences varies considerably. Within cultural studies, cultural geography, and politics, particularly in parts of Europe, you may well find a similar situation. Venture, however, into economics, psychology, or – as Faria (this volume) explores – architecture departments, and the picture will be very different.

4 We might see forms of reduction as 'abstractions', in the terms outlined by the philosopher Alfred North Whitehead.

5 Research is also always the opposite, namely expansive, in the sense that each research project, each piece of writing, adds something to the world that wasn't there before. Research inevitably does both: reducing the world to a selection of relevant terms and observations and expanding the world by adding to the existing set of ideas. Even the most 'reductionist' theory works against itself, since with its publication the world is not reduced but enlarged.

6 An overview of the latest round of FP7 (Framework Programme 7) research projects can be found here <http://cordis.europa.eu/fp7/ssh/project_en.html>, and those funded by the European Research Council can be found here <http://erc.europa.eu/erc-funded-projects>.

BIBLIOGRAPHY

Bendix, R., 'Concepts and Generalizations in Comparative Sociological Studies', *American Sociological Review*, 28 (1963), 532–39

Boltanski, L., and L. Thévenot, *De La Justification. Les Economies de La Grandeur* (Paris: Gallimard, 1991)

Bryant, L. R., 'Latour's Principle of Irreduction', *Larval Subjects*, 2013 <http://larvalsubjects.wordpress.com/2013/05/15/latours-principle-of-irreduction/> [accessed 18 August 2015]

Clifford, J., 'Introduction: Partial Truths', in J. Clifford, and G. E. Marcus, eds., *Writing Culture: The Poetics and Politics of Ethnography* (Berkeley: University of California Press, 1986), pp. 1–26

Clifford, J., and G. E. Marcus, eds., *Writing Culture: The Poetics and Politics of Ethnography* (Berkeley: University of California, 1986)

Cook, I. R., and K. Ward, 'Relational Comparisons: The Assembling of Cleveland's

Waterfront Plan', *Urban Geography*, 33 (2012), 774–95

Dickens, D. R., and A. Fontana, *Postmodernism and Social Inquiry* (New York: Guilford Press, 1994)

European Union, 'Regulation (EU) No 1291/2013 of the European Parliament and of the Council of 11 December 2013 Establishing Horizon 2020 – the Framework Programme for Research and Innovation (2014–2020) and Repealing Decision No 1982/2006/Ec', *Official Journal of the European Union*, L (2013), 14–172

Friedman, S. S., 'Why Not Compare?', in R. Felski, and S. S. Friedman, eds., *Comparison: Theories, Approaches, Uses* (Baltimore: Johns Hopkins University Press, 2013), pp. 34–45

Gingrich, A., and R. G. Fox, 'Introduction', in A. Gingrich, and R. G. Fox, eds., *Anthropology, by Comparison* (New York: Routledge, 2002), pp. 1–24

Halewood, M., A. N. Whitehead and Social Theory Tracing a Culture of Thought (London: Anthem Press, 2011)

Haraway, D., Primate Visions: Gender, Race, and Nature in the World of Modern Science (New York: Routledge, 1989)

Harding, S. G., *The Science Question in Feminism* (Ithaca: Cornell University Press, 1986)

Jensen, C. B., 'Comparative Relativism: Symposium on an Impossibility', *Common Knowledge*, 17 (2011), 1–12

Keane, W., 'Estrangement, Intimacy and the Objects of Anthropology', in G. Steinmetz, ed., *The Politics of Method in the Human Sciences: Positivism and Its Epistemological Others* (Durham, NC: Duke University Press, 2005), pp. 59–85

Latour, B., *An Inquiry into Modes of Existence: An Anthropology of the Moderns*, C. Porter, trans. (Cambridge, MA: Harvard University Press, 2013)

——Reassembling the Social: An Introduction to Actor-Network-Theory (Oxford: Oxford University Press, 2005)

——*The Pasteurization of France* (Cambridge, MA: Harvard University Press, 1988).

Law, J., and J. Hassard, *Actor Network Theory and After* (Oxford; Malden, MA: Blackwell/Sociological Review, 1999)

Longxi, Z., 'Crossroads, Distant Killing, and Translation: On the Ethics and Politics of Comparison', in R. Felski, and S. S. Friedman, eds., *Comparison: Theories, Approaches, Uses* (Baltimore: Johns Hopkins University Press, 2013), pp. 46–63

McFarlane, C., and J. Robinson, 'Introduction – Experiments in Comparative Urbanism', *Urban Geography*, 33 (2012), 765–73

Peacock, J., 'Action Comparison. Efforts towards a Global and Comparative yet Local and Active Anthropology', in A. Gingrich, and R. G. Fox, eds., *Anthropology, by Comparison* (New York: Routledge, 2002), pp. 44–69

Radhakrishnan, R., 'Why Compare?', in R. Felski, and S. S. Friedman, eds., *Comparison: Theories, Approaches, Uses* (Baltimore: Johns Hopkins University Press, 2013), pp. 15–33

Robinson, J., 'Comparisons: Colonial or Cosmopolitan?', *Singapore Journal of Tropical*

Geography, 32 (2011), 125–40

Scheffer, T., and J. Niewöhner, eds., *Thick Comparison: Reviving the Ethnographic Aspiration* (Leiden; Boston, MA: Brill, 2010)

Steinmetz, G., 'Odious Comparisons: Incommensurability, the Case Study, and "Small N's" in Sociology', *Sociological Theory*, 22 (2004), 371–400

—— 'Scientific Authority and the Transition to Post-Fordism: The Plausibility of Positivism in U.S. Sociology since 1945', in G. Steinmetz, ed., *The Politics of Method in the Human Sciences: Positivism and Its Epistemological Others* (Durham, NC: Duke University Press, 2005), pp. 275–323

Stengers, I., 'Comparison as a Matter of Concern', *Common Knowledge*, 17 (2011), 48–63

Strathern, M., *Gender of the Gift* (Berkeley: University of California Press, 1988)

Tyler, S. A., 'Post-Modern Ethnography: From Document of the Occult to Occult Document', in J. Clifford, and G. E. Marcus, eds., *Writing Culture: The Poetics and Politics of Ethnography* (Berkeley: University of California Press, 1986), pp. 122–40

Ward, K., 'Towards a Relational Comparative Approach to the Study of Cities', *Progress in Human Geography*, 34 (2010), 471–87

SECTION ONE

LOGICS

2

COMPARATIVE RESEARCH: BEYOND LINEAR-CAUSAL EXPLANATION

Monika Krause

THEORETICAL CONVERSATIONS ABOUT COMPARISON IN THE SOCIAL SCIENCES have been dominated by a relatively restrictive view as to what comparisons are good for, and what kinds of comparisons are legitimate. This view takes various forms in different research contexts, and we should not oversimplify when we engage with it. Nevertheless, it can be briefly characterised as based on the premise that comparison can be avoided; that one must compare 'like with like'; that comparison aims at causal explanation; and, one should add, that it aims at a very specific type of causal explanation.

The practice of comparison in the social and human sciences has, of course, always been more diverse. Comparison is an aspect of any kind of practice that invokes knowledge in the sense that all information implies some version of comparison to other possible realities; comparison of a formal and relatively more self-conscious kind has always been used to various ends in academic practice. However, the diverse practices of comparison have rarely found their way into textbooks on methodology – if comparisons have made it into textbooks at all.

In this context, this paper aims to free the academic practice of comparison from its theory. Or rather, the aim is to free the theory of comparison from itself so that it can better do its job of providing reflection on existing practices of thinking and research, and perhaps improve them. Recently, there have been efforts to rediscover diverse forms of comparison in different disciplines (Fox and Gingrich 2002; Dear 2005; Pickvance 2001; Brubaker 2003; Robinson 2004; Jensen 2011; Scheffer and Niewöhner 2010; McFarlane and Robinson 2012). This work provides thoughtful reflection and exemplary pieces of research, and I am building on it here.

Nevertheless, more work can be done: building on these efforts can move broadly in three directions. Firstly, we can work towards a more differentiated understanding of the 'old'. Both textbooks and critical accounts have tended to overstate the homogeneity of traditional practices of comparison. We can benefit from examining the assumptions that have been associated with comparison in the past in more detail, and, in particular, from examining the diverse material research practices that have been involved. Secondly, and relatedly, we can develop a better sense of how diverse practices of comparison have always been in the history of different disciplines. This can provide us with exemplars of good research and help us direct our energies beyond overstated claims of newness in ongoing work. And thirdly, we can work on reflecting on (and perhaps shedding) some of the normative baggage of the debate. Traditional discourses of comparison have tended to put the weight of 'science', 'reason', and 'progress' on choosing the right kinds of comparisons. In some of the newer work, this baggage is sometimes simply reversed: the aim is to avoid 'traditional' or 'hegemonic' practice at all cost. In some of the rhetoric around alternative ways of doing comparison, every research project has to bear at least the weight of innovation – if not resistance or transcendence – in a way that is not realistic or helpful.

This paper discusses comparison based on attention to research practices and on their different ends. It asks what comparisons can be useful for, and in what ways. I begin with the observation that comparison has been identified with one specific aim: that of causal explanation, and in particular that of linear-causal explanation. It is commonly said that 'one cannot compare apples and oranges'. This sentence only becomes intelligible in the context of linear-causal explanations, and I will suggest it only becomes intelligible in the context of the hold clinical trials have had on the methodological imagination of the social sciences. I will then discuss a few other ends that comparisons can be useful for, such as description, concept development, critique, and different kinds of explanation. Lastly, I will discuss a few forms of comparison that can be recognised as being useful once we broaden the ends that comparison can legitimately be used towards.

COMPARISON AND LINEAR-CAUSAL EXPLANATION

There are many different ways in which 'old' understandings of comparison can be described and named. The way one labels what one is departing from of course has implications for how one frames the limitations of previous research, and for the kind of alternatives that can be imagined. Some textbooks have equated comparative research with cross-national comparisons, and some critical reflections also associate traditional comparisons with specific units of analysis such as 'cross-national' or 'cross-cultural' comparison (see Brubaker 2003). Others take a broader view: alongside the obviously polemical labelling of common assumptions concerning comparisons as 'hegemonic', 'mainstream', or 'orthodox', we find seemingly more theorised notions such as 'generalising', 'deductive', 'positivist', or 'universalist'.

In what follows, I explore the benefits of one specific way of analysing what may unite some traditional ways of talking about comparisons. I will argue that in the theory of comparisons, comparisons have long been associated with one specific end: they were thought to serve causal explanation, and, more specifically, the kind of causal explanation associated with general linear reality (Abbott 1988; Abbott 2005). What is characteristic of this vision is not so much a deeply held positivist (or universalist) conviction – whatever that would mean – but a set of implicit assumptions which privileges a clear separation between cause and the outcome, conceived as things and a linear model of causality. In addition, it is usually thought to be important to establish how important variables are in relation to other variables.

We can characterise the tradition in terms of a specific philosophy of science; a vision of scholarly work that draws on the model of mechanical physics that has shaped representations in the traditional history of science and philosophy of science, in other disciplines, and the public.[1] But rather than address the issue on the level of ideology, I am interested in work that identifies specific practices and research problems that are at the origin of different regimes of doing comparison. Looking at practices has two advantages: 1) it allows us to investigate regimes of legitimising comparisons in their diversity, and 2) it allows us to take into account the original usefulness of specific assumptions about comparisons.

Isabelle Stengers (2011) does a brilliant job of analysing the preconditions of comparability in experimental physics, but another practice which has perhaps been even more important for the social sciences is the clinical trial. The aim of clinical trials has been to establish the efficacy of different kinds of treatment. For example, Iain Chalmers quotes a seventeenth-century physician who issues the following challenge to his 'competitors':

> If ye speak truth, Oh ye Schools, that ye can cure any kind of Fevers [...] come down to the contest ye Humorists: Let us take out of the hospitals, out of the Camps, or from elsewhere, 200 or 500 poor People that have Fevers, Pleurisies, etc. Let us divide them in halves, let us cast lots, that one half of them may fall to my share and the other to yours; I will cure them without blood-letting [...] but you do as ye know [...] we shall see how many Funerals both of us shall have: But let the reward of the contention or wager be 300 Florens deposited, on both sides (2001: 1157).

In this vision, a comparison is like a race between two horses. Or rather, if the treatments are the horses, the comparison is the racetrack. The comparison is thus the staging ground of a competition, and the concern is for the competition to be fair. For this reason, the two groups (which are compared) need to be as similar as possible, except in regard to the treatment.

It would be interesting and important to sketch in detail the history of different research practices associated with comparison, and their impact across the social sciences. However, this is beyond the scope of this paper. I would hypothesise a process whereby specific research problems serve as 'model systems' (Creager, Lunbeck, and Wise 2007; Howlett and Morgan 2011) that have an impact on how research is imagined beyond their original application.

In sociology (like in other disciplines) certain cases have served as privileged reference points for certain objects or areas of research, and have shaped perceptions in unacknowledged ways (Guggenheim and Krause 2012). Similar processes may be at work with regard to research methods.

The clinical trial seems to be a prime example for such a privileged reference point for social science methods: it is on the one hand a very specific practice responding to a very specific research problem – the testing of medicines – with very specific units of analysis and elements such as individuals, diseases, and medical interventions. On the other hand, it has become central to how causality, and, by implication, explanation, is understood much more broadly.

The hold of the clinical trial on the social scientific imagination has, at times, been very explicit. Glenn Firebaugh, for example, writes in *The Seven Rules of Social Research*: '[t]he trick in causal analysis is to create those conditions by comparing like with like – through investigator-produced random assignment (as in controlled experiments), through naturally occurring random assignment or through some other means of matching' (2008: 163). Regression analyses, but also fixed-effect models and sibling models, are all attempts to simulate clinical trials for observed – as opposed to more self-consciously created – data (see Firebaugh 2008).

These types of comparison inherit the notion of causation as a form of competition among treatments. They imagine all types of causes as a form of 'treatment' and seek to establish their impact independently of all other factors. Regression analysis is used with individuals as units of analysis, but it is also used in quantitative forms of cross-national research in political science, and in cross-cultural comparisons such as those published in *Cross-cultural Research* based on the Human Area Relations File (see, for example, Deaner and Smith 2012; Martínez and Khalil 2012).

Echoes of the clinical trial are also audible in more qualitative work, if only in the form of a kind of defensiveness with regard to the trial-inspired notion of causality. More specifically, one hears echoes of the clinical trial whenever causality is conceived of as an analogy to the impact a 'treatment' might have, and whenever the causal effect of some phenomenon needs to be established in competition with all other factors.

These tendencies have been influential in American comparative-historical sociology, for example. This has shaped, for instance, the way the state has been conceptualised in American sociology (Skocpol 1979; 1985). In its attempts to prove the causal impact of its structures, the state had to be conceptualised as a separate 'thing' in a way that excluded cultural aspects; it also had to be constructed as entirely separate from economic forces and class interests. Attempts to prove the causal impact of culture in this particular way have similarly led to a definition of culture that makes it hard to understand how culture and other aspects of social practice intertwine (see, for example, Alexander and Smith 2001).

COMPARISON AND BETTER DESCRIPTION

I have argued that there is a widespread assumption that comparisons aim to establish linear-causal relationships. This assumption has obscured other ends of social analysis in general, and of comparison in particular. To the extent that linear-causal analysis is the aim, description and category-construction are only considered as a means towards an end. In clinical trials, description of the disease itself is only a preliminary step – though other medical research may explore symptoms in more detail and the definition of a disease may of course be problematic, especially in hindsight (see Bowker and Leigh Starr 1999). In regression analysis too, description or measurement is a preliminary step, important only as a means towards establishing correlation among observed values (Marradi 1990). By subordinating description and category construction to linear-causal explanation, the concern with linear-causal explanation has proliferated trivial forms of description and category construction, while precluding some of the yields that might result were these aspects of social science research considered as ends in themselves.

For pragmatic reasons (and because only explanation is really considered valuable) research has often focused on descriptions that can be easily collected about a large number of cases, and it has focused on descriptions that can be quantified. But description is important, and this is not just about 'getting the facts right', as is sometimes acknowledged in the quantitative tradition.

Description also situates a case with regard to sensitising concepts. Questions such as: 'What is it like? What are its properties? How does it work? What kind of pattern can we observe? How is something changing?' are descriptive and important, and comparisons are useful for answering them.

Some in the interpretative tradition emphasise the value of understanding the case in its particularity in opposition to the practice of comparison.[2] The trope that comparison hinders understanding keeps recurring: Estrid Sorensen, for example, notes that '[s]pecificities are likely to become invisible through comparison' (2008: 312). However, it has also repeatedly been pointed out from within interpretative traditions that even understanding a particular case is a comparative task (see Barnes 1973: 190; Kuper 2002: 146; see also Skocpol and Somers 1980).

All scholarly description involves selective forms of contextualisation and decontextualisation, and there are costs and benefits to different strategies. But we need to reflect on these costs and benefits in the context of concrete research projects, and we need to do so without implying two extreme positions which are misleading. Firstly, we need to avoid implying that description without comparison is possible. Any object becomes an object in relation to other objects – even an object considered holistically becomes a whole in relation to other wholes. A good repertoire of comparative cases also allows us to precisely characterise a phenomenon in its uniqueness and particularity. Secondly, we need to avoid implying that the only available form of comparison in the scholarly tradition is cross-national comparison, large-n linear-causal comparison, or cross-cultural comparison in the service of linear-causal explanation. The trade-offs do not seem to be in choosing between description and comparative practice, but between different kinds of comparative practices, and between different kinds of comparative practices maximised for different ends.

COMPARISON AND CONCEPT DEVELOPMENT

Like description, concepts are a means to an end in the linear-causal tradition. In clinical trials, the unit of 'patient' and the categories 'ill' and 'healthy' are the starting point of the analysis: the real interest lies in exactly how to randomise, and which treatment has better results. In the social sciences, this has led to a lot of work with received categories, and for pragmatic reasons to work with categories, in which the data is already coded.

The use of concepts as categories for linear-causal analysis also has follow-on costs – in some ways regardless of the quality of the category used: once a unit of analysis or a category is 'baked' into a linear-causal analysis, the practices involved in its construction slip under the surface. It can thus become harder to ask questions about the historical conditions of the unit of analysis, and about the specific ways in which description was achieved.

Linear-causal analysis also casts its shadow backwards into the way non-causal use of categories and comparative description is read. That is, if linear-causal assumptions are widespread, even a comparison that is purely descriptive can invite readings that treat the unit of comparison as an explanatory variable. Cross-national comparisons in particular seem to almost automatically be read in some corners in a way that turns the category of description into a causal hypothesis. If someone studies a social movement in Finland and in Norway, it is assumed that something about these countries can explain the observed difference. This assumption shapes expectations for EU-funded projects that combine field sites in different countries (Akrich and Rabeharisoa, this volume; see also Sorensen 2008).

But comparative description using concepts as categories does not have to be read as preparing linear-causal explanation (where the category is the explanans). It can be a provocation for further research and conceptual development. It could raise questions about further variation within the unit of analysis, particularly in view of partial data collection: an ethnography, for example, has rarely covered the whole unit of analysis; it usually studies a culture through a particular village (see Kuper 2002: 143). It could also raise questions about further differentiation within the descriptions pertaining to the unit of analysis.

What I am suggesting here is that some of the problems associated with categories have to do with their specific uses in linear-causal analysis. I want to suggest that categories are useful for description, and comparison is useful for improving categories. Indeed, I would argue that developing categories is the proper aim of theoretical practice, and in that sense, comparison is essential to theoretical practice (Krause 2010).

Some kinds of comparisons are especially useful for developing concepts. Comparisons that take their departure from existing units of analysis have played an important and useful role: that of comparing common units of analysis to their opposite. Rather than just compare individuals, social theorists have compared discourses that construct individuals with those that do not, thus asking how the individual has become the dominant unit of analysis (Weber 1964 (1904); Foucault 1978, 1979). Rather than just compare nation-states, we can compare them to other social forms such as hordes, the mafia, or city states. This has enabled Saskia Sassen (2006), for example, to break the nation-state down into some of its constituent elements and ask new questions about different combinations of territory, authority, and rights. Rather than just do a comparison between cities, we can compare the city to its supposed opposite in terms of density or size, and ask broader questions about forms of settlement (Gans 2009).

COMPARISON AND CRITIQUE

The most fundamental operation of critique is not to say 'this is bad', but rather to say: 'It is not necessary. It could be otherwise' (Calhoun 2001). Critique has been practised in different intellectual traditions and I would suggest that comparison is central to all of them. At its most modest, critiquing means to say 'this could be looked at in another way'. Unsettling established views of the world requires comparison, at least among ways of seeing the world. Critique can also use comparison between different cases to show that any given social phenomenon is not natural or necessary.

Though comparison is often associated with universalism in contexts where that is seen as a bad thing, comparison of course has an important role to play in challenging ethnocentric, or otherwise provincial, assumptions. Foucauldian (and Nietzschean) genealogy, for example, is a comparative practice: discourse analysis is holistic and imminent, but it also depends on juxtaposition. It asks the analyst to go back in time until he or she finds assumptions and practices that are significantly different from the present (Foucault 1977, 1978; Baert 2010).

This denaturalisation can also be an effect of comparisons in more conventional social science. Max Weber's comparison of the Protestant and Catholic work ethic, for example, can be read as an attempt to establish culture as a causal variable. But it has also shown that it is not natural for people to want to work as much as possible, or even to respond to incentives (Weber 1963 (1904)).

Critique in a stronger Marxian sense is at its best also not so much a denunciation, but a comparison. In other words, Marxian analysis is a comparison of contemporary society to a different social reality that is thought to be better and that is analytically specified. The analysis of capitalism as a mode of production based on private ownership of the means of production becomes possible only in conjunction with its imagined counterpart: a society based on the shared ownership of the means of production. This comparison allows Marxism to produce unique perspectives on the experience of work in capitalism, as well as on housing markets in capitalist cities, and on the state.

COMPARISON AND DIFFERENT KINDS OF EXPLANATIONS

To the extent that comparison is associated with explanation, it is generally associated with linear-causal explanation. But there are different approaches to explanation, and comparison is also useful for explanations of different kinds. Chris Pickvance (2001), for example, has argued that while comparison is often used to explain different outcomes, it is also useful for explaining similar outcomes with different causes and for functionalist explanation.

Comparison can also be used for explaining a phenomenon by listing its conditions of possibility. In this mode of investigation, a particular phenomenon is examined in comparison to other phenomena in order to specify its form.[3] In dialogue with other observations, we can ask: 'What would have to be different for this to be different from what it is?' In this version of explanation, analytical description and explanation – and critique in the sense discussed above – fall together.

One way to make sense of scholarship on the Holocaust, for example, is to list a number of conditions that were necessary to make this particular atrocity possible. Comparing the genocide to spontaneous, short-lived outbursts of violence, we can underscore the modernity of the event and highlight the role of bureaucratic organisations (Browning 1993), national boundaries, the nature of the modern state (Bauman 1990), indirect domination (Postone 1980, 1993), profit-driven organisations (Hayes 2001), and the logic of specialised professional practice (Benedict 2003). In making comparisons with other nation-states, we can mention the German heritage of anti-Semitism (Goldhagen 1996) and the complicated relationship with violence in German forms of selfhood (Elias 1996). Comparing hypotheses about social dynamics on different scales, we can single out situational factors such as the tendency to obey authority focused on by the Milgram (1974) experiments.

In another example based on research on humanitarian-relief NGOs, I argue the form that humanitarian relief takes today can be described as a market for projects (Krause 2014). Humanitarian relief agencies provide assistance to populations in need, and they do so in the form of projects. Agencies produce projects, and they strive to produce good projects. The pursuit of the good project develops a logic of its own that shapes the allocation of resources and the kind of activities we see independently of external interests, but also relatively independently of beneficiaries' needs and preferences. Agencies produce projects for a quasi-market in which donors are consumers. The project is a commodity, and with that, those helped become part of a commodity. The pursuit of the good project encourages agencies to focus on short-term results for selected beneficiaries. The market also puts beneficiaries in a position where they are in competition with each other to become part of a project.

We can identify this social form and what makes it possible by comparing it to other ways in which needs are produced, and in which populations are, or are not, provided with what they need. Historicising attention to distant suffering and comparing it to earlier times, we can identify means for learning about suffering and providing relief (Haskell 1985) as a condition of possibility of the market for projects. Making comparisons to responses from within the local community (which form part of existing political and religious structures), we can add the emergence of a specific form of humanitarian authority since the late nineteenth century, and especially since the 1970s. Comparisons to a situation where no one responds to distant suffering can identify Western governments' and Western publics' interest in relief of suffering, influence, and stability as a contributing factor. Comparisons to traditional welfare states allow us to identify competition between providers of different national origins and the fact that no organisation has a commitment to a specific population as an element of the market for projects. Making comparisons to a situation where all human communities would be able to provide for their needs themselves, we can identify different phases of primitive accumulation as contributing to the current form of humanitarian relief. For instance, the IMF-led restructuring of the 1980s and 1990s has contributed to the vulnerability of large populations, and is also a precondition for disaster relief.

Explanatory comparisons in the linear-causal tradition can tend to normalise what is common to the cases considered. If we are just asking, for example, why among 'modern' nations it was the Germans who organised the killing of Jews and other minorities on a large scale, the nation-state and other aspects of modernity do not come into view as factors contributing to the Holocaust.

Cross-national research can tend to focus on variation among policies that, on the world historical scale, are relatively similar. The mode of explanation presented here allows us to retain the significance of the phenomenon as a whole, and explicate it by listing and naming all conditions of possibility, including features common across capitalist nation-states, but not universal across social forms more broadly.

Naming conditions of possibility does not allow us to assess the relative impact of competing factors. The Holocaust emerges both as a particularly modern, and a particularly German, phenomenon. However, it gives us an overview of differences to other phenomena and possible analytical, as well as political, leverage points. This allows us to situate practical proposals within the full range of conditions which it might be possible to affect.

KINDS OF COMPARISON: LIKE WITH LIKE/LIKE WITH UNLIKE OR DIFFERENT TYPES OF SERIAL COMPARISON

If all things can be described in terms of both similarities and differences (and if a shared category can always be found), the distinction between comparing 'like and like', and comparing 'like and unlike', collapses. The admonition to compare 'like with like' does not, as such, have meaning. It follows that the term 'comparable' also does not, as such, have meaning – nor does the term 'incomparable' (be it used as a prohibition or in rebellious embrace). Rather, we need to investigate how, and in which practical context, the rule to compare 'like with like' has assumed meaning, and what kind of similarity and difference have been meant?

There have always been both similarities and differences involved in comparing 'like with like'. The question under discussion has been about how many differences a given research project can handle at the same time (see Macfarlane and Robinson 2012). We have seen that in a clinical trial, the comparison is a competition and the concern is for it to be fair. The two groups included in the comparison need to be as similar as possible, except in regards to the treatment. Comparing 'like for like', then, means we need to hold all other sources of variation constant.

For description, concept development, and critique, it can also be useful to compare objects that are expected to be the same in some or most respects. It might allow us to better focus in on specific differences that we want to describe or conceptualise. If we are comparing men's and women's experiences of unemployment and we have limited resources, for example, we might want to construct sample groups of men and women that have a similar socio-economic status or cultural location. It can also be useful to compare cases with only one similarity and as many other differences as possible. If we are studying cities or professions or a certain type of organisation, we might construct a sample that contains the largest number of differences within it. One may also compare one case to as many other cases that are different in as many different ways as possible.

One important difference between comparisons that are maximised for linear-causal explanation and comparisons that are maximised for description, concept formation, or analytical explanation is that they envision a different kind of seriality in their ambitions. Linear-causal comparison aims at repeating the same comparison many times to achieve statistical significance. In other words, the comparison between treatment group and control group is designed to be the same comparison multiplied by the number of people in the group. Whenever we count the number of comparisons involved in a study by the term 'n', we are implying that any additional comparison does not add a qualitatively new dimension.

Other aims are better served by many separate comparisons in succession with objects that are the same, and different, in various ways. We may want to compare a nation-state to an empire, to the Mafia, to an NGO, and so on. Serial comparison of this kind can eventually erode some of the undesirable consequences of category construction. For example, with the kind of seriality that repeats the same comparison multiple times, every additional comparison naturalises the unit of comparison and obscures its condition of possibility. In contrast, with the kind of seriality that strings together many different kinds of comparisons, every additional comparison questions, but also clarifies, the unit of analysis.

THE ASYMMETRICAL COMPARISON

To me, the assumption that seems to most limit current practices of comparison in the social sciences is the assumption that all compared cases need to be given equal amounts of attention. In writing and assessing explicitly comparative research designs, we spend a lot of time thinking about which case(s) should be considered. Meanwhile, most qualitative designs still consider only one case, and both single-case and explicitly comparative studies spend too little time thinking about other relevant cases and literatures (or about the larger diversity in the world), which could be considered by drawing from information that is widely available, or on research that is less in-depth.

The expectation of symmetry is related to certain assumptions about the purpose of comparison. If the concern is for the comparison to be a staging ground for a fair competition, then it seems natural to treat all competitors in the same way. The assumption of symmetry also ties in with underlying assumptions about the nature of measurement or description. First, symmetry of attention appears as the default if measurement has no costs because one is working with existing data sets. Second, if measurement is unproblematically assumed to be either true or false, it makes sense to exclude data that is very poor.

Most social science research encounters more complicated questions of measurement, however, and it encounters trade-offs between different aims of the research – among them quality of information and various strategic aims of the research. Though we tend to not make them explicit, a lot of different kinds of comparisons go into conceptualisation and description – and most of them are asymmetrical. Of course, good research has to contribute new in-depth knowledge on some case or cases, but such research can be enriched with information about other cases from secondary sources (and even by pure thinking exercises). Asymmetrical comparison enhances the interpretation of findings in any study – whether that study has formally been comparative or not.

The assumption of symmetry leads to the defensiveness of single case designs that do not look left or right, and it leaves the potential insights of comparative studies as underexploited. This leads to duplication of efforts among researchers. The seriality that I outlined above potentially undermines the distinction between comparative and non-comparative designs, and between included and excluded cases.

HYPOTHETICAL COMPARISON

In order to take the asymmetrical comparison to one of its conclusions, comparisons can also of course be made with hypothetical cases. Firstly, cases that are considered in relation to a specific question need not be real. Secondly, information about cases considered for comparison need not necessarily be true. Moreover, it is not always essential to know if a case is real, or if our information about it is real, if we present our analysis in measured ways as the result of a hypothetical comparison.

Counterfactual imagination has a long tradition in social science work. That is, we can ask: 'What are the kinds of things that could be happening but are not? Did they ever happen? What would have to be different for them to be happening? How might this phenomenon be different under various analytically specified circumstances? How might this be different in the best, or in the worst, of worlds?' Making comparisons with hypothetical cases is an element of all theoretical work. We use hypotheses produced by theories, and then test them against the data. This has also long been known in quantitative work. Regression analysis is based on comparisons of patterns in actual data to different kinds of models, based on equations.

One distinction I want to draw here is between hypothetical comparisons that aim to find a close match to reality, and those that aim to engage with the imagination in order to identify new forms of possible similarities and differences. Borrowing from Tilly (1984), we might call the latter 'the variation-finding hypothetical comparison'.

In network analysis, for example, comparison to hypothetical cases is used to better describe patterns, and to explore the consequences of assumed, observed, and other possible patterns. Bearman and colleagues, for instance, analyse 'reports of relationships among adolescents in one town [...] and compare the structural characteristics of the observed network to simulated networks' (2004: 44). They thus compare network structures, but the simulations also allow them to map the implications of different network-structures for the spread of sexually transmitted diseases.

This type of work stands out in the degree to which the language for capturing variation between and among different social worlds (real and simulated) is formalised. However, more qualitatively-oriented work can also draw more broadly on fiction, history, and anthropology for cases of comparison. It may be hard to be fully knowledgeable about historical and geographically distant cases. Getting the facts right is important in social science research, but so is challenging parochial taken-for-granted assumptions through comparison. According the status 'hypothetical' to comparisons with cases outside the researchers' first-hand expertise may encourage the social scientific imagination of diversity. Qualitative social scientists have been reluctant to create their own fictions, though these could be created with analytical goals in mind (see Guggenheim 2009).

THE UNDIGESTED COMPARISON

Lastly, I would like to mention the undigested comparison. A digested comparison, with either a different case or a competing analysis, is one where a comparison has been thought through in a way that fits the goals of the project: the relevant similarities and differences have been identified; the observed similarities and differences have been used to at least discover the shared or non-shared category; and the conceptual framework has been thought through in response to the comparison (see Lazarsfeld and Barton 1951). If explanation is an aim, perhaps the implications of the comparison for relevant relationships among phenomena under investigation have been thought through.

A different form of comparison is one usually introduced by 'but see' in footnotes. This can either point to an empirically different case, an empirical parallel, or a difference in interpretation. The 'but see' can indicate that the comparison has not been fully assimilated into the author's conceptual framework; perhaps if it were fully assimilated, a major point might not result. While in general it might be good advice to try to improve academic writing by trying to fully incorporate the material from the footnotes into the main text, it is up to discussion whether any given work contains the right amount of digestion to warrant publication or sharing.

Celebrating the undigested comparison that owns up to being such also means looking at the undigested comparisons hiding in all types of other analytical operations. It is certainly preferable to have an openness towards undigested comparison, rather than practise the 'bitchy footnote' – if we follow Grafton (1999), this is the very origin of the footnote – where footnotes are used to dismiss competing interpretations in a way that suggests more digestion than has actually been accomplished.

Another example of an undigested comparison that is not acknowledged as such is metaphorical re-description, where one case serves as a metaphor for others without actual comparison. This is often what happens when cases become theories and are applied to other cases, instead of being compared. Foucauldian scholars, for example, can tend to apply Foucault's account of the prison, the school, and the hospital to all other types of setting that they then identify as forms of 'governmentality'. Perhaps no school-in-formation is exempt from this tendency. In recent years, for example, it has become popular with the growth of science and technology studies to call all kinds of practices and settings 'laboratories' without much attempt to consider differences, as well as similarities, between the different cases (see Guggenheim 2012).

CONCLUSION

The project to free the theory of comparison from itself has become the project to free it from the theory of clinical trials. There are, of course, epistemic and political stakes to debates about comparison in particular – and to debates about methods in general; but we should pay just as much attention to the mundane constraints of research practice.

These constraints matter as much, and they matter in ways that are not always articulated. Methods seem to draw on specific research problems as their models. Assumptions that make sense in one context get transferred from one research context to another. What makes sense as a practice for comparing treatments may bring some strange assumptions to the examination of national histories.

Reflection on the ends of comparison can have several advantages: it brings us back to specific people and specific practices. It can also remind us of the kinds of things an academic paper can and cannot achieve. That is, it suggests a sort of balancing act among different ends and limited resources, rather than a clear path with rivers full of crocodiles on both sides. The theory of comparison in the service of linear-causal explanation has clearly instilled a fear of 'getting it wrong', which still shapes the debate on different sides.

It can be uncomfortable to discuss the quality of research beyond 'right' or 'wrong', and beyond the content of intellectual positions. Nonetheless, it might be that on top of epistemological and practical research differences, there is a joint enemy to the different sides in the debate about comparison – which we might simply call 'intellectual laziness'. We all encounter different kinds of laziness and our frustrations may be shaping interventions in implicit ways, and they may also produce misunderstandings. There is, on the one hand, the laziness of work that uses un-reflected units or categories of comparison (often shaped by available data in unacknowledged ways). There is, on the other hand, the laziness of works that are descriptive in a way that merely illustrates existing 'theory' – in a context where this sometimes just means 'well-known arguments by authors who happened to have become famous'. There is also the laziness of comparisons that are not suited for linear-causal analysis, and do not clearly articulate how they add value on any other dimension.

I do not think we are looking for one new 'right' way of doing comparison, but we might want to have a conversation about desirable directions as we individually and collectively try to do the best work possible. I would suggest that every piece of information has to be, in principle, 'accountable' to all possible comparisons that could be made. We can use comparisons to constantly question and improve our categories of analysis and description. With the kind of serial comparison I am proposing, this can include asymmetrical and hypothetical comparisons, while considering one or more cases through original research.

We can, of course, not make the demand that every piece of information should be accountable to any comparison to any given talk or paper. All papers, talks, and books are preliminary results and legitimately works in progress. Some contributions add a lot to the conversation among scholars in other ways by showing material connections between cases: for example, those that can form the basis of constructing new units for comparative analysis. However, we can make this demand of intellectual ambitions and of shared standards of conversation. 'Accountable' here means 'in principle answerable to'. The answer to 'what do you make of a possible comparison to x', should never be 'I did not include x in my research'. It has to be, at least: 'that might be interesting because…'

We have historically disproportionally demanded this type of accountability of 'non-typical' cases, which has meant in the current environment that non-US and non-UK cases have had to be justified in English-speaking journals, whereas UK and US cases have at times been analysed as though their interest was self-evident and as though other countries and research on other countries do not exist (see Stöckelová, this volume). Nonetheless, I think the appropriate answer is not to refuse to engage in comparisons, but to insist that everyone makes the particularities of their assumptions and cases explicit as much as possible.

ACKNOWLEDGEMENTS

This paper benefitted from comments received by Joe Deville, Jennifer Robinson, and the editors of this volume. I am also grateful to the participants of two workshops on comparisons at Goldsmiths College: one organised by the editors, and an earlier workshop organised by the editors with Rebecca Cassidy, Claire Loussouarn, and Andrea Pisac.

NOTES

1   See Mayr (1982) for a provincialisation from a biologist's perspective.
2   See Steinmetz (2004) for an extended discussion on the origins of these arguments.
3   See also Ragin's (1992) notion of casing (see also Ragin and Rubinson 2009).

BIBLIOGRAPHY

Abbott, A., 'Transcending General Linear Reality', *Sociological Theory*, 6 (1988), 169–186
—— 'The Idea of Outcome in US Sociology', in G. Steinmetz, ed., *The Politics of Method in the Human Sciences* (Chapel Hill, NC: Duke University Press, 2005), pp. 393–426
Akrich, M., and V. Rabeharisoa, 'Pulling Oneself Out of the Traps of Comparison: An Auto-ethnography of a European Project', this volume
Alexander, J., and P. Smith, 'The Strong Program in Cultural Theory: Elements of a Structural Hermeneutics', in J. Turner, ed., *Handbook of Sociological Theory* (New York: Springer 2001), pp.135–150
Baert, P., *Social Theory in the Twentieth Century* (Cambridge: Polity Press, 2010)
Barnes, B., 'The Comparison of Belief-Systems: Anomaly Versus Falsehood', in R. Horton, and R. Finnegan, eds., *Modes of Thought: Essays on Thinking in Western and Non-Western Societies* (London: Faber, 1973), pp. 182–198
Bauman, Z., *Modernity and Ambivalence* (Cambridge: Polity, 1990)
Bearman, P. S., J. Moody, and K. Stovel, 'Chains of Affection: the Structure of Adolescent

Romantic and Sexual Networks', *American Journal of Sociology*, 110.1 (2004), 44–91

Benedict, S., 'Caring while Killing: Nursing in the "Euthanasia" Centers', in E. R. Baer, and M. Goldenberg, eds., *Experience and Expression: Women, the Nazis, and the Holocaust* (Detroit: Wayne State University Press, 2003), pp. 95–110

Bowker, G. C., and S. Leigh-Starr, *Sorting Things Out* (Cambridge, MA: MIT Press, 1999)

Browning, C. R., *Ordinary Men: Reserve Police Battalion 101 and the Final Solution in Poland* (New York: Harper Perennial, 1993)

Brubaker, R., 'Beyond Comparativism: Theory and Research in Comparative Social Analysis', *EScholarship UCLA*, (2003) <http://www.escholarship.org/uc/item/7t52j73w> [accessed 4 February 2014]

Calhoun, C., 'Critical Theory', in G. Ritzer, and B. Smart, eds., *Handbook of Sociological Theory* (London: Sage, 2001), pp. 179–200

Chalmers, I., 'Comparing Like with Like: Some Historical Milestones in the Evolution of Methods to Create Unbiased Comparison Groups in Therapeutic Experiments', *International Journal of Epidemiology*, 30.5 (2001), 1156–1164

Creager, A. N., H. E. Lunbeck, and M. Norton Wise, eds., *Science without Laws: Model Systems, Cases, Exemplary Narratives* (Durham, NC: Duke University Press Books, 2007)

Deaner, R., and B. Smith, 'Sex Differences in Sports across Fifty Societies', *Cross-Cultural Research*, 47.3 (2013), 268–309

Dear, M., 'Comparative Urbanism', *Urban Geography*, 26.3 (2005), 247–251

Elias, N., *The Germans: Power Struggles and the Development of Habitus in the Nineteenth and Twentieth Centuries* (Cambridge: Polity Press, 1996)

Firebaugh, G., *The Seven Rules of Social Research* (Princeton, NJ: Princeton University Press, 2008)

Foucault, M., *Discipline and Punish: The Birth of the Prison* (New York: Pantheon Books, 1977)

——*The History of Sexuality* (New York: Pantheon Books, 1978)

Fox, R. G., and A. Gingrich, eds., *Anthropology, by Comparison* (London: Routledge, 2002)

Gans, H. J., 'Some Problems of and Futures for Urban Sociology: Toward a Sociology of Settlements', *City & Community*, 8.3 (2009), 211–219

Goldhagen, D. J., *Hitler's Willing Executioners. Ordinary Germans and the Holocaust* (New York: Knopf, 1996)

Grafton, A., *The Footnote. A Curious History* (Cambridge, MA: Harvard University Press, 1999)

Guggenheim, M., 'The Science Fiction of Science Studies', unpublished manuscript, 2009

Guggenheim, M., and M. Krause, 'How Facts Travel: The Model Systems of Sociology', *Poetics*, 40 (2012), 101–117

——'Laboratorizing and Delaboratizing the World: Changing Sociological Concepts for Places of Knowledge-production', *History of the Human Sciences*, 25.1 (2012), 99–118

Haskell, T., 'Capitalism and the Origins of the Humanitarian Sensibility, Parts 1 and 2',

The American Historical Review, 90.2/3 (1985), 339–61

Hayes, P., *Industry and Ideology: IG Farben in the Nazi Era* (Cambridge: Cambridge University Press, 2001)

Howlett, P., and M. S. Morgan, eds., *How Well do Facts Travel?: The Dissemination of Reliable Knowledge* (Cambridge: Cambridge University Press, 2011)

Jensen, C. B., ed., 'Comparative Relativism: Symposium on an Impossibility', *Common Knowledge*, 17.1 (2001), 547–566

Krause, M., 'Theory as the Practice of Hunting Variables', paper presented at the *105th Meeting of the American Sociological Association*, Atlanta, USA, 2010

——*The Good Project: Humanitarian Relief NGOs and the Fragmentation of Reason* (Chicago: Chicago University Press, 2014)

Kuper, A., 'Comparison and Contextualization', in R. G. Fox and A. Gingrich, eds., *Anthropology by Comparison* (London: Routledge, 2002), pp. 143–176

Lazarsfeld, P., and A. Barton, 'Qualitative Measurement in the Social Sciences: Classification, Typologies, and Indices', in D. Lerner, and H. D. Lasswell, eds., *The Policy Sciences* (Stanford: Stanford University Press, 1951), pp.155–192

Marradi, A., 'Classification, Typology, Taxonomy', *Quality & Quantity*, 24.2 (1990), 129–158

Martínez, P. R., and H. Khalil, 'Battery and Development: Exploring the Link between Intimate Partner Violence and Modernization', *Cross-Cultural Research*, 47.3 (2012), 231–267

Mayr, E., *The Growth of Biological Thought* (Cambridge, MA: Belknap Press, 1982)

McFarlane, C., and J. Robinson, 'Introduction: Experiments in Comparative Urbanism', *Urban Geography*, 33.6 (2012a), 765–773

McFarlane, C., and J. Robinson, eds., 'Experiments in Comparative Urbanism', *Urban Geography*, 33.6 (2012b)

Milgram, S., *Obedience to Authority: An Experimental View* (New York: Taylor & Francis, 1974)

Mill, J. S., *System of Logic: Ratiocinative and Inductive: Being a Connected View of the Principles of Evidence and the Methods of Scientific Investigation* (London: Longmans Green, 1898)

Pickvance, C. G., 'Four Varieties of Comparative Analysis', *Journal of Housing and the Built Environment*, 16.1 (2001), 7–28

Postone, M., *Time, Labor, and Social Domination: A Reinterpretation of Marx's Critical Theory* (Cambridge: Cambridge University Press, 1993)

——'Anti-Semitism and National Socialism: Notes on the German Reaction to "Holocaust"', *New German Critique*, (1980), 97–115

Ragin, C. C., '"Casing"' and the Process of Social Inquiry', in C. C. Ragin, and H. S. Becker, eds., 'What is a Case? Exploring the Foundations of Social Inquiry' (Cambridge: Cambridge University Press 1992), pp. 217–226

Ragin, C. C., and C. Rubinson, 'The Distinctiveness of Comparative Research', in T.

Landman, and N. Robinson, eds., *The Sage Handbook of Comparative Politics* (London: Sage, 2009), pp. 13–34

Robinson, J., 'In the Tracks of Comparative Urbanism: Difference, Urban Modernity and the Primitive', *Urban Geography*, 25.8 (2004), 709–723

Sassen, S., *Territory, Authority, Rights: From Medieval to Global Assemblages* (New Jersey: Princeton University Press, 2006)

Scheffer, T., and J. Niewöhner, eds., *Thick Comparison: Reviving the Ethnographic Aspiration*, vol 114 (Leiden: International Studies in Sociology and Social Anthropology, 2010)

Sewell, W. H. Jr., 'Ideologies and Social Revolutions: Reflections on the French Case', *Journal of Modern History*, 57.1 (1985), 57–85

Skocpol, T., 'Cultural Idioms and Political Ideologies in the Revolutionary Reconstruction of State Power: A Rejoinder to Sewell', *Journal of Modern History*, 57.1 (1985), 86–96

—— *States and Social Revolutions: A Comparative Analysis of France, Russia, and China* (Cambridge: Cambridge University Press, 1979)

Skocpol, T., and M. Somers, 'The Uses of Comparative History in Macrosocial Inquiry', *Comparative Studies in Society and History*, 22.2 (1980), 174–197

Sorensen, E., 'Multi-sited Comparison of Doing Regulation', *Comparative Sociology*, 7.3 (2008), 311–337

Steinmetz, G., 'Odious Comparison: Incommensurability, the Case Study and Small Ns in Sociology', *Sociological Theory*, 22.3 (2004), 371–400

Stengers, I., 'Comparison as a Matter of Concern', *Common Knowledge*, 17.1 (2001), 48–63

Stöckelová, T., 'Frame against the Grain: Asymmetries, Interference and the Politics of EU Comparison', this volume

Tilly, C., *Big Structures, Large Processes, Huge Comparisons* (New York: Russell Sage Foundation Publications, 1984)

Weber, M., *The Protestant Ethic and the Spirit of Capitalism* (London: Unwin 1968 (1904))

3

CROSS COMPARISON: COMPARISONS ACROSS ARCHITECTURAL DISPLAYS OF COLONIAL POWER

Alice Santiago Faria

WHEN I FIRST BEGAN TO RESEARCH NINETEENTH-CENTURY COLONIAL STATE architecture in Goa, comparing the architecture of Portuguese and British India was part of my original work plan.[1] Currently (as in the nineteenth century), Goan people frequently make comparisons between *Estado da India* [Portuguese India] and the British Raj, and undoubtedly this is one reason I decided to consider this comparison. However, soon after starting my work, I concluded that a systematic traditional comparison of the state architecture of Portuguese and British India was not feasible. There were several reasons for this. Fundamental differences existed between the two colonial administrative systems, meaning that their respective public buildings were different in nature. Furthermore, the relationship between architecture and power in these two empires during the nineteenth century also seemed too different to allow for any form of proper architectural comparison. The main reason for this was that Portugal and Britain were in two different imperial cycles: whereas *Estado da India* had been in decline for some time, in British India this was the period when the Raj became firmly established.

Some time later, while reflecting on this during a talk at Goldsmiths (University of London), I stated that I had arrived at a hypothesis that would allow a comparison of the architectures of Portuguese and British India involving comparison *across* time, using a realigned timeline to match periods when the relationship between architecture and colonial power was similar. In other words, this meant times when architecture was used to affirm and establish colonial power, and when specific types of buildings became symbolic representations of the empires that had built them. Which buildings would therefore best represent the Portuguese and British empires in India and their power relations?

The Portuguese empire hinged on trade and profit, but was inseparable from religion. Religion and religious conversion were essential to Portugal's control over *Estado da India*. Even today, churches are the key architectural reference when it comes to discussing the Portuguese presence in India, or the Portuguese presence in the world. Established first as a diocese, Goa became an archdiocese in the mid-sixteenth century, with a jurisdiction that stretched from the east coast of Africa to China and Japan. The cathedral in the city of Goa was the home of the archbishop of all Catholics in the Orient, and therefore the most important and representative building of the Portuguese empire in that part of the world.

The British Raj was based on trade and profit, but was also inseparable from technology – especially the railway, as this was fundamental to Britain's ability to control the Indian subcontinent. Eventually, every Indian was more or less forcibly 'converted' to technology – the religion of the nineteenth century. It is not by chance that one of the main ideological pillars of Gandhi's movement was the return to manufacturing and pre-British rural life, or that he protested against British technology.

Bombay (Mumbai) was not the capital of British India, but was one of the most important presidencies, along with Calcutta (Kolkata), and Madras (Chennai). However, the opening of the Suez Canal (1869) established Bombay as the main point of entry to India. By 1872, rail links to the hinterland and the major cities in the territory confirmed the status of Bombay as the centre of modern India, even if it was not its political heart. Not surprisingly, therefore, the Victoria Terminus (VT, or Chhatrapati Shivaji Terminus as it is now known) is considered by many as 'the central building of the entire British Empire – the building which expresses most properly the meaning of an imperial climax' (Morris and Winchester 2005: 133).

Consequently, if these two buildings – the Cathedral in the old city of Goa (the sixteenth-century capital of the *Estado da India*) and the Victoria Terminus in Bombay – were the buildings most representative of the imperial powers that had built them, comparison appeared feasible. However, in practice, would such a comparison reveal that both had a similar aim – of displaying imperial power – and that both were designed to fulfil that same purpose? Would it reveal common ground in terms of the relationship between architecture and power in the two empires by displaying similar characteristics?

Challenged to think about the practical problems arising from this comparison, this chapter represents my personal path through the paradox described by Fox and Gingrich in the introduction to *Anthropology, by Comparison*:

> A familiar paradox currently haunts attitudes towards comparison [...] If considered from afar, comparison seems to be the fundamental research tool it always has been, so self-evident that some scholars may not regard it as worthy of closer examination. But when comparison is exposed to close examination, a contradictory intellectual reaction often comes into play, and comparison appears not simple and self-evident but rather as a topic and a method impossible to think about, dissolving into dozens of other issues, pieces and fragments (2002:1).

This chapter begins by analysing how the comparative method has been used in architectural history, reviewing key authors in its historiography. The second part returns to India to explain my hypothesis and choices for establishing a comparison between two things I had thought could not be compared. Subsequently, the buildings are compared in order to analyse the various contexts in which similarities can be identified, and to explore the difficulties of the comparative act in practice.

In examining and exploring the process of comparison, I aim to show that although comparison is a widely used practice in architectural history, its full potential is not exploited as much as it could be if more time were spent reflecting on such practices and engaging with them more creatively. In addition, this chapter aims to contribute towards understanding the role of architecture in establishing empires, showing that its importance and characteristics are similar in distinctive empires in time and history, such as in the Portuguese and the British empires. It suggests that the role of architecture in history (and in particular in the history of empires) could be better understood by comparing across building types, empires, countries, or communities, and across time. 'Comparing across' shows that architecture, societies, cultures, and powers are entangled, and can reveal some of the many different effects. While intending to reveal another perspective on the comparative act, it also emphasises that overall, there is nothing simple, linear, or banal about the practical making of comparisons.

THE 'COMPARATIVE METHOD' IN ARCHITECTURAL HISTORY

Comparison is a method common to the interconnected fields of architecture, art history, and architectural history. Although it is assumed to be a fundamental research tool, in practice architectural historians do not, nowadays, seem very interested in reflecting on it. Comparison thus seems to be both everywhere and nowhere, ranging from systematic comparisons to visual descriptions, and it is unsurprising that, as in other disciplines, a multitude of practices have emerged. This section aims to provide a brief overview of the history of comparison in architectural history: as it will demonstrate, the main purpose of using comparison in this field has been to compare buildings that have similar formal, stylistic, or typological characteristics. In addition, it will examine how architectural history deals with the problem of time, especially since this was one of the first questions that emerged when I began to think about the comparison I was working with.

The comparative method in architectural history has its roots in the restructuring of the French schools at the end of the eighteenth century, when it shifted towards a more technical approach to teaching that was more rational and less attached to the Beaux-Arts.[2] Jean-Nicholas-Louis Durand (1760–1834) – teacher from 1795 and later director of the architecture course at the Polytechnic School in Paris – was one of the most important figures in this movement. Durand's search for a systematic approach to architecture is best seen in his *Summary of Architecture Lessons Given to the Royal Polytechnic School* (1802).[3] However, he had already applied this systematic method to history in his *Survey and Parallel of all Buildings, Ancient and Modern, Remarkable for their Beauty, Size, or Singularity, Drawn on the Same Scale* (Durand 1799).[4]

Prior to Durand, Fischer von Erlach,[5] in *A Plan of Civil and Historical Architecture* (1725), had already used images where different buildings of the same type were visually compared.[6] Von Erlach's book is considered by many to be the first book on architecture to use the comparative approach. However, his goal was to produce a survey of monuments rather than a comparative study (von Erlach 1725: Preface). Although he does display images side by side, he does not explicitly compare them in the accompanying text. He uses building types (e.g. Roman triumphal arches, Roman temples, Chinese bridges, and Greek temples) or building elements from a specific period or region (e.g. doors from temples in Syria). Similarly, J.D. Leroy in *The Ruins of the Most Beautiful Monuments of Greece* (1770)[7] juxtaposes plans of temples drawn on the same scale.[8] Although this process of creating visual parallels (i.e. juxtaposing buildings or parts of buildings of the same kind – used by both Leroy and Fisher Von Erlach) was much closer to the process of classification used in the natural sciences than a systematic practice of comparison (Madrazo 1994: 12–13), they were nevertheless important predecessors to Durand's works.

Durand's comparative purpose is clearly expressed in the title of his book, *Survey and Parallel of All Buildings of All Types,* and was reinforced in a letter reproduced in the first volume of the 1799 edition. In the letter, Durand states that he had found a way of deepening his knowledge by comparing, which meant comparing buildings of the same *kind* and drawing them on the same scale. For him, this was the easiest and most useful form of comparison. He describes a systematic typological method which involves using buildings of the same 'kind' and drawing them in 'parallèle' (i.e. in parallel or side by side on the same scale).[10] Comprising two volumes (the first containing the text and the second the drawings), Durand uses comparison in both, albeit sometimes different, ways. For example, in the comparative visual tables (examples of which

FIG. 3.1 Triumphal Arches (comparing by building type), J.N.L. Durand, 1799[9]

are shown above), Greek and Roman architecture is usually separated, while in the text, Greek and Roman temples are compared. Moreover, in the comparative drawings, Greek constructions are presented side by side with those of the Egyptians, Indians, and Turks (in a table of tombs, for example). Again, in the introductory text to the volume of drawings, Durand reiterates his view on how comparisons should be made by selecting the same kind of buildings and drawing them on the same scale – adding that they were juxtaposed according to their degree of similarity.

The practice of defining buildings as 'the same kind' might be debatable, and it is difficult nowadays to understand the use of 'public building' as a type as Durand does[11] when he presents town halls and courts side by side (Table 17), or hospices, lazarettos, caravanserais,[12] and cemeteries (Table 30). In the first example, Durand explained in the text that for him, town halls and courts are used for the same purpose, meaning they have the same function – public service (1799: 23). In the second example, Durand establishes the relationship between the buildings in terms of form (1799: 38). Likewise, the definition of a 'global history' of architecture used by Durand and the way in which he separates East and West is controversial today, to say the least. Nevertheless, the point here is that Durand compares buildings where he can find common grounds for comparison based on form, function, or both, even if the relationship is not always finely balanced. It is in this way that this comparative practice relates to my hypothesis.

As Madrazo points out, throughout the ninety comparative tables Durand ascertains the role of design in architectural history, or what would nowadays be called 'research by design' (1994: 12). Following Durand's work, comparing buildings of the same type by juxtaposing them on the same scale became established as the systematic undisputed method of comparison (which is well recognised within the discipline, but used without serious reflection).

However, it was only at the end of the nineteenth century and in the early years of the twentieth century that the comparative method appeared as a recognisable and explicit methodological approach. It was also when architectural history emerged as a modern discipline. The *History of Architecture on the Comparative Method* by Banister Fletcher and Banister F. Fletcher (first published in 1896) was the key reference in the English-speaking world and is still the book that immediately comes to mind today when referring to the comparative method in the history of architecture.[13] Like Durand's work, the Fletchers' book is an attempt to produce a global architectural history. Although its reception has varied greatly over the years, the book has been revised twenty times and has expanded considerably since it was first published.

The Fletchers' comparative method gradually moved away from textual explanations to more visual comparisons, and illustrations became more important and occupied more space in the later editions. The principles of the first editions were maintained: analysing and contrasting the most basic elements of buildings – plans, walls, openings, roofs, columns, decorations, and so on – both textually and according to their design, by drawing the different elements side by side. Although drawings were not always presented on the same scale, the presence of a graphic scale still ensured that systematic comparison by design was possible.

In the fourth edition (published in 1901), the book was divided into historical (Western) and non-historical (non-Western) architecture, although no direct comparisons were made. In each section, comparisons were made between buildings of the same type and style from the same country. In the non-Western section, comparisons were also made between the basic constructive components of the buildings with ornament, and in particular were compared with respect to design, including comparisons of Chinese and Japanese ornament (or the form of arches). Sometimes the focus was narrowed down to comparisons between different works by the same author (as in the case of the Renaissance examples by Palladio), where the building types were mixed – presenting drawings of the Basilica and the Villa Capra Vicenza[14] alongside each other. Although this is an exception in the book and Fletcher does not compare the buildings or their parts textually, he does provide an insight into comparison across building types, establishing authorship as the common ground. The extraordinary survival of Fletcher's book as a key text up to the present day is not directly related to its comparative method. Rather, it is, above all, related to the attempt to produce a global history of architecture and to the quantity and quality of the illustrations, which cover a vast range of buildings. Furthermore, the discussions and the controversy surrounding the work of the Fletchers (see Çelik 2003; McKean 2006; Nalbantoğlu 1998) hardly ever centre on the way in which comparison is used, making it seem as if this does not merit serious debate.

Heinrich Wölfflin's methods and principles were an essential contribution towards systematising architectural history and establishing it as a modern historical field (Kultermann 1996: 241–246; Leach 2010: 1–2, 23–25, 36–40, 44–48).[15] Wölfflin's *Principles of Art History* defined five principles through contrast, as seen in the following chapter titles: Linear and Painterly; Plane and Recession; Closed and Open Form; Multiplicity and Unity; Clearness and Unclearness (1950 (1915)). By contrasting and comparing, and presenting images side by side in his lectures and books, he created the basis for formal comparison in art history. Despite the fact that over the years architectural history and art history have progressively diverged (Payne 1999; Jones 1981; Jarzombek 1999), the methodology and formal comparison, in particular, are still very evident in architectural history today.

In the age of the Modern Movement, the typological approach to architecture was dismissed. At that time, the history of architecture was concerned with key individual buildings, not method. These buildings were unique examples of art (Oechslin 1986: 38), and the early historians of the Modern Movement, such as Pevsner (1936), Kaufmann (1933), or Hitchcock (1929, 1932, 1958), rarely engaged with comparison explicitly. However, since they emerged from the German tradition of art history (with the exception of Hitchcock), they did use photographs to create more implicit forms of comparison. These were presented side by side to show the formal relationships between buildings or other constructions.

During the 1950s and 1960s, a new generation of architectural historians (i.e. architects-historians) emerged, changing the scene of the discipline into a more complex theatre. By 1970, when the great masters of the Modern Movement had disappeared, method, typological approach (Madrazo 1994: 23), comparison, and global history emerged once again.[16]

All these examples indicate the enduring presence of comparison in architectural history through a wide range of practices which emphasise the importance of visualisation in either formal or more systematic comparison. They also show that the use of comparison in the history of architecture (whether it be buildings, parts of buildings, or just form) generally signifies comparing 'like to like'. It is a process that rarely involves discussion, since it is considered 'simple to the point of banality' (Venturi, Izenour, and Brown 2000 (1977): 114).

One important exception to the work of the historians of the Modern Movement[17] was Giedion's *Space, Time and Architecture* (1941).[18] Comparison is very evident in the book and is assumed to be an essential process for studying architecture (Giedion 1968: xiii). Despite the fact that Giedion considered architecture to be a complex organism – emphasising that it is not only a question of style, form, or social and economic context, but that architecture has an existence of its own – Tournikiotis has stressed that Giedion's comparisons were also based only on visual similarities between constructions which he labelled 'visual descriptions' (Giedion 1968: 24–25; Tournikiotis 1999: 48). For example, in the fifth edition of his book, published in 1967, Giedion compares a Neolithic gravestone with le Corbusier's Ronchamp Tower (Fig. 3.2), presenting photographs of each right next to each other.

344a. Stele at the neolithic monumental "Tomb of the Giants" in Sardinia.

344b. LE CORBUSIER. Pilgrimage Chapel of Notre Dame du Haut, Ronchamps, 1955. View from the west. A Mexican architect, R. Barragan, pointed out the secret affinity of the tower of Ronchamps with a prehistoric cult structure in Sardinia.

FIG. 3.2 Neolithic gravestone vs. Corbusier's Ronchamp tower, S. Giedion, 1968[19]

Tournikiotis' critical comment on this famous comparison is that it

> relies solely on a morphological likeness [...] There is no other connection, either social or technical, capable of linking works so different from one another and so distant from one another in time (1999:48).

Tournikiotis does not consider form in isolation to be a crucial aspect of comparison, thereby challenging the interest in visual/formal analysis alone in architectural history.

Space, Time and Architecture is nonetheless important for the particular way it deals with time. Since realigning a timeline means, in practice, to compare across time, one of the first questions I had was how architectural history approaches time. A conventional, chronological, or historical account is generally concerned with the same 'architectural period' or 'style', which may involve relatively short or longer periods of time, but always in reference to clearly defined periods. Nevertheless, there are many cases in which time is used differently. For example, working with a building type (like Durand) or a specific building element (like Fletcher) normally implies much longer periods of time. Giedion's importance to the debate on the theme of time and architecture is undisputable. For him, history is dynamic and continuous: 'The past cannot be disentangled either from the present or the future [...] [They] are all part of a single, irreducible process' (Tournikiotis 1999: 45). Time is what Giedion calls 'the eternal present' (1968: xix–xx), and this consequently poses no problem for making comparisons.

Like Giedion, Spiro Kostof is one of the most important and pioneering authors of architectural history.[20] Engaging in a cultural history of architecture, Kostof does not compare architecture in different cultural contexts, but uses similar items from the same chronological period and cultural region. In his opinion, comparison across time is not very useful, and he argues that much better results can be achieved by comparing buildings built at the same time and across geographies (Kostof 2003 (1959): 9–38). However, breaking with the usual historical practice, he displaces architects from their 'chronological time' in order to maintain the study of a particular place (Kostof 2003: 10). This means that the book is mostly organised by geography, and not chronologically by authors, which would be a more conservative way to do it.

Thus, I soon realised that comparing across time was not a concept alien to architectural historians, even when dealing with more conventional accounts of time than those of Giedion or Kostof. Even though my hypothesis does not displace buildings from their chronological time, it was through Kostof that I understood that studying a specific architectural context (such as place or power), while comparing across time and moving things from their original time or synchronising periods of time,[21] should not represent a problem for architectural history.

COMPARING THE UNCOMPARABLE

This section begins by exploring the notion of imperial cycles and their relationship to architecture. Exploring this concept will explain why – given that this relationship was so different in Portuguese and British India in the nineteenth century – I initially concluded that their public architecture was 'uncomparable'. Subsequently, it explains how, using the same concept, a hypothesis was established for comparing the architecture of these empires using two buildings as a case study; it also explains the reasons for choosing them.

It is easy to grasp the idea that empires pass through different stages in history (Bayly 2004). Although there are differences between ruling periods and the ways in which the powers themselves are imposed on others throughout the ages, it is possible to identify relatively similar periods of conquest, establishment, and decline in the life cycle of empires.[22]

The Portuguese arrived in India in 1498 and conquered the city of Goa in 1510. In just two decades, Goa became the Portuguese capital in the Orient, ruling over territory extending from Mozambique to Timor. The sixteenth century and the beginning of the seventeenth century were periods seen by historiographers of the Portuguese empire as the golden age of the Portuguese in India. However, this only lasted for a short period, as the new colonial powers (namely the British and the Dutch) were arriving in the area.

From the second half of the seventeenth century onwards, *Estado da India* faced huge difficulties. Its northern territories in India were eventually lost, and the country was reduced to Goa, Daman, and Diu. Its territorial configuration survived with more or less the same structure from the mid-eighteenth century until 1961. Likewise, the political influence of India would also change dramatically in the mid-eighteenth century, with Goa losing its power over Mozambique, Macau, and Timor a century later.

The British arrived in India one century after the Portuguese. In 1612, the East Indian Company established the first factory in Surat, in the state of Gujarat. The company increased its control over the territory in the eras that followed, although by the end of the eighteenth century the British government had begun to take over. Nevertheless, it was only after the 1857 rebellions that power was completely transferred to the Crown. During this period (known as the Raj) India became the jewel in the British Crown, with its supremacy almost uncontested until 1918. After the First World War, the situation began to change, and independence was granted in 1947.[23]

Architecture has always been one of the foremost means of establishing, representing, and upholding authority in empires. However, the lengthy presence of the Portuguese in India transformed this relationship between architecture and colonial authority. After three and a half centuries, there were few European Portuguese in Goa. The colonies were only of very limited importance to a country immersed in a civil war from which stability only emerged in 1853, and only for a short period of time. The entire nineteenth century was marked by political instability, a financial crisis – with the state having to repeatedly resort to external help – and colonial rivalries with other imperial powers, notably England. However, in the late nineteenth century, the colonial issue became more important to Portuguese society and the Portuguese colonial state tried to regain some authority; the truth was that in Portuguese India the colonial state was crumbling and was being challenged on a daily basis by the Goan elites. Furthermore, each time Lisbon tried to impose its authority, the Goan elites would resist. The only real power in Goa was the Catholic Church, which had an established authority dating back many centuries.

During the nineteenth century, the public administration and most sectors of Goan society (such as the legal system, medicine, engineering, and even the Church) were mainly, if not completely, controlled by Goan Catholic elites (some of whom were descended from the Portuguese, and others from Hindu converts). As elsewhere, the territory was completely transformed, largely in the second half of the century. The major strategies for these transformations were decided by Lisbon, which, while facing pressure from other colonial powers, made half-hearted colonising efforts. During the nineteenth century, almost every urban development and building constructed in Goa was planned or designed – and built – by people born and educated in the territory who were engineers or overseers of public works trained in the military schools of Goa (Faria 2010; 2012).

Moreover, the Portuguese state was bankrupt, which meant that many public buildings were old residential houses that had been renovated and public administration departments constantly changed their head offices, sometimes working in rented properties. Therefore, it is easy to understand why Portugal did not affirm its imperial rhetoric in Goa through architecture during the nineteenth century; this had been the role played by religious architecture in the sixteenth and seventeenth centuries (Faria 2010), in marked contrast to the *imperial vision* of architecture during the British Raj (Metcalf 2002 (1989); 1995).

This provides a challenge for comparison geared to comparing 'like with like', as is the usual case in architectural history. The logic of comparing similar elements, such as building types, fails in this case. Moreover, it is a challenge that relates not only to architectural history, but also to general theories of comparison that insist on comparing like with like.

From this perspective, I thus concluded that the architecture of Portuguese and British India in the nineteenth century could not be compared, meaning that any systematic comparison of buildings of the same type (such as churches or train stations) was unfeasible. One of the main reasons was the difference between the administrative systems. Public buildings are erected by an institution (the state) to represent it, and at the same time provide public services (functions). Representing the state is an intrinsic part of the function of a public building and the relations between architecture and the state are entangled, therefore they cannot be ignored (Hise 2008). However, town halls, for example, did not have the same function in both systems, even if they shared the same name. Consequently, even public buildings from Portuguese and British India that shared the same name were not of the same type, since they did not fulfil the same functions (see for example, Figs 3.3 and 3.4).

Consequently, I decided not to carry out a systematic or explicit comparison, since I thought that in this case neither form nor function would establish common ground for comparison. On reflection, however, I came to realise that comparison was always present in my work, which probably explains why I returned to it.

Since the mid-twentieth century, architectural history – including, as we have seen, the work of Giedion, Venturi, and Kostof, among others – has examined

FIG. 3.3 General Post Office, Calcutta, designed by W. Granville, 1864–1868[24]

FIG. 3.4 Central Post Office, Panjim, Goa, designed by PWD, 1893[25]

architecture in more diverse ways, moving closer to many other fields in the social sciences such as sociology, anthropology, and cultural studies. A shared conclusion emerging from the recent literature in a number of these fields is that there exists a fundamental 'capacity to compare everything with everything else' (Jensen et al. 2011:5). This includes comparing with a specific purpose and establishing relationships between the entities being compared.

If the relations between architecture and state are so relevant to the production of architecture (or vice versa), where they may hinder comparison in a similar architectural context (e.g. architecture used to affirm and establish colonial power), it should be possible to compare different 'architectures of power'. However, if Portugal and Great Britain were in different phases of their colonial cycles in the nineteenth century, the timeline (i.e. the chronological history) would have to be realigned or synchronised in order to do so.

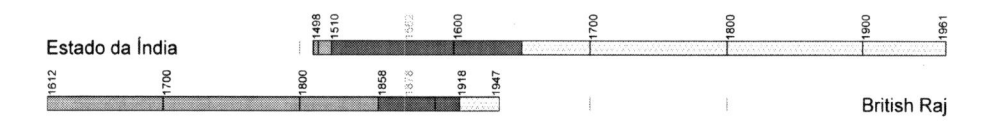

FIG. 3.5 Synchronised Timeline (establishment period shown in darker grey)

For this case study, this meant synchronising the periods when the relationship between architecture and power did not constrain comparison, namely the period in which they had achieved a state of establishment (see Fig. 3.5). This was a time when the architecture of both states was produced with a specific goal: to convey a message of supremacy and display imperial power. As seen at the beginning of the second part of this chapter, in terms of the Portuguese empire in India, this period would extend from the early sixteenth century to the second half of the seventeenth century, whereas for the British Raj it would be the period between 1857 and 1918. As previously argued, in practice this meant comparing the cathedral in the city of Old Goa (started in 1562) – the home of all Catholics in the Orient – and the Victoria Terminus (started in 1878) in Bombay. Both buildings date from the period when the respective empires were well-established, and as constructed forms were representative of the two mainstays of the colonial power that built them: religion and technology. Therefore, they were the two perfect case studies to use to compare the empires.

I am not certain when it was first said that railway stations were the cathedrals of the nineteenth century, but as Meeks shows (quoting the nineteenth-century *Building News and Engineering* journal), this idea recurs throughout the second half of that period. The text specifically states (noting that cathedrals were the model for the construction of railway stations): 'Railway termini and hotels are to the nineteenth century what monasteries and cathedrals were to the thirteenth century' (2012 (1956: 90). Gothic cathedrals, in particular, were a reference for railway stations since they were seen as an example of technological expertise. This shows how people at the time thought about these buildings and what was expected of them. It was not a matter of cathedrals and railway stations having different functions, but of them having the same significance and importance.

(STATE) POWER + (STATE) ARCHITECTURE: AN ASSEMBLER OF RELATIONS

In the third part of this chapter, I intend to re-examine the stages in the actual comparison of the cathedral in the old city of Goa and the Victoria Terminus in Bombay (Mumbai) in British India. I will show that even though there are some constraints, there are nevertheless a variety of contexts within which these buildings can be related. What kind of relationships based on similarities emerged from the actual comparison?

The relationship between (state) power and (state) architecture is the central subject of my work; it is my assembler of relations, or comparator. In this regard, I follow Deville, Guggenheim, and Hrdličková, around which a number of possible frameworks have been assembled (this volume). Each of these contexts is a unique component of the assembling device, and in addition, each context has its own specificities.

Both similarities and differences can emerge through comparison. Some similarities have already been presented, as they were the starting point of this

FIG. 3.6 Cathedral, Old Goa (sixteenth century)[26]

FIG. 3.7 Victoria Terminus, Bombay (nineteenth century)[27]

work. The objects are both buildings – architectonic bodies – and they were both designed with the aim of becoming central features of the empires that built them. There were, of course, also differences. When I began my research, differences immediately emerged within the historiographical context. There were no problems in ascertaining the main facts relating to the Victoria Terminus (i.e. the author, the date when it was built, etc.), whereas in the case of the Goa Cathedral, the three main authorities on the subject – Rafael Moreira (1995), António Nunes Pereira (2005, 2010), and Paulo Varela Gomes (2011) – do not always agree on the facts. I decided to follow Varela Gomes, the most recent author (although my own concern was not with a detailed discussion of the historical facts which are argued and reasoned by him (2011:54–65)).

Since the main aim of this comparison was to identify relations of similarity between the Goa Cathedral and the Victoria Terminus, the focus was on the similarities found, and on analysing them individually to show how they all highlight the interactions between architecture and imperial power.

Urban location

The cathedral is located in a central urban area of Goa which already existed when the Portuguese arrived. Although, to the best of my knowledge, it is not possible to ascertain what stood in this location in 1562, there is a strong possibility that it was the site of an existing temple.[28] Nevertheless, the location (which is near the Inquisition headquarters established in Goa in 1560) was a reminder of the presence of the new powers in the city – as Nunes Pereira notes (2010: 246). The Victoria Terminus was built in a central area of the city of Bombay, in the exact location of a former Portuguese church built in 1570 that had been already relocated to a different part of the city.

The location of the buildings within the urban systems, therefore, shows that both constructions were planned in existing central sites in the cities. There is also a strong probability that both buildings replaced existing constructions symbolic of former powers, thus displaying the presence of the new imperial authorities.

Authorship

The royal order to build a new cathedral arrived in Goa in 1562, and the construction work began in the same year. The King's architects probably designed the plan in Lisbon (as in the case of the other cathedrals), with an architect based in Goa adapting the plan locally. Rafael Moreira proposed the hypothesis that Inofre de Carvalho, a Portuguese architect living in Goa from 1551–1568, was the author of the cathedral. However, in Gomes's account, the building of the cathedral was suspended from the 1570s to the end of the 1590s because of the economic, political, and military crisis in *Estado da India*. The situation only changed in 1597 with the arrival of D. Francisco da Gama, when work recommenced (albeit subject to economic restrictions). With him travelled Julio Simão, the chief engineer to *Estado da India*, who was to replace the Italian architect who had previously held the position.[29] In Gomes's opinion, Simão designed everything in the cathedral except the plan, and was Flemish, German, or English, with Italian training. Moreover, at the time of his death, Simão was considered the author of the building, as this is inscribed on his headstone and can be found inside the cathedral.

The Victoria Terminus was designed by the British architect Frederick William Stevens in 1878, and opened in 1887 to celebrate Queen Victoria's Golden Jubilee. Born in Bath, England, in 1848, Stevens became an engineer in the Indian Public Works Department in 1867, after five years of work in England. After working in Poona for a year, he was transferred to Bombay. Following the success of the Victoria Terminus building, he set up his own practice in Bombay, where he died in 1900. Stevens's reputation as the author of several buildings in the 'Bombay Gothic' style (or Indo-Saracenic, as some authors describe it) was already established when he was commissioned to design the Victoria Terminus, described as the largest and most extensive architectural work in India at the time.

Although there are many uncertainties surrounding the origins and life of Simão, it is safe to assume that both men had similar profiles. They were European architects from the metropolis who, by the time they were commissioned to design the buildings, were employed in the public works department of the imperial state. In addition, both were established experts with a knowledge of the place where they were going to work.

Ornament

According to Gomes, Simão was responsible for 'everything having to do with the architectural articulation in the cathedral, every order, every moulding, every ornament' (2011: 58). In his opinion, all the works attributed to Simão were different from anything built in Portugal at the time. Pereira goes even further, underlining, on the one hand, the plan's similarity to that of the Cathedral of Portalegre in Portugal, and, on the other, the uniqueness of the ornament, stressing that it represents the 'Goan synthesis of European influences' (2010: 246).

Philip Davies, in *Splendours of Raj*, does an excellent job describing the Victoria Terminus:

> It is a highly original work albeit one rooted firmly in the tradition of Ruskin, Scott and Burges [...] It is the supreme example of tropical gothic architecture. With only a subtle hint of Saracenic motifs; a riotous extravaganza of polychromatic stone, marble and stained glass (1987: 172).

Even if Davies considers that the ornament and skyline 'invoke comparison' with St. Pancras Station in London, he explains that most of the ornament 'was designed by the Bombay School of Art with Stevens, who conceded that it was quite the equal of anything to be found in Europe' (1985: 172–178, 257).

Comparison of the ornament in the two buildings reveals an unusual (exotic) style in both, more evident in the decoration than in the general forms. It was an ornament of a kind never before seen in the metropolis, even though it had strong links with what was being produced in Europe, reflecting a synthesis or fusion that, in both cases, aimed to display a knowledge of local traditions on the part of the colonial powers. Since knowledge was power, displaying this ornament was therefore a display of power (Metcalf 2002: 5, 24–54).

Significant similarities thus emerged through the Goa Cathedral and Victoria Terminus comparator: European architects, each working for an imperial state but established in India for a considerable time, designed both buildings. In both cases, they were built at times when expectations for the empire were high, and both buildings were intended to be key imperial symbols. They were built in central urban locations previously occupied by the powers that these empires replaced, and both featured ornaments that were unusual for Europe.

CONCLUSION: ON THE ADVANTAGES OF CROSS COMPARISON

The aim of this chapter was to consider the practice of comparison within the disciplinary context of architectural history. Key examples were used to demonstrate that comparison is an enduring practice in the field. Although used extensively as a methodical tool, there is no serious reflection on its practices, resulting in a rather limited exercise instead of a unique 'event' that must be thought through (Stengers 2011: 49–50).

Attempting to compare things that were, to me, *uncomparable*, made me reason through a series of topics that constantly appeared, ranging from issues concerning type, time, style, historiographical and historical aspects, to aspects of architecture, architecture, and art history, the history of empires as academic disciplines, and the importance of design as a research tool. Thinking and reasoning through all these aspects made me see the importance of 'comparativism as a method of learning' (Stengers 2011: 62) rather than just as a tool.

Architectural historians are judging comparability too fast and without questions, mostly because comparison is being done between like with like. In this process, comparison and architecture are not looked at using their full potential. Still, it is not always considered with the same weight of importance when thinking comparatively. Architectural historians should free themselves from constraints imposed by disciplinary fields. Is it really not worthy to compare the Parthenon in Athens with Chartres Cathedral in France (Kostof 2003: 36)? 'Why not?' should be the first thing one ought to ask.

Comparisons across time, across empires, and across building types reveal that the relationship between architecture and the state (state power) is stable and that there are constant indicators of these relations: authorship, a central location in urban space, purpose (function), and unusual locally inspired ornaments. These are all comparable contexts that confirm common aspects of the relationship between architecture and state power during the establishment periods of Portuguese and British empires, also confirming that the Goa Cathedral and the Victoria Terminus had common ascribed meanings. This helps us to better understand not only the buildings themselves, but also the people that built them, and attests to the advantages of cross comparison in understanding the important role of architecture in the history of empires. Furthermore, the conclusions confirm that results can be obtained by thinking about comparability and uncomparability in a more creative way.

Cross comparison, in any area of study, means comparing things that are not identical and thus are not immediately identifiable as comparable using a traditional approach. Comparing comparative practices across disciplines (as described in this volume) helps us to understand similarities and differences and can open up new perspectives on the way in which we engage in research. Comparing in these terms amounts to much more than a tool; it is a process through which we understand our research subjects better, whatever they may be. And so, for me, comparison will never be simple again.

ACKNOWLEDGEMENTS

This research is supported by a postdoctoral fellowship on the project 'Building the Portuguese Empire in the 19th century'. Public Works across the Indian Ocean and the China Sea (1869–1926) (SFRH/BPD/76090/2011) financed by Fundação para a Ciência e a Tecnologia (FCT) through national funds from Ministério da Educação e Ciência.

NOTES

1 I would like to thank the late Paulo Varela Gomes for his comments and conversations on this theme.

2 I follow the views of Benevolo and Middleton concerning the French rationalist tradition (Benevolo 1999: 54–64; Middleton and Watkin 2003: 7–34).

3 *Précis des leçons d'architecture données à l'École polytechnique.*

4 *Recueil et Parallèle Des Édifices de Tout Genre Anciens et Modernes, Remarquables Par Leur Beauté, Par Leur Grandeur, Ou Par Leur Singularité, et Dessinés Sur Une Même Échelle,* published in 1799–1800.

5 Johann Bernhard Fischer von Erlach (1656–1723), an Austrian architect, sculptor, and historian of architecture.

6 *Entwurf einer historischen Architectur,* dated 1721 but only published in 1725.

7 Julien-David Leroy (1724–1803) was a French architect, professor of architecture at the French *Académie* (until it closed in 1793), and later at the *École Spéciale d' Árchitecture,* and the *Institut de France.*

8 *Ruines des lus beaux monument de la Gréce* [*The Ruins of the Most Beautiful Monuments of Greece*] was from an edition dating from 1770 (the text was first published in 1758).

9 Durand, Jean-Nicolas-Louis; Legrand, Jacques Guillaume, *Recueil et parallèle des édifices de tout genre anciens et modernes, remarquables par leur beauté, par leurgrand eur, ou par leur singularité, et dessinés sur une même échelle,* Paris, 1801, Plate: 21, Sign: C4892 GRO RES, Heidelberg University Library.

10 '[J]'ai trouvé que le plus sûr était de rapprocher, pour en faire la comparaison [...] principalement si je rapprochais, comme je l'ai fait, les uns des autres les Monumens d'une *même espèce,* en les dessinant sur une *même échelle.* Qu'ainsi, la comparaison en deviendrait bien plus facile, beaucoup plus prompte, et serait d'une bien plus grande utilité' (Durand 1799: 1–4, Letter to J.G. Legrand, emphasis added). It is arguable whether one should translate 'parallèle' as parallel or comparison, as there are differences and similarities between the two words. Nevertheless, in this context I think Durand uses the words synonymously.

11 I use the word 'type' and 'building type' in the same sense as Pevsner (1997 (1976)). 'Type' relates to form (materials, styles, organisation, etc.) and function. However, this use is not at all consensual. On the concept of type and typology in architecture, see Markus 1993; Madrazo 1995; Teyssot 2003.

12 Caravanserais or canvansarais were structures on the main trade routes where travellers could rest and replenish their supplies. They existed mainly in Persia, but they could also be found along the main trade routes between south-east Europe and Asia.

13 Banister Fletcher (1833–1899) and Sir Banister F. Fletcher (1866–1953), father and son, were both historians of architecture.

14 Usually known as 'La Rotonda'.

15 Heinrich Wölfflin (1864–1945) was born in Switzerland and was a very influential

art historian with a sound reputation in his time. He was a teacher at the University of Berlin and the University of Zürich, and had several famous students of art history and architectural history.

16 The examples and different approaches are many, and I will just mention a few. It is still Pevner's *History of Building Types* that somehow resumes Durand's 'survey of types' (Pevsner 1997 (1976): 6–7). Two decades later, Thomas Markus's *Buildings & Power* (1993) was among the best examples of a new typological approach to architecture. Comparison is not present in these works as an explicit method. Looking at specific types of building, Anthony King's *The Bungalow* (1985) studies the social production of the buildings and uses comparison in that context. Spiro Kostof (1985), and more recently Ching, Jarzombek, and Prakash (2006) are examples of attempts to do a global history of architecture in very different ways. Both books use visual and textual comparisons.

17 George Kubler's *The Shape of Time* was also significant for art history. For Kubler, the comparative method was also the essence of art history, although he mainly used metaphors for his comparisons – comparing works of art with examples from nature, mathematics, etc.

18 Sigfried Giedion (1888–1968) was a Swiss art historian and student of Heinrich Wölfflin in Munich. He taught in Zurich, Switzerland, and at Harvard in the US. His book *Space, Time and Architecture* is one of the most important books on the history of modern architecture, and is still used in architecture schools today, running to five editions. More recently, Claude Mignot has also argued for the importance of a continuous timeline in architectural history, as opposed to time cuts using 'centuries, kings, or styles' (2005:4).

19 The authors and publishers have made every effort to contact the copyright holders for permission to reprint the images shown here. Any copyright holders should contact the publisher, who will endeavour to include appropriate acknowledgements and corrections in future editions of the book.

20 Spiro Kostof (1936–1991) was an architectural historian born in Turkey, but he moved to the US in 1957. He was a teacher in several universities in the US, including Yale, Berkeley, MIT, and Columbia.

21 A term used by Ching, Jarzombek, and Prakash (2011) to refer to comparison across time.

22 The idea of cycles appears in several global historiographies and also in the current historiography of Portugal, which divides Portuguese colonial history into three main periods: the first is the Oriental empire; the second is when the attention turned to Brazil; the third (African empire) was when attention was focused on Africa from the independence of Brazil up to 1975. For a general history of Portugal and the Portuguese empire in English, see, among others, Disney (2009). For a more comprehensive picture of the various stages of the Portuguese empire, see Bethencourt and Chaudhuri (1998); Serrão and Marques (1986–2006).

23 The bibliography on British India is vast; for an overview, see the classic work by Percival Spears and for more recent views, the *New Cambridge History of India*.

24 Photo by Alice Santiago Faria, 2005. No rights reserved.
25 Photo by Alice Santiago Faria, 2005. No rights reserved.
26 Photo by Alice Santiago Faria, 2005. No rights reserved.
27 *Victoria Terminus, G.I.P. Railway.* Approximately 1905. Special Collections, University of Houston Libraries, University of Houston Digital Library, July 20, 2014 <http://digital.lib.uh.edu/collection/p15195coll29/item/21>
28 There are several references in the historiography of the Portuguese in India to the construction of churches on sites where temples had previously stood. Among others, see the various entries on Goan churches in the volume by José Mattoso and Walter Rossa (2011) and C. Boshi (1998: 429–455).
29 This may not have been the first time he had worked in India, where he lived until he died.

BIBLIOGRAPHY

Nalbantoğlu, G. B., 'Toward Postcolonial Openings: Rereading Sir Banister Fletcher's "History of Architecture"', *Assemblage*, 35 (1998), 7–17 <http://www.jstor.org/stable/3171235> [accessed 3 August 2012]

Bayly, C. A., *The Birth of the Modern World, 1780–1914: Global Connections and Comparisons* (Malden, MA: Blackwell Publishing, 2004)

Benevolo, L., *Historia de la Arquitectura Moderna*, 8th edn rev (Barcelona: Editorial Gustavo Gili, 1999)

Bethencourt, F., and K. Chaudhuri, eds., *História Da Expansão Portuguesa*, 5 vols (Lisbon: Circulo de Leitores, 1999)

Boshi, C., 'Estruturas eclesiásticas e Inquisição', in F. Bethencourt, and K. Chaudhuri, ed., *História Da Expansão Portuguesa, vol. 2* (Lisbon: Circulo de Leitores, 1998), pp. 429–455

Çelik, Z., 'Editor's Concluding Notes', *Journal of the Society of Architectural Historians*, 62 (2003), 121–24 <http://www.jstor.org/stable/3655089> [accessed 3 August 2012]

Ching, F. D. K., M. M. Jarzombek, and V. Prakash, *A Global History of Architecture* (Hoboken: Wiley, 2011)

Davies, P., *Splendours of the Raj: British Architecture in India, 1660–1947* (London: J. Murray, 1985)

Deville, J., M. Guggenheim, and Z. Hrdličková, 'Same, Same but Different: Provoking Relations, Assembling the Comparator', this volume

Disney, A. R., *A History of Portugal and the Portuguese Empire. From Beginnings to 1807*, 2 vols (Cambridge: Cambridge University Press, 2009)

Durand, J. N. L., *Recueil et Parallèle des Édifices de tout Genre Anciens et Modernes Remarquables par leur Beauté [...] avec un Texte Extrait de l'histoire Générale de l'architecture, par J.-G. Legrand* (Paris: impr. de Gillé fils, 1799) <http://gallica.bnf.fr/ark:/12148/bpt6k85721q> [accessed 11 August 2012]

—— *Précis des Leçons d'Architecture Données à l'École Polytechnique* (Paris: Chez l'Auteur, 1802) <http://archive.org/details/prcisdesleon01dura> [accessed 11 August 2012]

—— *Recueil et Parallèle Des Édifices de Tout Genre Anciens et Modernes, Remarquables Par Leur Beauté, Par Leur Grandeur, Ou Par Leur Singularité, et Dessinés Sur Une Même Échelle* (Paris: 1800/1801) <http://digi.ub.uni-heidelberg.de/diglit/durand1802> [accessed 11 August 2012]

Faria, A. S., 'L'Architecture Coloniale Portugaise À Goa: Le Département Des Travaux Publics, 1840–1926', PhD Thesis, Doctorat de Université, Université Paris I, 2010

—— 'O Papel Dos Luso-Descendentes na Engenharia Militar e nas Obras Publicas em Goa no Longo Século XIX', in A. Teodoro de Matos, and J. Teles e Cunha, eds., *Goa: Passado e Presente* (Lisbon: CEPCEP e CHAM, 2012)

Fox, R. G., and A. Gingrich, *Anthropology, by Comparison* (London and New York: Routledge, 2002)

Giedion, S., *Espacio, Tiempo y Arquitectura: el Futuro de una Nueva Tradición*, 2nd edn (Madrid: Editorial Científico-Medica, 1968)

Gomes, P. V., *Whitewash, Red Stone. A History of Church Architecture in Goa* (New Delhi: Yoda Press, 2011)

Hise, G., 'Architecture as State Building: A Challenge to the Field', *Journal of the Society of Architectural Historians*, 67 (2008), 173–77 <http://www.jstor.org/stable/10.1525/jsah.2008.67.2.173> [accessed 17 January 2012]

Hitchcock, H. R., *Architecture: Nineteenth and Twentieth Centuries* (New Haven, CT: Yale University Press, 1987)

Hitchcock, H. R., and P. Johnson, *The International Style Architecture since 1922* (New York: W. W. Norton, 1995)

Jarzombek, M., 'The Disciplinary Dislocations of (Architectural) History', *Journal of the Society of Architectural Historians*, 58 (1999), 488–93 <http://www.jstor.org/stable/991543> [accessed 17 January 2012]

Jensen, C. B., et al., 'Introduction: Contexts for a Comparative Relativism', *Common Knowledge*, 17 (2001), 1–12 <http://commonknowledge.dukejournals.org/content/17/1/71> [accessed 3 August 2012]

Jones, D., 'Architecture as a Discipline of the Humanities', *JAE*, 34 (1981), 18–23 < http://www.jstor.org/stable/1424661> [accessed 14 June 2013]

Kaufmann, E., *De Ledoux a Le Corbusier: origen y desarrollo de la arquitectura autónoma* (Barcelona: Gustavo Gili, 1985)

Kostof, S., *Historia de La Arquitectura*, 3 vols (Madrid: Alianza Forma, 2003)

Kultermann, U., *Historia de la Historia del arte. El camino de una ciencia* (Madrid: Ediciones AKAL, 1996)

Leach, A., *What is Architectural History?* (Cambridge: Polity Press, 2010)

Leroy, J. D., *Les Ruines des plus beaux monuments de La Grèce considérées du côté de L'histoire et du côté de L'architecture*. Seconde édition corrigée et augmentée, Paris, 1770 <http://www.purl.org/yoolib/inha/6651> [accessed 11 August 2012]

Madrazo, L., 'Durand and the Science of Architecture', *Journal of Architectural Education*, 48 (1994), 12–24 < http://www.jstor.org/stable/1425306> [accessed 3 August 2012]

——'The Concept of Type in Architecture: An Inquiry into the Nature of Architectural Form', PhD Thesis, Swiss Federal Institute of Technology (Eidgenössiche Technische Hochschule, Zürich) ETH, 1995 <http://dx.doi.org/10.3929/ethz-a-001503629> [accessed 24 August 2012]

Markus, T. A, *Buildings & Power: Freedom and Control in the Origin of Modern Building Types* (London and New York: Routledge, 1993)

Mattoso, J., and W. Rossa, eds., *Asia, Oceania. Portuguese Heritage around the World: Architecture and Urbanism*, vols III, IV (Lisbon: C. Gulbenkian Foundation, 2011)

McKean, J., 'Sir Banister Fletcher: Pillar to Post-colonial Readings', *The Journal of Architecture*, 11 (2006), 187–204

Meeks, C. L.V., *The Railroad Station: An Architectural History* (New York: Dover Publications, 2012)

Metcalf, T. R., *Ideologies of the Raj* (Cambridge and New York: Cambridge University Press, 1995)

——*An Imperial Vision: Indian Architecture and Britain's Raj* (New Delhi: Oxford India Paperbacks, 2002)

Middleton, R., and D. Watkin, *Architecture of the Nineteenth Century* (Milan, London and New York: Electa Architecture, 2003)

Mignot, C., 'Le Temps n'a pas de frontières: le cas de l'histoire de l'architecture (1570–1670)' in *Collections électroniques de l'INHA. Actes de colloques et livres en ligne de l'Institut national d'histoire de l'art* (Paris: INHA, 2005) <http://inha.revues.org/655> [accessed 15 October 2009]

Moreira, R., 'From Manueline to Renaissance in Portuguese India', *Mare Liberum*, 9 (1995), 401–7

Morris, J., and S. Winchester, *Stones of the Empire* (Oxford and New York: Oxford University Press, 2005)

Oechslin, W., 'Premises for the Resumption of the Discussion of Typology', *Assemblage*, 1 (2006), 37–53 <http://www.jstor.org/stable/3171053> [accessed 3 August 2012]

Payne, A. A., 'Architectural History and the History of Art: A Suspended Dialogue', *Journal of the Society of Architectural Historians*, 58 (1999), 292–99 <http://www.jstor.org/stable/991521 > [accessed 3 August 2012]

Pereira, A. N., *A Arquitectura Religiosa Cristã de Velha Goa: Segunda Metade do Século XVI Décadas do Século XVII, Orientalia*, 10 (Lisbon: Fundação Oriente, 2005)

——'Sé Metropolitana de Goa e Damão' in J. Mattoso, and W. Rossa, eds., *Asia, Oceania. Portuguese Heritage around the World: Architecture and Urbanism*, vol III (Lisbon: C. Gulbenkian Fundation, 2011), pp. 244–246

Pevsner, N., *A History of Building Types*, 5th edn (New Jersey and London: Princeton

University Press, 1997)

Serrão, J., and A. H. de Oliveira Marques, eds., *Nova História Da Expansão Portuguesa*, vols xi (Lisbon: Editorial Estampa)

Stengers, I., 'Comparison as a Matter of Concern', *Common Knowledge*, 17 (2011), 48–63 < http://commonknowledge.dukejournals.org/content/17/1/48> [accessed 12 June 2013]

Teyssot, G., 'Norm and Type. Variations on the Theme', in A. Picon, and A. Ponte, eds., *Architecture and the Sciences. Exchanging Metaphors, Princeton Papers on Architecture* (New York: Princeton Architectural Press, 2003), pp. 141–73

Tournikiotis, P., *The Historiography of Modern Architecture* (Cambridge, MA: MIT Press, 1999)

Venturi, R., S. Izenour, and D. Scott Brown, *Aprendiendo de Las Viegas. El Simbolismo Olvidado de La Forma Arquitectónica. GG Reprints* (Barcelona: Editorial Gustavo Gili, 2000)

von Erlach, F. J. B., *Entwurff einer historischen Architectur.* (Leipzig: [s.n.], 1725) <http://archive.org/details/Entwurffeinerhi00Fisc> [accessed 18 August 2012]

Wölfflin, H., *Principles of Art History: The Problem of the Development of Style in Later Art* (New York: Dover, 1950) <http://archive.org/details/princarth00wlff> [accessed 19 August 2012]

SECTION TWO

COLLABORATIONS

4

SAME, SAME BUT DIFFERENT: PROVOKING RELATIONS, ASSEMBLING THE COMPARATOR

Joe Deville, Michael Guggenheim, Zuzana Hrdličková

INTRODUCTION: WHAT IS A COMPARATOR?

OUR EXPERIENCE OF WORKING ON A COMPARATIVE PROJECT ENTITLED 'Organising Disaster: Civil Protection and the Population', whilst trying to find the 'same, same but different',[1] has directed our attention to the practicalities of undertaking social scientific forms of comparison, as well as to some of the ethical and political questions that arise from its use.[2]

Much has been written about the latter question: as we detail in the book's Introduction and touch on again below, comparison has been critiqued within social science from a variety of quarters. These concerns range from the unwarranted reduction of complex social and cultural phenomena by researchers through the imposition of comparative practice, comparison's complicity with sometimes dubious political and methodological projects (e.g. European colonialism, strident methodological positivism, the creep of market-oriented ranking practices), and even the meaninglessness of invoking comparison as a distinct practice, given its apparent ubiquity in other settings.

What has received far less attention are the ways in which comparisons of all sorts come into being through an entity that we call the 'comparator'. We respond to this absence by asking and answering two questions: 'Who, or rather, what, is the comparator? And, how does the comparator affect a researcher's relationship with the objects being compared?'

Conventionally, the term 'comparator' is understood as a standard against which an object is compared. The comparator (in this sense of the word) is therefore a static benchmark – and it is the quality of being both *fixed and known* that allows the act of comparison to take place. However, there is also a type of microchip called the comparator that is more active and interventionist – it sits in electronic circuits and measures incoming voltages from different sources, switching on or off as a result of its act of *doing* comparisons between fixed and variable voltages (Fig. 4.1).[3] The comparator, in our appropriation of the word for social science, is therefore an assemblage that undertakes comparative *work*. As occurs with the comparator chip, social scientific comparison has to be assembled from diverse entities according to specific forms of knowledge and expertise. In order to produce the comparative output, these assembled parts have to actively intervene and provoke relations between previously

FIG. 4.1 A comparator chip[5]

uncompared inputs.[4] For obvious reasons, the comparator in social science is vastly more complex and heterogeneous than the comparator chip. As we will show, it is not a single thing, but an assemblage of researchers, funders, and research technologies – including entities such as databases and software, legal regulations and theories, and methods. When it is put to work, the comparator creates comparison(s) by shaping and being shaped by the world around it.

The creative figure of the comparator is largely absent from literature focused on comparison as a specifically qualitative social scientific practice. In recent discussions, its place is taken by much debate about the epistemological problems associated with comparison. It has therefore been observed that although comparisons have fallen out of favour, doing social research is always comparative (if only in implicit ways), and should be reconsidered (Gingrich and Fox 2002). The revived interest has led to renewed discussions of a number of old questions: Is it legitimate to compare this with that, or what is the *tertium comparationis* – the quality that the things being compared have in common (Steinmetz 2004; Wagner 2011)? What are the issues associated with the apparent undertaking of comparison and the construction of binary oppositions (Strathern 2011a)? What are the specific assumptions about relationality that inform Western ideas about comparison as contrasted to those from other areas of the world (Battaglia 2011; Candea 2011; de Castro 2011; Strathern 2011a; Strathern 2011b)? How might comparison, with its universalist historical baggage, be squared with contrasting approaches that have in some quarters been accused of relativism (see the various discussions in the special issue on comparative relativism, in particular Lloyd 2011; Holbraad 2011; Jensen 2011; Smith 2011)?

Meanwhile, in what is sometimes referred to as 'comparative urbanism', a number of authors have stressed that comparison would benefit if it became more adventurous and attentive to relational complexity. This might be achieved by moving away from the orthodox comparison of only large cities or nation-states, or towards understanding the rich variety of more complex relations and relationality informing a given urban setting (Cook and Ward 2012; Gough 2012; Jacobs 2012; McFarlane and Robinson 2012; Robinson 2011; Ward 2010). And, in a recent collection that aims to 'thicken comparison' (Scheffer and Niewöhner 2010), a range of authors discuss the difficulties of doing comparison, while frequently noting comparison's creative, transformative, and potentially pedagogical effects. However, by and large, the method shows the analytical productivity of making different, unusual, or richer comparisons, rather than exploring the situated assembly of the comparative social scientific act itself.

Comparison has also been subject to analysis by a number of writers working with concepts and methods drawn from Science and Technology Studies (STS). This has shown clearly the way in which comparison is inevitably a constructive, creative act, a dynamic bringing together of entities that are otherwise potentially either unrelated, or related in some other way. This is what Helen Verran (2011) and Isabelle Stengers (2011) variously refer to as 'comparison as participant'. However, despite being so good at looking at the methods and procedures of others, STS has often tended to be rather silent when it comes to its own practices and politics (see Haraway 1997). Thus, the empirical focus has tended to remain on the comparisons done by others, whether by scientists (Stengers 2011), medical practitioners (Mol 2002), or indeed non-human entities as diverse as pigs, neutrinos, and tornadoes (Brown 2011). Again, the figure of the social scientific comparator tends to remain invisible and undeclared. This is despite the fact that STS (along with much feminist research) has shown that ostensibly detached applications of logic can be deeply implicated in a range of unarticulated interests and influences. It is thus crucial to study the specific assembly of the comparative act as it involves the building of what Annemarie Mol (2002) calls the 'platforms of comparison'. Looking at medical practitioners, Mol draws attention to the specific situation that produces the comparison (*where* the comparison is made) and the consequences of putting these entities into relation. We are keen to extend this empirical problematisation of comparison to social science itself. For if comparisons are indeed omnipresent and inevitable (an inevitable 'matter of fact', as Stengers (2011) puts it), then what are the specific procedures, (human/non-human) situations, and effects that produce social scientific comparisons?

We aim to show, first, that achieving comparison is a complex process in which a comparator has to be actively assembled. In our case, this comparator is a group of people mediated by a number of research technologies. Second, we show that this comparator is shaped by (and shapes) the research object in a continual process. Finally, we explore the potential of an approach that explicitly seeks to *provoke* comparison – in which developments within our research result precisely from the specific way in which our comparator has been assembled.

We present comparison as we have experienced doing it, seeking it, and observing it, mainly within the first half of our four-year research project. This is a story of how the creation of a ten-page proposal became a research project with a life of its own, shaped by diverse personalities, experiences, knowledges, and technologies, as well as our research objects themselves. In doing so, we recognise that there is a fine line between navel-gazing and the constructive sharing of one's own experiences. We hope our paper achieves the latter.

THE PROJECT COMPARATOR

In our project, titled 'Organising Disaster', we are interested in exploring the ways in which disaster preparedness is produced. We analyse civil protection as a specific form of ordering society, involving modes of knowledge, technologies, and organisations intended to deal with disaster. We follow an assembly of organisations and organising technologies, and examine how they produce particular ways of preparing for disaster, and how this, in turn, has effects on the way that society is composed. To do so, we look at three national cases: India, Switzerland, and the United Kingdom.[6] From the very outset, the project has been explicitly comparative, with each team member taking responsibility for one of the three cases. The venture might thus appear to be conventionally comparative – another in the long line of research undertakings that has the nation-state as a unit for comparison. However, we are interested in the question of comparison precisely because we are uncomfortable with how it tends to be generally problematised. Our response in this paper is an '*eigen*-observation': we scrutinise our own organisational practices and modes in which our own knowledge is brought to, and shaped through, the objects we study.

The following observations give a sketch of the basic layout of one particular comparator. However, we maintain that any account of a comparator would need to cover a similar set of elements (see below). For this reason, our description can be taken as a first step towards understanding its generic features. A working comparator is always a complex assemblage, and never simply a tool, an operation, or a method.

In the first part of the paper, we describe the following elements of the process: the initial assembling of the comparator and its researcher constituent parts, the feeding of the comparator, and finally the calibrating of the comparator. Later, we show what happens when the comparator goes to work.

Assembling the Comparator

We, the comparator, consist of three human team members (Michael, Joe, and Zuzana) and a number of technologies. Michael, as the project lead, began building the comparator by writing a research proposal. The number of human actors was pre-defined by his proposal. Once he received the funding, adverts were placed, interviews conducted, and CVs assessed. And it is here that the project's initial process of assembling a comparator begins. Through this process of searching and weighing both imagined qualities and the potential fit into a team, there is a move from the fiction of a project as the outcome of a unified author towards the project as a contingent practice, dependent on the meshing and balancing of similarities and differences within a team. This selection procedure also highlights a strange imbalance in the comparisons at stake: the comparisons that emerge from the research project are founded on the comparison of academic CVs and first impressions in a carefully staged twenty-minute play called the 'job interview'. This process decides research routes taken and not taken. By bringing together these diverse individuals (Michael, in his decisions, and Zuzana and Joe in their accounts of themselves) who in our case were not previously known to each other, our comparator was born.

We can now go back to the proposal and read from it some crucial features of the particular comparator that were defined in it. The proposal suggests undertaking three case studies in three different countries. In other words, it sets up a three-way comparison that is in many ways unbalanced. By naming countries as the entities to be subject to comparison, the proposal, on the surface at least, resorts to a tried and trusted method of comparing at the level of the nation-state. However, already in the proposal it becomes clear that the nation-state is a placeholder for a multiplicity of organisations, practices, and places. This becomes even more obvious when we actually work on the project. As the project does not merely compare (national) policies, but rather actual exercise practices, it lets each case study itself make a variety of selections within the mixture of differing national disaster management practices. It is a central aim of the project to compare countries with very different frameworks: from India, with its highly professionalised approach, to Swiss civil protection, which is reliant on a draft system.

This uneasy form of comparison is not only a matter of our research object – disaster management – but it is also an outcome of Michael's particular training and exposure to organisational sociology, STS, and European anthropology. Combining an ethnography of organisations with an analysis of discourses produces the problem of how to relate the local and parochial to a wider set of social influences. Doing this in three countries in parallel inevitably brings up a multiplicity of specific empirical levels that do not obviously link up with each other.

Further, the proposal makes a crucial connection: it assigns one person to each case country. It creates a comparator in which persons are aligned with a particular level of comparison (the nation-state). However, one could imagine the same project with different persons being responsible for different levels of analysis. By pre-deciding to match persons with places, a particular kind of comparator was already envisaged in which local specialisation would be conceived of as located in persons, thus following a traditional model – at least in anthropology – in which knowledge about places and cultures is assumed to be located in researchers' minds and bodies. However, from the start, decisions were made that had significant effects on the relationship between researcher and place. For Michael, he decided that, despite being Swiss, he would research the UK, and not Switzerland. It was his personal way of acquainting himself with the country to which he had emigrated. As it happened, the other two project members (in typical 'anthropological' fashion) would also not conduct research in their native countries. While Zuzana (a Czech anthropologist specialising in South Asia) has had experience with conducting research in India, for the British economic and STS sociologist Joe, Switzerland was quite unfamiliar. The comparator then is very much one that deals with distributing the sensory apparatus of researchers over the world, and brings it back together to exchange what was gathered.

Feeding the Comparator: Cohesion and Autonomy

Once the comparator is assembled, its life can assume different forms and the comparison it produces hinges on the comparator having a certain cohesion. This is an often overlooked feature of comparison. Comparing is a practice of bringing material together and putting it in conversation, and not simply an assembly of empirical data with different characteristics. Only a comparator – able to hold the three in view simultaneously in a practice of commensuration – may eventually produce comparison. Before bodies can go into the field, they first have to be made part of the comparator.

Some models for achieving this kind of cohesion include: research and writing procedures involving constant struggles over theoretical or disciplinary hegemony; a very loose assemblage of individual author-subjects, each with their own voice and research practices that exist next to one another; and a hierarchical model in which some parts of the comparator are 'research assistants' that do what the team leader tells them, and in which their primary function is to act as extensions of his or her author-subject. Each of these approaches obviously has its own advantages and disadvantages. Our approach has been a mixture of these. We have a broadly flat structure, but one that is characterised by hierarchical 'moments' when Michael assumes the role of final decision maker. One such decision was to specify three parallel research projects associated with three different places, which inevitably reduced the autonomy of the other two team members. 'Hierarchy', then, is not so much a matter of an organigram, but an outcome of the fact that one person wrote the research proposal, and that, in implementing the proposal, Michael also decided to stick (broadly) to his original plans.

Our approach also involves two modes of doing research. The first is an autonomous mode, one more familiar to social scientists: this is the pursuit of individual research interests in relation to a particular object. Here, insight stems from the individual's personal relationship to that object, in which they feel able to bring their own particular set of skills and interests to bear. Based on our own experiences, we are confident that this mode is a crucial precondition for an individual researcher's ability to engage with an object creatively (an extreme opposite case would be the over-determined research setting where a researcher slavishly does the bidding of another). But we also see this autonomous, individual mode as one way of *feeding* the comparator. We will provide more examples of this below. For now, it can be summarised as a process of pedagogical and creative development: we are continually trying to make this heterogeneous, but at least partially unified entity, better able to compare than it could previously: individual insights about one case have the potential to allow the comparator to both learn (i.e. to compare better than it could before) and grow (i.e. to extend its reach), and to be able to comparatively connect research entities that it was not able to connect before. However, in order to be able to do so, the comparator has to be trained through a second, less familiar mode of engagement: calibration.

Calibrating the Comparator

The artist John Stezaker splices together portraits of men and women to form what he calls 'marriages'. In a recent interview, Stezaker said:

> I am often asked why I don't just get two people, pose them for photographs and splice the shots more accurately, but that misses the point. It's the imperfect match, the failure of unity, that makes us identify with these beings (Phillips 2012).

The image below (Fig. 4.2) of our team – and Zotero – as comparator is an homage to Stezaker's 'marriages'. What holds for his images also holds for the

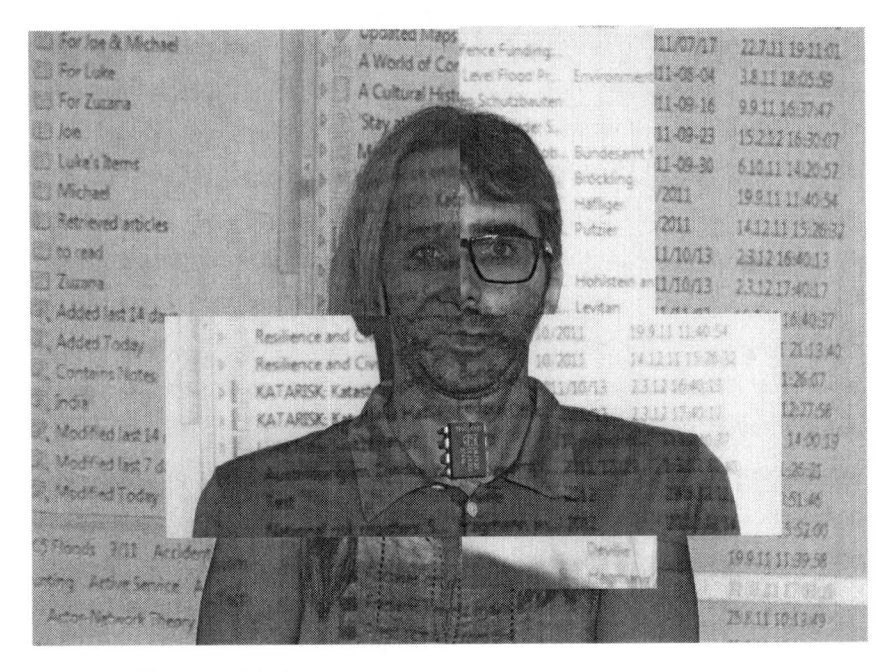

FIG. 4.2 The assembled comparator

comparator: it is the imperfect match *created by attempting unity* that creates a functioning comparator. Without the attempt at unity, there is no comparator. Further, and more importantly, even if a perfect match were possible, to strive after it would be to overlook the possibilities for creative tension generated by an imperfect unification.

Calibration is one way of deliberately moving towards this imperfect unity. It can be understood as an ongoing mutual adjustment – of each, to each other, as well as to our technologies, and our research objects. The first route we took was to calibrate some of our thinking through weekly reading seminars. This not only helped us read some of the more pertinent literature for our study, but it also helped to calibrate our ideas of what we are looking for and how we are thinking about what we are doing. Reading is in many ways a comparative practice which inevitably shapes how we see our cases, even if the topic is unrelated. It is very much the collective act of discussing the reading, in which pre-knowledge, or even guesswork about empirical material, is inserted and tested with regard to its comparative promise(s). The reading seminars also highlighted the very different ways in which we, the human parts of the comparator, are each influenced by our training and differently conceive of both ethnographic fieldwork and issues of comparison.

Another crucially important calibratory practice of ours is how we file what we have read. We process all our materials through another component of our comparator – Zotero, a piece of bibliographic software that makes referencing much simpler. Zotero is one part of the technological mix that feeds and calibrates our comparator (other crucial tools are shared qualitative data analysis tools (NVivo), shared online storage facilities, and communication tools that enable multi-way, remote communication – e.g. Skype conference calling). But more than its bibliographic function, it is Zotero's ability to become a shared database that is particularly powerful for us. All our notes, references, and PDFs of journal articles are automatically synchronised, with each team member having access to the materials that other team members have uploaded, read, excerpted, and annotated.

This process is a strange kind of putting what is normally 'private' and individually memorised into the hands of the research group. A researcher's unique trail of readings, similar to their engagement with ethnographic data, is usually assumed to be embodied. The conventionally conceived author-subject is in many ways understood as nothing else than a machine (albeit a nontrivial one) that rejigs past readings and combines these with 'ideas'. In its very design and promise, bibliographic software, as a recombination and sorting device, already implies a re-ordering of the author-subject (Krajewski 2012).[7] The resulting databases potentially become electronic filing cabinets with the (unacknowledged) status of a co-author. As Niklas Luhmann put it in his account of working with his own unique sorting system, 'The following is a piece of empirical social research. It is about me and another: my filing cabinet' (1981: 222).

However, using an ever-expanding bibliographic database as a group adds a further dimension to this aspect of research practice: texts appear, with little sense of the logic that accompanied their insertion. At its most practical, this means that some of the more mundane work of the comparator can be distributed across multiple parties: key relevant sections can be excerpted for others to use, and key facts and figures are highlighted. Further, since Zotero does not show (unless manually inserted)[8] who authored a note on a text, these notes could be written by any team member. Especially if some time has passed since the text was noted, this can generate a strange sense of self-misrecognition as the reader wonders: 'Did I write this?' Often, it is not possible to be sure, and thought processes and ideas start to blur. This is another step away from a unified author-subject and towards a distributed but cohesive comparator.

Moreover, Zotero itself materialises the comparator as a cohesive unity. As a unified entity, comparators need to perform processes of differentiation in order to make comparison possible. In a bibliographic database, any item or note could potentially be a unit of comparison with any other. The result is that, to keep comparison stable, the database ends up mirroring and reinforcing the project structure. In our own case, this happens in two-ways. First, as we created folders for primary and secondary source materials for each of the three countries being researched, Zotero reproduced the national case study structure. All references relating to India are in a folder titled 'India', and so forth. But, second, we also created folders for each person, and these were meant to contain any material deemed important by him/her. This dual structure then shows that, through its operations, the comparator, understood as dependent for its success on forms of communication between team members (and between team members and Zotero), produces a multiplicity of possible alignments: people come to be aligned with places and certain references, but this happens precisely because Zotero is in principle neutral and non-aligned. In practice, it is perfectly possible for Zuzana or Joe to check material contained in a folder called 'Michael'.

Further mutual calibration occurs in the writing process, although different types of writing generate different comparative modes. Collective papers explicitly provoke comparison, as the writing of this article has revealed to us. This text only partially reveals the numerous (sometimes difficult) processes of calibration we have undertaken as we have tried to adjust to the ambitions, ideas, and writing styles of others – with each category having the potential to be compared according to values which can be understood very differently between authors. This is one of the most explicit sites where negotiation emerges as an important calibratory tool. In our struggles for a coherent (but not unified) voice, as articulated through texts – as well as in our meetings and conversations – comparison becomes contingent on the success of ongoing processes of comparative negotiation.

Autonomous, individual papers can also quickly be pulled towards comparison. We decided from an early stage that any member of the team could use another's data as required. We have even written down this sharing principle as a kind of contract. The need for this arose from various issues we discussed at the start of the project related to the possibility of people leaving the project. On the face of it, this was not related to the comparator; however, it automatically contributed to the particular form that the comparator took. The agreement stipulated that in the case of a team member leaving, all of his or her materials would remain with the project, but they could also be used by the person who was departing. The remaining team could further use this material for publications, but that would make the leaving member an author on publications substantially based on these materials.

We have also each given conference presentations where one of us has used another's materials for their own comparative purposes. We have frequently found comparing our national cases helpful, often as an explanatory device. Of course, this implies a high degree of leniency on the part of the producers of the material. It also reveals to us (as well as sometimes to others) that the comparator is something assembled. The assumption in a conference is that what is said is backed by the embodied experience of the speaker. But our creative 'borrowings' from others are not 'citations': they do not draw on material produced and claimed by another author as settled facts. Instead, our new author – now an independent (socio-technically distributed) comparator in its own right – lays claim to 'data' without being able to fully qualify its use. This becomes most obvious when (during conference presentations) one is required to answer questions on the other, less familiar cases.

We aim to reach productive (im)balances through our comparisons, where, on the one hand, they hold the potential to make team members think, but, on the other, are neither so strange and different as to repel, or simply baffle. To be only able to draw on partially shared understandings of what it means to do what we do has the extremely challenging effect that, before and while we compare, we also compare our modes of working. When working as a team, comparison does not therefore automatically emerge, as it needs to be actively calibrated, with materials being constantly reframed through different theoretical and methodological lenses.

There is one further actor that plays a crucial role in changing the composition of the comparator, which we have so far only touched on briefly: our research objects themselves. What then happens when we take the comparator and its calibratory apparatus into the field and into dialogue with the people and things we encounter there?

A comparator is not only calibrated in relation to the persons that compose it, but also in relation to the settings and objects it attempts to compare. Much has been written about the way that comparison changes the outcomes of both qualitative and quantitative research. Less attention has been paid to the inverse relationship between the research object and comparison itself. In examining this, we follow three ways in which the comparator is shifted by the entities it encounters. The first concerns access – that is, how and when we were able to obtain entry to our respective field sites. In order to provide a sharp contrast, we will focus on just two of our three cases in this instance: Switzerland and India. These can be said to represent opposing poles in the varying trajectories of access we have observed over the course of our project. The second shift concerns those moments when a particular set of objects in one site shifts comparative attention in another. Here we begin to draw all three of our cases into dialogue. We continue in this vein to examine the third and final set of shifts. These are enacted not in relation to a particular set of objects, but in relation to practices – comparative practices, in fact. We examine what we can learn from the comparisons of others, as well as how we might compare these to our own social scientific comparisons.

Access Shifts the Comparator

As noted, most discussions of comparison conceive of it as if it were a smooth and transparent practice in which the comparator is in full control. This is equally true of those who critique comparison as being oppressive for forcing entities together. This overstates the power of social research and (particularly for ethnographic research) is often far from the case: the comparator is dependent on what is usually called access to the field. In our project, each researcher ideally needs to gain access to at least some parts of each country's civil protection organisation. Given the conception of the comparator we have outlined, we might rather call it not access, but 'the extension of the comparator to our interlocutors' (for reasons of practicality we do, however, use the former in what follows). These extensions are based on innumerable contingencies that in turn, shape the comparison. While in non-comparative research these simply change the course of the project, for a comparative project each contingency has repercussions for the whole comparator. Each field note in one site raises a potential question about the respective field note in the other site(s), and each movement of the research trajectory in one site adds tension to the overall direction of the comparator. To assume that the comparator has the power to force ethnographic sites into one comparative framework would ignore the fact that each negotiation with a field site has its own trajectory that can only partly be influenced by the needs of the comparator.

Of our three cases, Switzerland provided the quickest and smoothest journey of a researcher into the field. Joe heard a radio interview in which a key member of the governmental apparatus that coordinates Swiss civil protection was speaking about a major forthcoming exercise. A letter of introduction to the person was drafted and Joe received a reply two days later, informing him that the request had been forwarded to press relations. A week after that, another reply arrived from the head of press relations, informing him that after consultation with the head of the exercise, access had been granted. Two months later, he was in the field, observing one of the largest command and control exercises that had been staged in Switzerland in recent years. There, he was able to meet key players and develop contacts that would facilitate many additional fieldwork visits over the next year and a half, including to meetings surrounding a second major exercise. He was also eventually able to obtain schedules detailing when and where all the exercises involving central government would take place, allowing him to plan and coordinate his fieldwork accordingly.

Gaining access, then, was relatively straightforward. With the benefit of hindsight, we can reflect on how this part of the comparator benefitted from at least two broad sets of helpful circumstances. The first are the relationships between the background of the researcher, the framing of the project, and the history of Swiss civil protection. It was Joe's distinct impression that his position as an outsider helped smooth his access. Within Switzerland, there is some sensitivity about the role played by civil protection.[9] However, being a British researcher and thus ostensibly disconnected from these debates, as well as being able to frame the research as part of a wider European interest in civil protection (given the project was funded by the EU), may have helped allay fears that the research was being conducted with unstated political objectives. The second is the particular organisational culture that is a feature of Swiss civil protection. Chain of command is rigorously respected, perhaps even more so than in some other Swiss organisations, given that a significant number of its personnel continue to be involved in Switzerland's militia army.[10] There is also a pervading culture of organisational efficiency: people are almost never late for meetings; meetings themselves closely follow pre-planned agendas; emails rarely go unanswered; events are organised in good time and often months in advance – even years, in the case of large exercises; the relevant IT infrastructure allows shared access to key documents; emergency organisational action plans are rigorously worked over and scrutinised; and so on and so forth. For the Swiss field site, numerous materials existed and were readily available, and access to it was smoothed through the very same organisational routines that were part of the research object. In other words, the comparator could be fed because the organisation itself had certain features that helped to feed it.

Compare this to the labour involved in gaining access to the Indian field site. This involved at least four sets of challenges. First, a particular bureaucratic actor had to be enrolled: the research visa.[11] A major consequence of this was to delay the entry of the comparator into the Indian field site by ten months.

The second challenge was that the frequent transfer of people between different parts of the Indian administrative apparatus rendered any negotiated access temporary. In one instance, Zuzana had to liaise with four different heads of the same force, all of whom had different opinions about 'letting her in'. Whenever one left, she had to seek new permission from the next. The first two gave an oral commitment to support her, while the third 'head' even went ahead and formally authorised her access. This, however, turned out to be not enough. Upon Zuzana's return to India for a planned six-month stay (now accompanied by a full research visa), the new (fourth) organisational head revoked the access granted to her by his predecessor and asked that she obtain authorisation from the Home Ministry. This involved temporarily enrolling the Czech embassy (given Zuzana's nationality), who were required to issue further supporting documents until she finally gained access.

The third issue was the central position of personal and informal relationships with key people that often determined the degree and type of access. Many of Zuzana's initial contacts were brokered by fellow academics either from Puducherry or New Delhi. After another promising research lead fell apart due to a change in personnel, fellow researchers in Puducherry put her in touch with someone near the very top of the local hierarchy.[12] This opened a new door to a research site perhaps better than that which was now inaccessible. Increasing familiarity with Zuzana and the project amongst key figures in the Indian state hierarchy also played a role. For instance, towards the end of her stay in India, officers (who had initially been adamant about strictly following official hierarchical processes) became more willing to exert what agency they could within their realm of responsibility to make her research possible. For example, she was given tips about upcoming events that did not require official permission, allowing her to collect perhaps the most important data of her research so far.

The fourth issue is that disaster management falls under the responsibility of the Home Ministry. One consequence of this is that access to disaster response bodies is considered a security issue as they are manned by personnel from paramilitary forces. To venture into such a highly sensitive field site without the correct authorisation in India would be unwise, as it could lead to charges of espionage and imprisonment.

Compared to Switzerland, the Indian part of the comparator had to become connected to a far more heterogeneous and ever-changing set of actors. Zuzana had to be prepared for the terrain of potential comparison to constantly shift, or for a new actor to be integrated into the processes of calibration and stabilisation necessary for comparisons to occur. Of course, this experience may itself in due course be integrated into a comparative analysis of organisational differences between our respective cases; the question of how we gained access is itself part of an ethnography of how these organisations relate to particular parts of the public. What will likely be absent from such accounts (because of norms of academic self-presentation), however, are the asymmetries involved in preparing the ground for such comparative work.

There is a further effect which relates to the temporal and spatial *trajectory* of comparison. This concerns the variations in how access is achieved, and when and where it happens. Each can shape the overall comparative career of the project: access in one site may open up questions in another before any field research has even been possible. Or, a denial of access in another site may prompt a change of strategy in yet another, resulting in a move towards a different type of data which, in turn, may reflect back on the work planned (or being undertaken) in one or more of the other sites.

In the Swiss case, early field research showed, for instance, that there is a significant blur between state institutions and the population when it comes to civil protection. This is because of the sheer number of people that are enrolled into its dedicated, militia-based, state-led[13] civil protection force.[14] After an initial two-week training period, participation in this force can last years, even if it only involves attending a few days' worth of refresher courses every year. This opened up an opportunity for comparison and a shift in the research strategy in India: during the period in which access to state institutions was problematic, Zuzana shifted her attention to the localised training of the population, in work that is often effectively subcontracted by the state to NGOs. Here too, then, was an instance of the population being enrolled into civil protection procedures.

As access to the NGOs was far less challenging, Zuzana could learn about the disaster management arrangements within the local administrative structure and observe localised disaster preparedness training practices in several communities. The work being done in these communities exhibits numerous parallels with forms of training we have observed in Switzerland, and has generated a range of comparative questions: What relations of similarity and/or difference might the comparator be able to establish between these two forms of disaster response training? What constitutes the population in these instances? What constitutes the organisation of disaster response? Despite the pre-definition of the comparison, the comparator's gaze had thus shifted to take in a more diverse range of entities. A process of calibration was exposing different forms of organisational delegation and negotiations at the interface between civil protection organisations and populations.

Only a Comparator Can Produce Absence

In any research project, certain entities may emerge that come to possess a particular allure. These are the entities, for instance, that surprise, that are unusual, that 'force' our thought (see Stengers (2010)). In our project, one such entity, which also shifted the comparator's gaze, has been an object: the shelter – a category of building designed to protect its inhabitants from danger. This object produced a move that can only be achieved by a comparator, namely rendering visible an *absence*. Not only did shelters become objects to be researched, but also their prominence in one site prompted questions as to the reasons for their absence in other sites. It is only by moving through a comparator (either ours or someone else's) that presences in one site can trigger an attention to an object that does not exist in another. Absence became visible here as data; as something that can be positively discussed only because it is relevant somewhere else.

Our interest in shelters initially emerged during documentary research into the Swiss case. Switzerland is a country where now, following Cold War government policy, there are enough nuclear-proof bomb shelters to house almost 100% of the population.[15] This marks Switzerland out as a country whose response to the threat of the atomic bomb was, and is, unique in at least offering its population the possibility of survival after a nuclear attack (what Elaine Scarry (2011) calls the 'right of exit'). Despite the end of the Cold War, the Swiss shelter system is an ongoing project: shelters continue to be built and continue to be maintained (even if not to the same degree). As we have explored elsewhere, these shelters continue to have a direct impact on the conduct of preparedness practice, in part because their sheer material awkwardness means that they will not fit cleanly into contemporary civil protection paradigms (Deville, Guggenheim, and Hrdličková 2014).

We could have left the object in Switzerland. However, one of the features of being in a comparator is that entities in other settings tend to offer themselves up for comparison. This initially occurred in the UK. When we (the 'we' here being mostly Michael's end of the comparator) looked for shelters in the UK, the entity we found was actually not a material presence, but a material absence. At a relatively early stage in the Cold War (partly for reasons of cost and partly because of their possession of a nuclear deterrent) the UK decided against any comprehensive nuclear shelter building programme. Instead, the British population were more or less left to their own devices, being only provided with instructions on how to improvise shelters in their own homes and gardens.[16] For us, this absence was particularly striking given that, in Switzerland, bomb shelters were (and continue to be) something of an overwhelming presence (Berger Ziauddin 2010; 2012). We also quickly found that this absence had played a role in the sometimes contested history of British civil protection. This was, in part, a historical issue – the very lack of shelters for the population having arisen as an issue in the anti-war protests of the early 1980s. But it also resonated in the present: we argue elsewhere that the very absence of Cold War material preparedness practice may have made it *easier* for the UK to adopt certain post-Cold War forms of expertise than was the case in Switzerland (Deville and Guggenheim, 2015).

A comparison had thus been established and, in the process, the comparator had shifted to incorporate the relationship between these organisations and their history of building preparedness – as well as what was absent. This points to a more general observation about absences: it is impossible to specify absence if one cannot use a comparator to specify the presence of what is absent somewhere else in the world (obviously, the 'somewhere else' is not necessarily spatial. It could also be temporal, whether historical or utopian, or social and cultural). Without a comparator, there are no absences, only presences. The comparator, through producing absence, can then also help to produce new presences: what fills any absences (the answer can never be simply 'nothing')? This question, in turn, highlighted some of the more general moral and political questions that are tied up in all preparedness practice. How should a country protect its population? Who is to be included in protective measures, and who is excluded?

Our two-way comparator was therefore achieving a measure of stability. But again, a comparator can have something of a life of its own and can begin to demand questions of us. The existence of a seemingly neat two-way comparison begged the question: what about shelters in India? As we started thinking about this, our comparator also began to question both the level of comparison and the *tertium comparationis* (see also Sörensen (2008) on this point). What were we comparing when we were comparing shelters? Were we comparing material structures designed to defend civilians against disasters, or were we comparing the role and meaning of bunkers as a response to the threat of nuclear war? If it were the latter, then India shows similarities to the UK: nuclear bunkers are similarly absent, although some exist for key government officials.[17] What, however, if the comparison at stake is something else, namely the way ideas about protection against disasters are materialised?

In the course of looking for shelters in India, Zuzana came across the cyclone shelter. These shelters are the main purpose-built buildings designed to protect the population against cyclones, although people are also encouraged to move to other so called 'life-line' engineered buildings, seen as strong enough to withstand a cyclone, like schools. Fieldwork in Puducherry and Tamil Nadu showed that only people who normally live in thatched structures (i.e. they are poorer) use cyclone shelters, so hiding in specially designed shelters during a cyclone becomes a matter of socio-economic status. The Indian coast is also marked with some completely dilapidated shelters that have become the hub of what the Indian authorities conceive of as anti-social behaviour and are not used by the public in case of disaster. This failure to protect is ascribed in the general discourse of NGOs and the authorities to the lacking sense of community ownership. Therefore, the more recently built shelters are actually disaster-resistant buildings that have other primary functions – for example, serving as a local community hall or a school.

Thus, the comparator has shifted from the disaster to be protected from (in the case of Switzerland), to the relationship between shelters – as a category of purpose-built buildings – and the surrounding lives into which they become entwined. In the process, its focus intensified on questions such as what the politics of entry and exclusion sheltering implies, and the relationship between sheltering and the presence of a threat, including the other life of a shelter when it is not being used for protection. The comparator had become interested in the way the state administration conceives of its own role, how it understands disaster, and how it sees the population and its needs. Some of these interests pre-existed the Indian research as under-articulated ideas. However, by following the comparison of an entity that was present in two of the cases to the third, the comparator was provided with another powerful lens, both through which to consider the relationship between civil protection and the population, and to enrich our thinking. As we bounce around our cases, the comparator is being fed.

The Field Shifts the Comparator

We – and our devices – are not the only comparator in the research project, however. Our comparative project has encountered a world populated by a myriad circulating comparators. And these comparators have shifted our own.

It is not a simple case – as has often been observed – that thinking is always comparative, and that this thus also includes ordinary members of society. When we refer to the circulation of comparators, we refer to the use, by others, of explicitly deployed forms of comparison. These are the kinds of comparisons undertaken by academics and a range of other interest groups, including part-activists/part-academics,[18] policymakers,[19] and our informants.

In India, for instance, Japan is frequently mentioned – an idolised 'Other', whose disaster preparedness (with its technology, discipline, and civilian awareness of appropriate behaviour in earthquakes) represents practices to aspire towards. In Switzerland, Japan is also brought into the comparative frame, however, for a precisely opposite set of reasons: the events surrounding the

Fukushima nuclear disaster following the earthquake and tsunami (including the placement of its reactors in risky locations and the subsequent response by disaster response professionals) become a lesson in what *not* to do. At the same time, some respondents have held up the presence of the shelters as a legitimation of the Swiss approach to civil preparedness: even if there *were* a nuclear event (the argument goes), the Swiss population would still be able to retreat to their shelters.

We are drawn to such 'field comparators'. They open up potential important questions about the people, organisations, and things we are studying. In the above examples, for instance, we are able to see how our respondents invoke very particular (and quite conflicting) versions of Japanese disaster management. Field comparators, then, very often have a transparent political agenda. Indian disaster managers would like the population to be as well prepared for earthquakes as the Japanese are. With such ambitions, their disaster management organisation can continue to grow to reach a wider public. On the other hand, by invoking Fukushima, the Swiss want to justify and prolong the existence of their bunkers. By pointing at Fukushima, they are suggesting that although the Cold War is over, the risk of a nuclear incident, however small, cannot be eliminated. Thus, people may well at some point need to use the nuclear shelter. So, the comparisons of others further fed our comparator by providing fundamentally important insights. Our comparator became, then, quite a greedy thing.

Our attraction to field comparators is also based on the very fact that these comparators are so different from our own. First, field comparators are fast because they operate with minimal justifications invoking norms of empirical proof and theoretical rigour. Ours is cumbersome, as it relies on all the various steps we have described in this article in order to make it work and for it to conform to ethnographic and academic standards. Field comparators do not rely (to anywhere near the same degree) on this sometimes troublesome infrastructure. Actors in the field can invoke any comparison they like, often without the need to justify it or to calibrate a comparator first. They are likely neither to have to read extensive amounts of background literature, nor to justify what their *tertium comparationis* is, nor to write a research proposal that justifies why a comparison makes sense.

Second, our comparator is mainly built as a tool to understand differences. As a social scientific comparator, it attempts a degree of symmetry by holding one example against another, and accounts for various absences and presences, varying value judgements and operations grounded in historical routines. It simultaneously adds analysis on either side of the entities being compared, and tries to keep each case similarly thick.

The field comparators that we have encountered tend to operate in a more asymmetrical way, and are chosen strategically to make a political point. The asymmetric comparator proceeds by taking its own case as fully known and understood, while the other provides a standard to enable the comparator to make a judgement against it – based on a simple set of assessments. Comparison here is an evaluation composed of binary values: there is a simple yes or no: Japan is good at preparedness; we must strive to become like them; and Japanese nuclear power plants break; ours can (or cannot).

One consequence of this is that when we integrate the field comparator into our own, it becomes 're-symmetrised' and re-politicised in ways that may run counter to its use in the field. Without our own comparator, our field comparators' interventions through comparison would be not much more than the invocation of the comparative facts of another situation to make a political point. With our comparator, this comparative fact looks rather different: it draws our collective attention to the political composition of the comparators it absorbs. And, in so doing, it highlights particular aspects of the political composition of preparedness: what function does the idolisation of another's preparedness practice serve for the idolisers? Does the continued maintenance of Swiss shelters really have anything to do with the very particular kind of disaster that befell Japan in 2011?

CONCLUSION

As we have seen, comparison is not simply a practice that is imposed onto the field. Comparison proceeds by fits and starts, and it is just as much moved by the field as it moves the field. Following our own comparator as it has grown, changed, and shifted its focus, all the while absorbing other technologies of comparison and the comparisons of others, we have seen it traverse quite different analytical, political, spatial, and temporal domains.

We have also highlighted some peculiar features of comparison: the comparator is highly contingent on its composition, but the very practice of assembling it – ranging from job interviews and applications, internal hierarchies, to the technologies that keep it stable – is the part of it which is reflected upon the least within conventional comparative practice and never appears in resulting research articles. These conclusions are brought into sharper focus by the very fact that our comparator is made up of a team of researchers. A single-person comparator has the luxury of being able to proceed into the field far less encumbered by processes of calibration, and they can come out of the field without needing to develop ways to collectively think, analyse, and write. Nevertheless, being part of a collective comparator vividly exposes the precise mechanisms of comparison.

In this chapter, we have described a comparator that occupies one point on the spectrum between highly formalised types of comparative work and non-comparative ethnographic case studies. Since ours is only an auto-ethnography, we cannot compare our social scientific comparator to those of others. But as a reader, perhaps you now can, as this chapter now takes its home in a collection richly populated with other comparators. We ourselves are left to wonder about the comparator we have created and become: has our comparator been assembled in the right way? How might a differently composed comparator have produced different comparisons? How might we have calibrated differently? What if the contingencies of access had pointed us in different directions? What can our comparator see that others cannot?

Asking these questions with the comparator as its focus also allows us to conclude by reframing ongoing concerns about the ethics and politics of comparison, some of which we drew attention to at the start of the chapter and which we explore at greater length in the book's introduction. Much of the criticism of the use of comparison in the social sciences has stemmed from the observation that by forcing social and cultural phenomena into relation with one another, their complexity and specificity ends up being lost.

The argument, in effect, is that practising comparison is to practise a form of 'injustice'.

One way to respond to this challenge is to observe that the field never has comparison done 'to it' in any straightforward way. Comparison happens through what Isabelle Stengers calls the creation of 'rapport' between the entities being studied (2011: 49). This act of creation is neither a given, nor is this process ever disinterested. Our comparisons happen because of the way people, things, and organisations either smooth out or resist our progress and offer themselves up to the comparative work that we wish to do with them. This is, then, in part about the mundane features of much research practice – gaining access for instance – and in part about how entities push themselves into contention *for* comparison. For example, a shelter in one site pushes itself into our comparative reckoning, in part because of our desire to find a parallel, but also because it renders itself as relevant to be taken into account (through various formal similarities to other shelters, similarities of material, and so on). Enacting social scientific comparison is also not a matter of the unilateral and politically motivated imposition of comparison into the field (to which actors might object). Particularly in a field of research like ours, which is populated by experts and individuals in positions of considerable power (a typical case of 'studying up', in other words), many of the actors we study have more than enough authority and mechanisms at their disposal to establish their own, often highly authoritative, comparisons.

For this reason, another response, one echoed by other contributions to this volume (see in particular Gad and Jensen), is to pay more attention to comparison as it occurs in the field. However, we may wish to hesitate before delegating authority for comparison to these field comparators in its entirety. Many of the comparisons undertaken by actors in the field are unconcerned with the question of whether or not justice is done to comparative entities. That is to say, these are comparisons that are not constrained by the disciplinarily-specific demands of empirical rigour.

To understand the specificity of (social) scientific comparison as compared to the comparisons undertaken by many of the other actors in the world, we thus need to understand the differences in the modes through which the comparator operates. Many field comparators are mobile, adaptable, and quick. Our comparator, however, is slow and cumbersome. For this reason, it needs to do much of its calibration work independently of the field. The problem of comparison cannot, therefore, be solved by asking actors (whether organisation, individual, or non-human) in the field to choose the comparative entities on our behalf: not only would this elide the work that would have gone into choosing that actor in the first place, it would simply replicate the problem of comparison a level further down the line. One of the benefits of allowing social scientific comparators the authority to set up the comparison is that at least this authority is clearly defined: there already exist a familiar set of conventions and techniques for rendering aspects of the contingencies of comparative practice transparent. In this chapter, we have pushed this process of rendering transparent far further than is usually the case. The comparisons of the field, however, do not often have such complex comparators.

Comparison is thus never in itself an unjust, colonial, reductive, or violent enterprise. It can be; however, in such cases, our energies should be placed into demonstrating how, and in what ways, the calibration of the comparator was inadequate. We also cannot simply replace inadequate comparators with those of the field: there may be occasions when we may want to compare in collaboration with actors in the field (as we in many instances have), but there may be other occasions when we do not, or when we judge the comparators of the field to be an equally inadequate starting point for comparison. Rather, we need both to understand our comparators in more depth, and to set them up in more productive ways.

In assessing the quality of a comparison, the focus should thus be on the operations of the comparator (potentially by comparing it to other comparators) and not on the reactions that the comparison produces. This is not a call for each and every ethnographic comparison to dissect its comparator as we have, or to see auto-ethnographic reflexivity as providing a ready-made solution for the problem of comparison. It is rather a call for attending far more to the contingencies of both comparison and the operations of the comparator. The question of the ethics and politics of comparison, then, cannot be answered by judging what is compared (or not), but rather how comparators operate. It has to be answered by assessing – whether by selecting the particular cases, by assembling, calibrating, and feeding the comparator in the way that we have (i.e. with care, with integrity and with a sufficient degree of skill). When assessing comparison as a social scientific method, we are thus not assessing a unitary thing, but rather a diverse and situated set of calibratory steps.

NOTES

1 Phrase used in South Asia meaning 'similar'.
2 Research for this article has been generously funded by a European Research Council (ERC) starting grant (number 263731).
3 The comparator chip performs two functions: 1) it measures currents coming into it from two different sources, and 2) on the basis of this comparison (and according to predefined thresholds) it switches either on or off. See: <http://www.brighthubengineering.com/robotics/60941-the-lm3-voltage-comparator-chip/> [accessed 21 January 2014]
4 It goes without saying in social research that this input-output process should be seen as dynamic, and involving a plethora of feedback loops.
5 Photo by Joe Deville. No rights reserved.
6 Our three cases have been selected because of points of continuity and discontinuity in their preparedness practices. For example, both India and Switzerland are, to varying degrees, dependent on civil protection mechanisms that are organised from the 'top down' and are also homogenous, with both having professional civil protection forces on call. The UK, by contrast, has no centralised, professional disaster response organisation, but is instead dependent on the coordination of diverse actors, ranging from the police, to the army, and to the fire service, whose precise deployment depends on the particular disaster at hand. Further, in the original proposal, the three cases were tied together by a shared disaster object: floods. This was chosen in part because of the fact that this is a disaster event relatively common to all three countries.
7 Luhman's monumental filing cabinet is a more nuts and bolts example – he famously said that, with its help, books effectively 'wrote themselves' (Luhman 1981).
8 We decided it was not necessary to insert the author of the excerpt.
9 This is in part because of its connection to the nationwide proliferation of nuclear shelters – as explored in the next section. This was accompanied by a dedicated civil protection force [*Zivilschutz*] which was composed mainly of men who were unable to serve in the conscript militia army (this situation has now changed – see the following footnote). In the 1980s in particular, this project became the object of political protest: although ostensibly a 'defensive' measure, protesters argued that it was ultimately a militaristic project that lent unwarranted legitimacy to the Swiss army (see Albrecht et al. 1988). After the end of the Cold War, many saw the maintenance of the shelter system,

the Swiss military, and a dedicated civil protection force as expensive and unnecessary.

10 The exact proportion of personnel working within the country's civil protection system (this is an umbrella organisation that includes the army, emergency services, *Zivilschutz*, and other organisations) who either continue to be involved in the Swiss army, or who were formerly, is unknown. Experience from the field, however, indicates that the proportion is substantial: perhaps as much as 50%, perhaps higher (given compulsory military service is restricted to men, this also indicates how male-dominated the organisation is).

11 Specific administrative regimes apply to foreign researchers, including a lengthy process of research visa application and registration.

12 Even here, reciprocal relationships played their part. This new contact was following a PhD programme led by the academic who put Zuzana in touch with him.

13 This was state-led despite the fact that the responsibility of leading this work was largely delegated to the cantons. Because of Switzerland's federal structure, these are clearly appendages of the state.

14 This is because of the close relationship between civil protection and the Swiss military. This is an organisation with only a very small number of full-time professional personnel. The remaining manpower is provided by a militia force that (in the event of a conflict) would be called into service. This militia reserve is initially recruited through a process by which young men (usually at the age of 18) are given the option of either entering into military service, or undertaking a form of voluntary service, or – and this is what concerns us here – entering the dedicated civil protection force (*Zivilschutz*).

15 At the end of 2010, the Federal Office for Civil Protection put the figure at 95% (Bundesamt für Zivilschutz 2010).

16 Some nuclear shelters were built; however, they were only done so for key government and military officials. See Deville et al. (2014).

17 The Indian case is more extreme than the UK, for in India there is a lack of even the pretence of protection for its population, should it be subject to a nuclear attack. These cases can be used to make a combined argument: just because there is a nuclear threat, it does not follow that a country needs to protect its population. Or, seen from another angle, it highlights the paranoiac quality of some aspects of Swiss civil protection. On a more general level, it leads to an important theoretical insight: risks do not explain preparedness, but preparedness has a logic in its own right that uses risks to legitimate its actions.

18 In the case of civil defence research, this can be seen in comparative literature, such as Lawrence J. Vale's (1987) *The Limits of Civil Defence in the USA, Switzerland, Britain and the Soviet Union: The Evolution of Policies Since 1945*, which is both an object of research, and academic study for us. Vale – who also did a comparative study – is not simply a precursor of ours, but the book is an indicator that, within the field of civil defence, a comparative view was very much part of the practice of civil defence.

19 For example, a policy paper on civil defence in India compares civil defence structures in the UK, Singapore, and Australia (Singh 2006).

BIBLIOGRAPHY

Albrecht, P., et al., *Schutzraum Schweiz: Mit dem Zivilschutz zur Notstandsgesellschaft* (Gümligen, Bonn: Zytglogge, 1988)

Battaglia, D., 'Of Archipelagos and Arrows', *Common Knowledge*, 17.1 (2011), 51–54

Berger Ziauddin, S., 'Wahre Schweizer Architektur ist unterirdisch – oder wie die Schweiz im Kalten Krieg zum Schutzbaumusterland wurde', paper presented at *Kolloquium DIALOGO*, Historisches Institut, Universität Stuttgart, 2010

—— 'Apocalypse Now? Swiss Bunkers as (In)effective Transition Spaces into the Postnuclear World', Paper presented at the *Organising Disaster Advisory Board Workshop*, Goldsmiths University, 2012

Brown, S. D., 'Rats, Elephants, and Bees as Matters of Concern', *Common Knowledge*, 17.1 (2011), 71–76

Bundesamt für Zivilschutz, 'Schutzbauten', <http://www.bevoelkerungsschutz.admin.ch/internet/bs/de/home/themen/schutzbauten.html> [accessed 23 December 2010]

Candea, M., 'Endo/Exo', *Common Knowledge*, 17.1 (2011), 146–50

Cook, I. R., and K. Ward, 'Relational Comparisons: The Assembling of Cleveland's Waterfront Plan', *Urban Geography*, 33.6 (2012), 774–95

De Castro, E. V., 'Zenos Wake', *Common Knowledge*, 17.1 (2011), 163–65

Deville, J., and M. Guggenheim, 'Vom nuklearen Krieg zu all hazards. Die Katastrophe versprachlichen, materialisieren und berechnen', in S. Marti, and D. Eugster, eds., *Das Imaginäre des Kalten Krieges. Beiträge zu einer Wissens- und Kulturgeschichte des Ost-West-Konfliktes in Europa* (Essen: Klartext, 2015), pp. 267–295

Deville, J., M. Guggenheim, and Z. Hrdličková, 'Concrete Governmentality: Shelters and the Transformations of Preparedness', in M. Tironi, I. Rodriguez-Giralt, and M. Guggenheim, eds., *Disasters and Politics: Materials, Preparedness and Governance* (Sociological Review Monographs, London: Wiley, 2014), pp. 183–210

Gingrich, A., and R. Gabriel Fox, eds., *Anthropology, by Comparison* (New York: Routledge, 2002)

Gough, K. V., 'Reflections on Conducting Urban Comparison', *Urban Geography*, 33.6 (2012), 866–78

Haraway, D., *Modest_Witness@Second_Millennium. FemaleMan©_Meets_ OncoMouse: Feminism and Technoscience* (New York and London: Routledge, 1997)

Holbraad, M., 'Raising the Anti-, or Relativism Squared', *Common Knowledge*, 17.1 (2011), 31–36

Jacobs, J. M., 'Commentary – Comparing Comparative Urbanisms', *Urban Geography*, 33.6 (2012), 904–14

Jensen, C. B., 'Comparative Relativism: Symposium on an Impossibility', *Common Knowledge*, 17.1 (2011), 1–12

Krajewski, M., 'Paper as Passion. Niklas Luhmann and His Card Index', in L. Gitelman, ed., *Raw Data* (Massachusetts: MIT Press, 2012), pp. 103–120

Lloyd, G. E. R., 'Multidimensional Reality', *Common Knowledge*, 17.1 (2011), 27–30
Luhmann, N., 'Kommunikation mit Zettelkästen', in H. Baier, H. Mathias, and K. Reumann, eds., *Öffentliche Meinung und sozialer Wandel/Public Opinion and Social Change* (Opladen: Westdeutscher Verlag, 1981), pp. 222–28
McFarlane, C., and J. Robinson, 'Introduction – Experiments in Comparative Urbanism', *Urban Geography*, 33.6 (2012), 765–73
Mol, A., 'Cutting Surgeons, Walking Patients: Some Complexities Involved in Comparing', in J. Law, and A. Mol, eds., *Complexities: Social Studies of Knowledge Practices* (Durham, NC: Duke University Press, 2002), pp. 218–57
Phillips, S., 'John Stezaker's Best Photograph', *The Guardian*, 8 August 2012 <http://www.theguardian.com/artanddesign/2012/aug/08/john-stezaker-best-photograph> [accessed 5 January 2015]
Robinson, J., 'Cities in a World of Cities: The Comparative Gesture', *International Journal of Urban and Regional Research*, 35.1 (2011), 1–23
Scarry, E., *Thinking in an Emergency* (New York: W. W. Norton and Co., 2011)
Scheffer, T., and J. Niewöhner, *Thick Comparison. Reviving the Ethnographic Aspiration* (Leiden and Boston, MA: Brill, 2010)
Singh, K. M., 'Revamping of Civil Defence in the Country: National Policy Approach Paper. High Power Committee Report', government report, National Disaster Management Authority, Government of India, 2006
Smith, B. H., 'The Chimera of Relativism: A Tragicomedy', *Common Knowledge*, 17.1 (2011), 13–26
Sørensen, E., 'Multi-Sited Comparison of "Doing Regulation"', *Comparative Sociology*, 7.3 (2008), 311–37
Steinmetz, G., 'Odious Comparisons: Incommensurability, the Case Study, and "Small N's" in Sociology', *Sociological Theory*, 22.3 (2004), 371–400
Stengers, I., 'Including Non-Humans in Political Theory: Opening Pandora's Box', in B. Braun and S. Whatmore, eds., *Political Matter Technoscience, Democracy, and Public Life* (Minneapolis: Minnesota University Press, 2010), pp. 3–34
——'Comparison as a Matter of Concern', *Common Knowledge*, 17.1 (2011), 48–63
Strathern, M., 'Binary License', *Common Knowledge*, 17.1 (2011a), 87–103
——'What Politics?', *Common Knowledge*, 17.1 (2011b), 123–27
Vale, L. J., *The Limits of Civil Defence in the USA, Switzerland, Britain and the Soviet Union: The Evolution of Policies Since 1945* (Basingstoke: Macmillan, 1987)
Verran, H., 'Comparison as Participant', *Common Knowledge*, 17.1 (2011), 64–70
Wagner, R., 'Vújà De and the Quintessentialists' Guild', *Common Knowledge*, 17.1 (2011), 155–62
Ward, K., 'Towards a Relational Comparative Approach to the Study of Cities', *Progress in Human Geography*, 34.4 (2010), 471–87

5

PULLING ONESELF OUT OF THE TRAPS OF COMPARISON: AN AUTO-ETHNOGRAPHY OF A EUROPEAN PROJECT

Madeleine Akrich and Vololona Rabeharisoa

PROLOGUE

A COUPLE OF MONTHS AGO, MADELEINE WAS INVITED TO AN ACADEMIC workshop on patients' organisations (POs) and health activists' groups. Her talk was based on our three-year EU-funded research project called 'European Patients' Organisations in Knowledge Society' (EPOKS). The project examined the variety of practices developed by POs to collect experiential knowledge and compare it with credentialed knowledge, and reflected on how these practices transform the governance of knowledge and the governance of health issues these POs deem relevant. In all, we looked at POs concerned with four specific conditions (rare diseases,[1] Alzheimer's disease, Attention Deficit Hyperactivity Disorder (ADHD), and childbirth) in four countries (France, the UK, Ireland, and Portugal).

After Madeleine's presentation, one participant raised three interrelated questions:

> 1) To what extent do conditions and/or national contexts determine POs' behaviours and actions?

2) How can one measure POs' successes and/or failures to change policies?

3) Are there general lessons to draw from our comparative project?

Madeleine confessed to Vololona that these questions came as a surprise. Indeed, she did not present EPOKS as a comparative project and did not mention the term 'comparison' at any time during her talk. In response to the participant's questions, she emphasised the complex and dynamic interplay between different elements such as the characteristics of conditions which are at stake, and the nature of credentialed expertise on these conditions in various countries. She also added that these should not be considered as mere external factors determining POs' activities, but rather elements which POs problematise throughout their activities. Moreover, she stressed the fact that what we were primarily interested in was diversity. This included the diversity of knowledge that POs engage with, the diversity of their knowledge-related activities, and the diversity of the effects of their practices on research and health policies.

Hmmm… It is likely that our colleague was not entirely satisfied with Madeleine's responses. This prompted us to ask ourselves the following questions: if we did not compare POs across the condition areas and national contexts we selected, then what exactly did we do? Why is it that we feel so uneasy with this issue of comparison? And how can we tackle this issue, given that it relates to the expectation that EU-funded projects should be comparative? To address these questions, we decided to revert back to our research practices and to the tools we set up for coordinating our project, extending from the writing of the research proposal to the drafting of scientific articles we submitted for publication. Our hope is that this retrospective auto-ethnography, based on a chronological retrieval of how and what we did, will clarify our approach to comparison, not only for our colleagues but also for ourselves.

INTRODUCTION

Why did we decide to apply to the EU call and to engage in such a multi-sited piece of research?[2] Our motives stemmed from previous research done on POs, as well as from the ongoing dialogue we have sustained with them for more than fifteen years. Firstly, Vololona and Michel Callon investigated why and how the French Association against Myopathies (AFM) got involved in biomedical research and came to consider research as a privileged route towards the social integration of people with neuromuscular diseases (Rabeharisoa and Callon 1999). They undertook this research at a time when very few STS scholars paid attention to patients' engagement in the production and dissemination of biomedical knowledge.[3] Vololona and Michel were repeatedly confronted by colleagues who emphasised the exceptionality of the AFM, its wealth, and the fact that neuromuscular diseases mostly affect children and are thus likely to provoke empathy in the general population. However, they intuitively felt that this engagement in biomedical research was not the preserve of the AFM, and they thus began to investigate other POs concerned with rare diseases. At almost the same time, Madeleine and our colleague Cécile Méadel began to study patients' and activists' electronic discussion lists. In reviewing their exchanges, they were able to witness patients' and activists' preoccupations with knowledge and, most importantly, the variety of knowledge that circulates through these lists (Akrich and Méadel 2002; 2007).

Secondly, throughout our research, we soon realised that POs were not happy about being passively studied. They put questions to us, raised issues we did not initially identify, and manifested their willingness to play an active part in our research endeavour. This was not always a comfortable exercise for us, but we learnt to translate their concerns into interesting research questions. This proved so worthwhile that we organised participatory conferences with them on various occasions in order to develop a collective and reflexive work that is attentive to our respective standpoints on the dynamics of patients' and health activism (Akrich, Méadel, and Rabeharisoa 2009).

Drawing on our previous research findings and observations, we made the decision to apply to the EU call with the following hypothesis: we wanted to put to trial the idea that different POs today build epistemic capacities and share political concerns about knowledge (both through the species of knowledge they engage with and the knowledge-related activities they undertake), with the view that the effects of these activities on POs and on their environments are diverse. More specifically, we seized the opportunity presented by the EU call to extend our sites of observation in order to confirm or disconfirm that

> 1) it is not only large and wealthy POs that are interested in knowledge (small and poorly endowed POs are too);
> 2) POs are not exclusively engaged in biomedical research. For instance, it is worth noting that some are also engaged in knowledge about medical practices or social sciences in less spectacular ways.

To be honest, we were not fully aware of what this decision committed us to. Of course, we did know that we would soon be confronted with the issue of comparison. However, at no point did we think that our multi-sited approach would raise methodological and conceptual difficulties that largely exceed the challenge of cross-national coordination. Applying to the EU call sounded like a good compromise between our intellectual interests on the one hand, and imperatives to 'internationalise' research and fund our activities on the other. At the risk of appearing naive, we did not anticipate that it would highlight, or at least expose us to, the 'national' dimension of comparison. Nor did we realise that engaging in this kind of comparative work would convoke a whole range of research traditions and practices. Eventually, it seemed like 'comparison' had an agency of its own, popping up like a mischievous spirit throughout the project and forcing us to make multiple adjustments.[4]

This paper is about our multiple encounters with this mischievous spirit of comparison. Indeed, while we thought that the research methodology we put together enabled us to master the issue of comparison in ways that suited us, this issue often reappeared out of the blue at unexpected moments of the project, very much like an evil spirit in a fairy tale. Though troublesome, this mischievous spirit was not all destructive, as it continuously fuelled our reflection on what exactly the issue of comparison entailed, and forced us to take our reasoning to its conclusion. In what follows, this paper will attempt to put the reader in the situation we had to face, and to recreate the surprises, uncertainties, and destabilising events we were confronted with. This is why the following text is in narrative form, starting with the drafting of our research proposal, and ending with the completion of academic articles drawing on the resulting research.

TO COMPARE OR NOT TO COMPARE? THE WRITING OF AN EU RESEARCH PROPOSAL

EU project applicants are often confronted with one main injunction: to demonstrate that their project will not simply result in the juxtaposition of a number of national case studies, but will bring in something more from their ordered confrontation. Indeed, an EU research project is expected to display similarities and differences between cases, and to determine explanatory factors for these according to the tradition of international comparisons (see for example Ragin 1981; Hassenteufel 2005; or Stöckelova, this volume). In our proposal, we were hardly able to escape this discourse, stating that

> [t]he provision of care and the organisation of health services greatly vary from one country to another, and sometimes result in divergent claims from nation-based organisations which are concerned with similar problems. Medical traditions are also diverse [...] As a case in point, the prominence of psychoanalysis in French psychiatry does make a difference in the way mental illnesses have been thought about, and results in specific claims from French patient and family organisations. Another important factor pertains to how certain issues raised by patient, user, and civil society organisations are valued by society at large. *Although cultural explanation should be handled cautiously, the absence of a Mad Pride movement in France, for instance, as compared to what happens in the UK (Crossley 2006), is a telling example of some sort of cultural difference between those two countries.* Finally, the maturity of civil society organisations, as well as their official recognition as stakeholders alongside institutions do matter. [Our emphasis]

In this excerpt, we clearly listed a series of variables usually related to the so-called 'national context' as potential factors which may explain the differences between POs, even though they are concerned with the same condition. One may notice, however, our own embarrassment with such an explanation when we mentioned the existence of a Mad Pride movement in the UK, and the absence of such a thing in France. Besides, out of the seventy-two-page proposal, this short paragraph is the only one where we detailed what the 'national context' is (supposed to be). We did not mention these elements elsewhere, and, most importantly, we did not consider them as factors to be searched in the methodology part of our project. Why not?

Undoubtedly it is because we did not intend to compare POs and explain similarities and differences between their behaviours and actions. This is in light of three particular variables which the literature on POs points towards: their organisational features, the nature of the conditions they are concerned with, and the national contexts within which they evolve (Huyard 2009; Löfgren, de Leeuw, and Leahy 2011). Indeed, prior to our EPOKS project, we coordinated an EU-funded specific action called 'Governance, Health and Medicine: Opening Dialogue between Social Scientists and Users' (MEDUSE), which consisted of a participatory workshop on POs' engagement with knowledge (Akrich et al. 2008). The dialogue with POs led us to two main statements:

1) POs, as organised entities, are irreducible to one another – each encounters its own problems and develops its own form of action to solve its problems.
2) Despite massive differences between POs in terms of their size, wealth, or proximity to biomedicine, they engage with strikingly similar, yet varied practices in regards to knowledge production and dissemination.

We were also struck by the discrepancy we observed between POs' practices and prevailing understandings of their role. The effect of this is that POs' involvement in knowledge-related activities is often ignored: a clear-cut separation between experts and laypeople continues to be maintained. This prompted us to publish a non-academic book based on testimonies gathered from a variety of organisations (Akrich, Méadel, and Rabeharisoa 2009). The book targeted biomedical practitioners and public health authorities, as well as POs themselves, highlighting the POs' multifaceted engagement with knowledge.

The EPOKS project took on the same conviction and aimed to explore the ways POs' knowledge-related activities emerge out of, and impact on, a *complex and dynamic interplay* between different elements. Some of these elements related to patients' conditions, others to the nature of credentialed expertise on these conditions, while some related to the missions POs endow themselves with (but whose list we, as social scientists, did not know in advance). The reason is that these are a result of POs' own analysis of which elements are relevant in their situations. As we explained in our proposal,

> the ways patients', users' and civil society organisations and movements intervene in the production of knowledge are not only diverse, but *depend on* national contexts, the causes that these organisations and movements stand for, as well as the web of expertise and issues in which they participate. EPOKS aims at deepening the understanding of this *contextualised character* of lay organisations' involvement in the co-production of knowledge, and its impact on health policy-making.
>
> The way lay organisations are involved with the production and circulation of knowledge *depends on* the causes they intend to defend. These causes *depend on* the characteristics of their particular conditions, *and on* the course of collective actions that various actors develop and that they decide either to join, or react to. [Our emphasis]

Let us expand a bit on the term 'depends on' in these excerpts from our proposal, as it actually denotes two different meanings. The first points to the singularity of every phenomenon, as it is captured by popular expressions such as 'It all depends'. It puts to the fore the fact that neither the actors nor we as social scientists can escape relativism. The second meaning is that every phenomenon is made of cascades of relations between heterogeneous elements, including those usually seen as exogenous factors, such as the provision of care in one given country. However, these relations do not predetermine the subsequent story, but rather result from the involvement and action of various actors. As social scientists, we should pay attention to the ways these relations are actively unfolded in the situations under study. This second meaning of 'depends on' points to 'relat-ionism', rather than to 'relat-ivism', the idea that 'anything goes'. The reasoning is that actors always situate themselves and act from somewhere, and so do we as social scientists (Haraway 1988). Therefore, this dual meaning of 'depends on' is exactly what the paradoxical expression 'comparative relativism' (Common Knowledge 2011) puts into discussion.

That being said, as we will see in a moment, we continued to talk about comparison, national context, and even typology throughout our proposal. There were obviously strategic reasons for this: after all, we applied for EU funding! The question then is how to work out the tension between this cumbersome injunction to proceed to international comparison, and our conviction that there is no such thing as a national context 'out there' which externally determines POs' behaviours and actions. Ultimately, it was through the design of our work plan that we tried to dissolve this tension. As will be shown, our work plan helped shift the focus of our analysis from comparison to multi-sited ethnography (Marcus 1995).

FROM COMPARISON TO MULTI-SITED ETHNOGRAPHY

Our project not only targeted POs in different countries, it also selected POs concerned with different conditions. Our objective was to observe a variety of sites and to highlight the fact that diversity does not contradict the existence of a phenomenon which crosses over these diverse sites, namely the crucial role that knowledge comes to play in POs' activities. Our approach stood on the opposite side of a comparative study of cases which share a number of controlled variables (i.e. POs' organisational characteristics, conditions they are concerned with) in order to evaluate the role of exogenous factors (i.e. factors other than the controlled variables – for instance, national contexts). This is because we did not hypothesise that the horizons of national POs are strictly delimited by national borders. In fact, it was quite the contrary, as from the outset we planned to analyse the complex networks of which POs partake, especially their transnational dimension. One objective of the project was indeed to reflect on 'Europeanisation from below' (i.e. the involvement of POs in networks of exchange and cooperation with European sister organisations), as well as 'Europeanisation from above' (i.e. the influence exerted by European umbrella organisations on national POs).

The final list of conditions that we decided to investigate was the result of discussions with colleagues we wanted to associate with in the research consortium, and all of these conditions intuitively seemed to be different enough to nurture the project. As mentioned previously, the list consisted of rare diseases, Alzheimer's disease, ADHD, and childbirth. We were of course aware that reviewers might ask: 'How did you choose these conditions?', and that 'intuition' was not an appropriate answer to the question. To borrow from Becker's motto: 'What is this the case of?' as recalled in Ragin (1992), we thus undertook rationalisation work in order to convince them, as well as ourselves, by addressing the question: 'What were the conditions the cases of?' The typology we produced contrasted with the POs' forms of engagement in knowledge according to two dimensions:

1) Their proximity/distance to biomedical knowledge and practices;
2) The degree of stabilisation of the network of expertise and issues related to their conditions.

We pictured and explained this typology as follows:

		DEGREE OF STABILISATION OF ISSUES	
		+	−
POs' ALIGNMENT TO THE BIOMEDICAL WORLD	+	CELL #1 RARE DISEASES	CELL #3 ALZHEIMER'S DISEASE
	−	CELL #2 CHILDBIRTH	CELL #4 ADHD

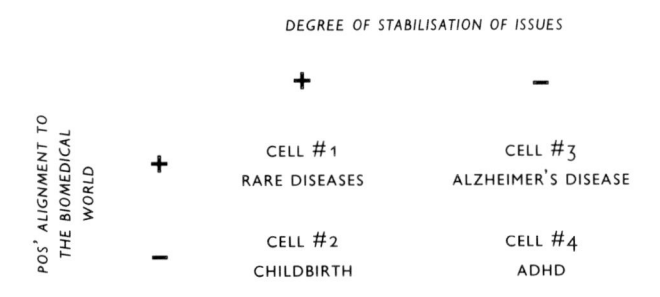

TABLE 5.1 Degree of stabilisation of issues vs. POs' alignment to the biomedical world

Preliminary research and discussion among the partners of the present project suggest that each of these four organisations or movements may stand as an exemplum for each of the four cells charted above. Besides, for each of these four organisations, there are similarities as well as important differences from one country to another. National contexts do matter for understanding the dynamics of these organisations or movements, as well as their framing of expertise and issues. This is why we put cross-national comparison at the core of the present project.

One can easily sense how ambiguous such a typology is. Our primary intention was simply to plead for the importance of examining a variety of sites. However, the graphical chart we adopted, and the distribution of POs between the four cells of the chart, unavoidably suggest a classification. Though we were cautious enough in saying that this is a 'proto-typology' (our word), which may well be modified in light of our observations, typology cannot but suggest a kind of metrics for contrasting different situations. Interestingly, as soon as we began our fieldwork, we abandoned this proto-typology (see Section 2). Retrospectively, we assume that this had to do with our work plan, which left no room for such a typology to be actioned.

We designed our work plan as follows. First, we defined four work packages, each devoted to one of the four conditions we chose. Each package consisted of case studies of POs which were active on the same condition in different countries. The cross-national analysis so dear to the heart of EU officials was therefore embedded into the design of the four work packages (WPs). The four WPs obeyed the same pattern that comprised a detailed description of the data collection, including an analysis of the relationships POs might have with one another and with transnational coalitions. This delineated the process for collectively discussing POs within the same WP, and POs from different WPs:

> It should be noted that, through their common involvement in common work packages, the partners will be constantly linked to each other all over the project, which is also a guarantee that the case studies will have a strong comparative dimension.

As one may expect, comparison was at the core of our work plan; however, it took up quite a different flavour here. First because we planned to establish a common interpretive framework for our observations, and second because all partner teams of the project were involved in different work packages and were invited to discuss collectively all case studies. Rather than contrast the different sites we studied, we decided to go through all of them and mobilise observations made on one site, as lenses through which to discuss what occurred in other sites. This is similar to what Henriette Langstrup and Brit Ross Winthereik (2008) did in their paper on the making of self-monitoring asthma patients in clinical trials and in general practices.

To recap, the writing of an EU research proposal comes with a very specific comparative injunction. That is, its aim is to find out similarities and differences between national case studies, and to explain how national contexts determine these similarities and differences. Unless one plans to proceed with such a comparative study, the writing of an EU research proposal rapidly turns into an equilibrium exercise. This is exactly what we experienced, as it involved constant navigation between the predicaments of comparison and alternative ways of looking at different sites. Retrospectively, it is clear, however, that we were not pursuing an international comparison which sought to explain differences and similarities through national contexts. Rather, we achieved this outcome by way of a transnational comparison (Hassenteufel 2005), which crossed various cases in order to bring more contrast and sharpness in the description of each, given that these cases are not supposed to belong to isolated planets.

PRODUCING AND TESTING COMPARATORS

However detailed it may be, a proposal is not sufficient to determine the actual conduct of a project. To study our different sites and to circulate amongst them, we had to refine constantly and transform our methodology. As Jörg Niewöhner and Philipp Scheffer (2008: 275) put it, the challenge was to 'exceed both the single case study and the contrasting of any number of multiple cases'. It was then crucial to find a way to create a 'rapport' (Stengers 2011) between chosen

POs and to look actively across them from a certain perspective. To borrow from Strathern (2011), we had to endorse a 'perspectivist' approach, which had a major practical consequence.[5] More specifically, in the habitual meaning of 'ethnography', we did not proceed towards multiple ethnographies in different sites. Rather, we set up a series of tools and procedures for cutting across the different sites we selected with one perspective: to observe POs' knowledge-related activities in light of the others'. To achieve this, we first went in depth into a common grid for data-gathering, and then we defined a protocol for discussing our observations in ways that each PO we studied (and/or partner team who studied it) served as a comparator to the others (Deville, Guggenheim, and Hrdličková 2013). Following Deville et al. (2013), we define a 'comparator' as the entity that does the work of comparison. In other words, the term 'comparator' designates one researcher, equipped with her/his embodied research experience, conceptual approach, and observations from fieldwork, and who puts her/his data and analysis to the trial of her/his project partners'. The comparator, therefore, is not a standard analyser out there; it emerges out of the comparative work it performs. In the following sections, we display the procedures we set up for turning not only each individual researcher, but also the project consortium itself, into a comparator.

THE MAKING OF A COMMON GAZE

How should we look at different sites to eventually produce a common interpretive framework? This was the purpose of the first meeting of the consortium (also called the 'kick-off meeting' in EU jargon), in February 2009. Though several partner teams had either an STS background or were sensitive to STS approaches, some also came from other disciplines, namely feminist studies, communication studies, and geography. Over the course of the meeting, however, we pragmatically put aside potential theoretical divergences. Our concern at this point was to define a shared protocol for data-gathering in ways that would permit us to look at the 'same sorts of things'. As coordinators of the project, we suggested a common grid for fieldwork which comprised three parts: 1) historical backgrounds of POs; 2) knowledge-related activities of POs; and 3) specific examples. Each of these were divided into a description of the objectives and a description of the methods. As an illustration, we reproduce the second part below:

- Knowledge-related activities of POs
- Describe the PO/Civil Society Organisation (CSO) knowledge-related activities
- The PO/CSO's role as co-producer of knowledge with specialists, as well as connector or translator between different worlds of expertise
- Its propensity to embrace or to challenge biomedical knowledge
- Content of information it produces (lay expertise versus experience-based expertise) and nature and scope of its targeted audiences
- Tools it mobilises for staging, shaping, circulating, and legitimating its expertise
- Participation in research projects and programs at national and European levels

Methods

- Collecting data through the PO/CSO website, publications (newsletter, brochures, leaflets, position paper if any), literature survey
- Identifying and interviewing key informants who are involved in knowledge-related activities[6]

This grid was clearly aimed at creating a common gaze on the POs we intended to study. It not only suggested how the fieldwork should be carried out, but also how to make it in ways that would later facilitate the crossing of our observations. This grid can therefore be a vehicle for circulating from one site to the next.

As science studies pointed out long ago, the manufacture of knowledge not only implies formal and explicit conventions, but also a shared culture resulting from repeated interactions between participants (Collins 1974; Knorr-Cetina 1981). We were soon reminded that social sciences do not make exceptions to the rule, especially when some partners raised questions about what exactly we meant by 'knowledge' and 'knowledge-related activities'. Despite our initial attempt to 'contain' potential conceptual divergences on what should count as 'knowledge', as coordinators of the project we had to post a long note to all partner teams after the meeting in order to clarify the articulation between lay knowledge and formal knowledge:

METHODOLOGICAL NOTE:

HOW TO MAKE CHOICES FOR FIELDWORK

As promised, here is a note, which is supposed *to clarify the way we should make choices regarding fieldwork.*

In the oral presentation, we may not have put enough emphasis on a central point of the project: the articulation between lay knowledge and academic expertise (i.e. medical expertise, but also economic expertise, health technology assessment, and so on). To tell it very roughly, we are interested in situations where:

- Patients' organisations try to push 'lay knowledge' in places where they are not normally considered relevant (i.e. in the determination of therapeutic strategies, in the elaboration of research programs or health policies, and so on).
- Patients' organisations participate in the production of 'expert knowledge' in order to achieve a number of goals and to strengthen certain claims.
- We are therefore seeking cases where there is an effort to build connections between different forms of knowledge, different worlds, and where some 'political issue', whether at individual or collective level, is at stake. (Unpublished note, 10 March 2009: 1)

We also had to restate our approach to the fieldwork after some partners' concerns with the use of ethnography. In the childbirth case for instance, we were really surprised at how similar knowledge-related activities exist within the five groups we studied, despite huge differences in their organisational features and initial motives for mobilising. That being said, the team which explored NCT UK recalled that the five groups are in fact very different. NCT UK, for instance, organises birth training sessions (which the other groups not do), and our colleagues who studied NCT UK suggested that it might be interesting at some point to do ethnography on the five groups. As coordinators of the project, we had to reassert that we did not intend to do ethnography on the POs, but rather to make observations that might help us to look at each of their knowledge practices in light of the others'. In the note mentioned above, we recommended that:

> *The word 'ethnography', which is used once in the project and has been used a few times in our meeting, should be taken in a very modest sense. 'Observations' should better describe what we mean:* if any of us has for example, the opportunity to assist general assemblies, board of directors meetings, scientific committee meetings, official commissions meetings (organised by administrations or health organisations), it might be interesting to do it; to grasp the nature of arguments which are used by participants and evaluate the role of specific knowledge. *But our approach is somehow heterogeneous and mainly pragmatic:* we need to identify right places, relevant documentation, key informants in order to tell stories that will allow us to describe and analyse what is at stake around knowledge-related activities in each organisation, and in relation to their strategies towards various actors.[7] [Our emphasis]

Retrospectively, despite the diversity of our backgrounds, we can fairly say that this recommendation played a crucial role in creating and maintaining a cohesive approach to our project. These notes certainly reinforced the creation of a common gaze on the sites we chose to explore. However, they achieved more than that: they settled down the premises of a common analytical frame by stating, for instance, that 'the very nature of (POs') self-help activities is not the focus of our research project'.

Most importantly, two elements from our research proposal, the proto-typology and the notion of national context, literally disappeared at this point. The vanishing of the proto-typology provides a clear indication of our approach to comparison. That is, we did not regard comparison as a classificatory method. Instead, we conceived comparison as a set of practices and tools for cutting across different sites with the same series of questions: what knowledge-related activities do POs undertake, for what purposes, and with what effects? Our ultimate aim was to test our hypothesis that knowledge indeed constitutes a strategic element of POs' activism, however diverse they are. As for the notion of context, we can reasonably say that we did not consider it to be an analytical concept for explaining why and how knowledge does or does not matter. Rather, we proposed to our partners that they should embrace the perspective of POs and identify how they actively partake in the definition of the context in which they themselves intervene. However, these exclusions remained implicit, leaving room for some tensions between theoretical backgrounds and research practices to accumulate until they popped up in the form of questions raised by our partners. Ultimately, the practice of comparison seems to have an agency of its own, fuelled by many micro-differences not only in the objects compared, but also in the comparators themselves, thus following a more sinuous path than the one we tried to predetermine through our recommendations to our partners.

WORKING OUT SINGULARITIES AND COMMONALITIES

Fixing the *modus operandi* for fieldwork was not enough, of course, for we also had to reflect on the way we would concretely combine the outputs of the fieldwork. Communication, exchanges, and modes of discussion were extensively reworked all along the project, the organisation of each meeting being the occasion to reflect again and again on the kind of comparative work we wanted to undertake.

After the kick-off meeting and up to the July 2010 meeting, partner teams involved in each work package visited each other and/or exchanged emails to discuss the observations they made. They thus began to look at each PO focusing on one given condition (in light of POs concerned with the same condition in other countries).

The July 2010 meeting was conceived in order to extend this comparative exercise to all POs and all partner teams along the following procedures. Based on preliminary data reports circulated amongst partners, the first day of the meeting was devoted to presentations organised by work packages:

> 1) Firstly, according to the common grid we circulated, each team working on one given PO reported on the data it collected and gave a few suggestions on how to characterise the PO's form of engagement with knowledge.
> 2) Secondly, those of us not involved in the work package (i.e. not concerned with the corresponding condition), were asked to display the similarities and differences s/he identified between the POs concerned with the same condition, and to bring in her/his views on these POs in light of what s/he observed in the case s/he studied.
> 3) Thirdly, a discussion took place where all partner teams commented on the analysis that emerged out of these presentations.

The second day of the meeting targeted the discussion of concepts, some of which drew on the literature, while others elaborated on the fieldwork to capture and make sense of the similarities and differences between the POs we studied.

Throughout this protocol, a dual process that put comparison at the heart of the research process was at stake: the objective was to ingrain the project as a 'whole' in the description of each case, as well to make the 'whole' emerge out of the diversity of cases. The expectation was that these repeated confrontations would produce a collective sensitivity to the specificities of each case, and that they would increase the relevance of our analysis on the common issue of the project (i.e. POs' modes of engagement with knowledge and their meaning).

However, as already stated, comparison came into play with its own agency, sometimes de-structuring what we thought had been stabilised for a while. For example, take the two groups of parents of children with ADHD in France and Ireland. In our presentation of the French group, we insisted on the fact that parents are assembling various species of knowledge in order to provide a multidisciplinary approach to the disorder and its treatment. Moreover, we mentioned the group of parents' contribution to the notion of cognitive disability, a category which is to be seen in the 2005 French Disability Act, but which does not exist in other countries. Our Irish partners also presented the variety of knowledge that the Irish National Council for ADHD Support Groups (INCADDS) and its member groups engage with. Although INCADDS embraces a biomedical definition for stating the fact of the disorder, it also pays attention to family therapies, as well as cognitive sciences and the promises of neurofeedback theory. It is most likely because of our focus on 'cognitive disability' as a French category that our colleague commented on the two presentations and was caught up with the question of the differences between the two groups. Almost automatically, the general discussion brought back the issue of 'national context' we thought we had neatly boxed as a manifestation of the 'differential agency of comparison'. This led us to ask: 'are there elements of these national contexts which may explain the differences between the two groups, and if yes, how do we account for these elements in our analysis'? It forced us to reopen the debate and to re-elaborate collective answers, which in this case translated into the idea that rather than talking of context, we should examine how each PO construes the disease.

Through the devices we progressively put in place over the project, we should say that instead of 'doing comparison' (i.e. comparing POs according a predetermined metrics that would be external to them), we were 'making comparison' (i.e. manufacturing comparators allowing to grasp from within POs' singularities and commonalities) (Deville et al. this volume).

FROM CASES TO CONCEPTS, AND BACK

The closing session of the July 2010 meeting was devoted to discussing a series of concepts to make sense of the observations we made, and to delineate the significant features of the knowledge-related activities which patients' organisations undertook, and which we planned to dig through over the coming months. As with any research project, our ultimate goal was indeed to publish, which implied that we had to disseminate our fieldwork to the space of academic production. This entailed another comparative endeavour, consisting of a twofold task: firstly, putting our case studies to the trial of relevant bodies of literature; and secondly, forging our own analytical tools to signpost how our approach might renew the understanding of patients' activism.

THE ACADEMIC ARENA: ANOTHER SPACE OF COMPARISON

Prior to the meeting, we circulated a list of concepts drawn from the literature. Some notions were coined by fellow researchers who investigated the upsurge of knowledge in the preoccupations of patients' organisations. This, for instance, was the case for Steven Epstein's 'therapeutic activism' (1995). Though very inspiring, this notion was too restrictive in regard to the variety of cases we examined, for it mainly targeted patients' organisations which engaged in biomedical research and aimed at fostering the development of new therapeutics. Other concepts were proposed by scholars to capture the transformative effects of certain health movements. Maren Klawiter's 'disease regimes' (2004) stood as an example, and raised much discussion amongst us. Some felt quite uneasy with this notion, due to the possibility that it might overshadow the multiple uncertainties in which certain conditions we explored were mired. Still, other concepts pointing to broad understandings of social changes were also on the list. This, for instance, was the case for the concept of medicalisation/de-medicalisation. We were pretty much cautious, however, about applying such an overarching concept to our fieldwork, for it might fail to account for the singular dynamic of each organisation we studied. Finally, we reflected on Sheila Jasanoff's 'civic epistemology', which she defined as 'the institutional practices by which members of a given society test knowledge claims used as a basis for making collective choices' (2005: 255). Jasanoff coined this notion to explain the differences between the politics and policy of life sciences in the USA, the UK, and Germany. Though intended to serve a comparative purpose, this notion did not match the methodology we put together. Indeed, we did not look at the commonalities of patients' organisations in one given country with an aim to compare these with the commonalities of patients' organisations in another given country. Our project was at odds with such an approach: it rather insisted on the existence of numerous links between patients' organisations of different countries, via European umbrella organisations, for instance, and questioned the circulation of models of activism between them.

To be sure, confronting our observations and epistemic orientations with those of other researchers is a classic academic game of sorts: colleagues expect you to consider previous studies on the same kind of empirical objects, and to discuss your analytical perspective in relation to existing ones. In retrospect, our playing of the game denotes two things. Firstly, we did it as yet another comparative trial extended to bodies of researchers/case studies we felt we were part and parcel of. Secondly, we did it to assert our collective agency by equipping ourselves with a shared reading of the literature. To strengthen this collective agency, we went a step further in elaborating a common interpretative framework grounded in our mutual understanding of the cases we studied and discussed.

ELABORATING A COMMON INTERPRETATIVE FRAMEWORK

Our critical reading of existing concepts was motivated by our willingness to contribute something original to the understanding of patients' activism. To achieve this, each of us was invited to propose descriptors which best translated what s/he observed and to question the others' case studies in light of these descriptors. However, this collective production and discussion of descriptors did not occur in a conceptual void. As mentioned above, we balanced the merits and limits of existing notions in light of our fieldwork, paying extreme attention to how and what extent these notions captured the singularity of the situations we explored. For instance, in order to highlight patient organisations' dual problematisation of what their conditions are, this prompted some of us to suggest moving from Klawiter's concept of 'disease regime' to the notion of 'cause regime,' and what these conditions are the cause of (i.e. what sort of issues they bring in). Eventually, we dropped the very notion of 'regime', for it was too constraining in regard to the multifarious trajectories of patients' organisations we studied. Instead of applying concepts from the outside, we were scrutinising if, and how, these concepts helped us to say something relevant about the specific issues which patients' organisations gave shape to, and to which they brought about concrete solutions. As a way of illustration, one of us concluded our discussion on medicalisation/de-medicalisation as follows:

> I feel like medicalisation/de-medicalisation is a highly situated issue [...]
> We should consider it (medicalisation/de-medicalisation) as one PO's concerns (amongst many others), rather than an analytical framework for us (EPOKS concepts 2009).

What then did our analytical framework look like? It articulated a series of descriptors of our own which enabled us to simultaneously dig around the similarities between the cases we studied, and to sharpen our attention to the specificities of each case. For instance, we clustered a series of descriptors under a common heading: 'Cause – Singularisation/Generalisation – Politics of numbers – Recombinant science'. This allowed us to underlie a common feature of the POs we observed, such as the dynamic and joint transformation of their motives to mobilise and the networks of alliances of which they partake. Moreover, as illustrated by the following note, it also allowed us to highlight how each PO engages in this process:

> Rare diseases patients' organisations explicitly engage in 'politics of numbers' that they voice as follows: 'Diseases are rare but rare diseases patients are numerous' [...] Recombining scientific knowledge constitutes another way to expand 'causes' [...] By mobilising, combining and confronting various multidisciplinary bodies of scientific knowledge, some rare diseases POs, although concerned with very different diseases, come to identify potential transversal issues [...] The French ADHD organisation recombines heterogeneous pieces of expertise and comes to ally with other collectives on this basis.

Now equipped with a common list of descriptors, each partner completed her/his study of POs' knowledge-related activities and reported to the team seven months later, in February 2011. As coordinators, we hesitated quite a lot between two modes of organising this subsequent meeting, and asked ourselves 'should we privilege conditions as entry points for presenting and debating our material, or the descriptors we put together'? We finally opted for the first option, fearing that the second one

> ... might constitute a too quick jump into a conceptual grid without paying enough attention to the *specificities* of each case, and lead to superficial exchanges [Our emphasis] (Email to the project team members, 16 December 2010).

We also envisioned parallel sessions, each on one given condition, but this did not prove feasible for each of us who were involved in different conditions. Furthermore, we explained to our colleagues that

> [w]e need to consider that each condition is only an entry point into the discussion, but that depending on the issues raised, it should involve material and analysis from other work packages (Akrich, email to the project team members, 16 December 2010).

We stated over and over again our priority was to make sense of each case in its singularity, while immersing it into a common atmosphere created by our shared methodology and common descriptive language. Everyone played the game of comparing a few descriptors with specific knowledge-related activities that s/he studied. The descriptors which were the easiest to express through empirical data were the most successful, and allowed the integration of different case studies with a common interpretative framework. This was notably the case for our notion of 'evidence-based activism', which captured striking similarities in our observations (i.e. the fact that knowledge is not a mere resource but an object of enquiry for patients' organisations, and that this affects their role in the governance of health issues in a variety of ways).

To recap, the process we went through was one of 'constant comparison' (Glaser and Strauss 1967) which took the form of a loop. The procedure started by travelling to each case individually, eventually returning to the original one with new lenses for augmenting its contrasts. The discussion about existing concepts and the production of original descriptors was embedded into this process, so much so that the group came up as an integrated comparator interlocking individuals, case studies, and notions. This has a crucial effect on the intellectual space we progressively designed: it is a space within which the analysis of each case is deepened through the circulation from one site to the next, thus suggesting a mode of generalisation which does not consist of extracting a few dimensions out of the singularity of each case, but rather thickens its singularity in light of the others. We will return to this point in our concluding remarks.

THE MULTIPLE TRAPS OF WRITING 'COMPARATIVE' PAPERS

After the February 2011 meeting, we decided to prepare a special issue of an academic journal on our notion of 'evidence-based activism', which appeared to encapsulate our findings the best. The issue was structured as follows:

> 1) An editorial recapitulating what we meant by 'evidence-based activism', and situating our notion vis-à-vis other concepts.
> 2) Four papers (one *per* condition) putting this notion to work and demonstrating how it renewed understanding of patients' and health activism in these condition areas.

Doing and making fieldwork, brainstorming our cases, and playing around with concepts is one thing. However, writing academic articles is quite another matter. So far, we have deployed ourselves within spaces whose contours we carefully demarcated, and staged a methodology which permitted us to debate research questions in ways which suited us. When it came to writing papers, our previous efforts for putting things under control were dramatically challenged. Writing an academic article is of course highly constraining, if only because the authors are required to order empirical material, concepts, and arguments in a standardised 10,000-word-piece! In addition, however, we encountered a series of difficulties: some we anticipated, others we did not. In particular, the issue of 'how to compare', which we thought we sealed in our methodological and conceptual box, resurfaced like an evil spirit at different moments of the writing and revising process. How we faced this process is the purpose of this last section.

STRUCTURING A COMPARATIVE ARTICLE AND FACING THE EVIL SPIRIT OF COMPARISON

As Hassenteufel (2005) rightly points out, writing a comparative article is a risky business. Either the author structures the article around a common interpretative framework and takes the risk of displaying the cases under comparison as mere illustrations of the concepts s/he puts forward, or the author details the cases s/he studies and concludes with a general discussion, an option which may undermine the comparative nature of the paper. We knew that we had to find our way through these two alternatives. What we were not fully aware of, however, was that the solution to this dilemma was very much dependent upon the number of cases we examined in each condition area, as manifested in the first version of our 'childbirth' paper (for which we investigated five activists' groups in four countries).

In the introduction of our 'childbirth' paper, we reviewed the existing literature on childbirth activism in order to situate our approach (i.e. the fact that we concentrated on practices rather than on ideological discourses on de-medicalisation of childbirth, and that we especially investigated knowledge-related activities with an aim to reconsider childbirth activists' groups' positions vis-à-vis medicine). We then had four sections, each focusing on the national groups we studied, *and* on specific sets of knowledge-related activities that these groups developed:

1) Making normal birth an operative category: statistical evidence about practices as a coordination device in the UK.
2) Producing evidence and defining causes: putting surveys at the core of Irish activism.

3) From scientific evidence to matters of concern: CIANE's participation in producing French guidelines.

4) International authoritative evidence as a source and a resource for the Portuguese childbirth movement.

Through this choice, we tried to hold together the internal coherence of each case and an analytical argument for the whole paper. The reviewers' comments made us realise that pooling together a juxtaposition of case studies and a substantial demonstration proved to hold nothing! They were sensitive to our prevarications, and although they recommended that our paper was worth being revised, they also raised a number of criticisms. The first reviewer, for instance, could not perceive that each empirical case was intended to make a specific point, and said that (s)he did not know 'how to work through the mountains of evidence presented to (him/her)' (excerpt from the letter sent by the journal editor to the authors).

In addition to the structure of our articles, we were confronted with a serious burden related to being adamant that singularities matter. As the reviewer above confessed, s/he was lost in 'the mountains of evidence' we provided. How to make sense of 'mountains of evidence' without sampling, sorting out, and arranging them into categories? This question takes up a salient feature when writing comparative papers, for readers somehow expect to find out explanatory evidence of the differences and similarities between cases. This was where the issue of 'how to compare' reappeared like an evil spirit, not only in exchanges between us as co-authors, but also in some reviewers' comments. Moreover, and this we did not fully foresee, it did so differently in each of the papers. Let us narrate how the evil spirit of comparison caught us, and how we pulled ourselves out of its traps in the three papers we co-authored.

THE TRAP OF TYPOLOGY

Because of the number of cases we studied – five groups in four countries – the 'childbirth' paper challenged us with the trap of typology. With five cases, one can hardly avoid typology readings, if only to ease the cognitive appropriation of the cases. In order to prevent such readings, we inserted quite a long discussion at the end of the first version, where the objective was to make sense of the differences between the cases (which any reader, even the most distracted one, could not miss), but without reifying explanatory factors of these differences. This puzzled the reviewers: the first found our paper too descriptive, whereas the second and the third read our piece as a preliminary step towards the elaboration of a typology that calls for further structural explanations, and they asked for more information on the organisations and countries. In effect, what we experienced was how difficult it is to report on multi-sited observations without inducing readings that escape the authors' control. This is because multi-sited observations inevitably suggest readings either in terms of typology, or in terms of 'global system-local situations'.

The solution we thus adopted was to revert to a more classic form of exposition: an articulation of the major claims in the introduction, an explicit and sustained argument in each part, the disentanglement of these arguments from specific case studies, and a clarification on the comparison issue. As we explained in our reply to the reviewers' comments,

> [t]he paper does not set out to undertake a comparison of the organisations or countries with a view to identifying variables that would explain their differences. It is now clearly signposted in the introduction that we focus instead on the capacity of the organisations to transform and redefine their environments by eliciting the emergence of new actors and new facts (Letter to the journal editor, 20 February 2013).

THE TRAP OF THE 'MODEL'

With the 'rare diseases' paper which involved France and Portugal, we were caught in quite a different trap: that of the 'cas d'école' model, 'golden event' (Lévi-Strauss 1958). This stemmed from the fact that our previous research on the AFM led us to conclude that this organisation may be considered as a 'cas d'école' of partnership between patients and biomedical communities. Subsequent quantitative surveys and ethnographic fieldwork provided evidence on this 'cas d'école' being turned into a model that a large proportion of French rare diseases patients' organisations, as well as the European Organisation on Rare Diseases (EURORDIS), endorsed. Because EURORDIS was very active in structuring umbrella organisations in Portugal, we confidently presumed that the French model of activism was disseminated in this country. Quite surprisingly, our quantitative and qualitative data disconfirmed our hypothesis: not only were Portuguese rare diseases patients' organisations not as proactively engaged in biomedical research as their French sister organisations, but some were very critical of the notion of rareness, arguing that it did not do justice to patients' and families' real life problems, such as disability and social exclusion.

These findings considerably complicated the drafting of the first version of our paper. On the one hand we were, and still are, convinced that there is something peculiar to rareness. On the other hand, it was pretty clear that the 'model of rareness activism' which we initially had in mind took a serious hit! The initial version of our paper tried to play around this tension. This did not escape one of the reviewers, who criticised our methodological inconsistencies:

> [The authors'] strategy of highlighting examples that contradict expectations is not the same as hypothesis testing.

Our mistake! After much discussion between the co-authors, we eventually decided to no longer posit the form of activism developed by French rare diseases patients' organisations as a model against which we measure their Portuguese counterparts. Instead, we focused our article on how the very notion of rareness was problematised and transformed in the local sites it crossed. We also considered Portuguese organisations' behaviours and actions as lenses through which to look back at French organisations, and, more fundamentally, questioned the very existence of a French model.

THE TRAP OF 'COMPARING COMPARISON'

With the 'ADHD' paper, which involved one group of parents in France and one in Ireland, the concept of medicalisation resurfaced. Though we considered that this concept could not serve as an analytical framework for us after the February 2011 workshop, we did not clearly realise at that time that we could no longer rely upon this concept for ordering our comparative writing. However, because the literature on ADHD largely mobilises this concept, we put too much effort into arguing that our notion of 'evidence-based activism' better captures the two organisations' epistemic efforts for extending and articulating a variety of evidence on the disorder (which go well beyond the realm of biomedical expertise). This was to such a degree that we did not find an intelligible way for highlighting how each organisation construed ADHD. Thus, as Stengers (2011) asserts, we were caught in the trap of 'comparing comparisons', and were too preoccupied with weighing the vices of the medicalisation frame on the one hand, and the virtues of ours in terms of 'evidence-based activism', on the other.

As we should have expected, it was precisely this issue of 'comparing comparisons' which the reviewers pointed out. They were all very enthusiastic about the richness of our empirical material, and just as much very critical of what they felt was an immoderate attack upon the concept of medicalisation. They suggested that we forced our empirical data into a restrictive analytical frame, and that somehow we were not fair enough in playing the game of 'comparing comparisons'. Consequently, they raised the issue of how exactly we compared the two organisations, and asked whether the national contexts into which they evolved might explain their differences, which our demonstration left little room to do.

While revising the paper, much discussion arose amongst the co-authors on how to handle this issue of national contexts. Eventually, we developed a twofold argument:

> 1) That the two organisations are preoccupied with aligning their politics of illness (i.e. ADHD is a multidimensional disorder which needs a multimodal

therapeutic approach) with their politics of knowledge (i.e. an interest in different species of credentialed expertise – biomedical, psychiatric, psychological, educational, etc.). Moreover, it appears that in order for this to be achieved, medicalisation is a starting point for the two organisations but not the end of the story.

2) That the two organisations' politics of illness/knowledge aims to transform the network of experts and professionals they ally with/oppose, and that these alliances/oppositions themselves result from the ways the two organisations problematise patients' and families' specific situations.

Subsequently, the second version of our paper tried to tighten more than we did initially:

1) The comparison between our approach to ADHD activism and alternative understandings of the same phenomenon.
2) The comparison between the two cases we studied.

In retrospect, it is clear that putting together our special issue was yet another device: a very demanding one which forced us to provoke once more the issue of comparison and to sharpen our view on what exactly we ended up with. Of course, the writing of academic articles is always a trial, if only because reviewers have their own embodied epistemic perspectives and political agendas which the authors may not share. The comments we got from the reviewers on the first drafts of our papers also reopened our comparative toolkit and brought back the question: how to compare without explaining differences and similarities between cases from the outside? As a matter-of-fact, reviewers' criticisms, as well as discussions between the co-authors over the writing and revising process, epitomised the 'differential agency of comparison', which manifested itself in a variety of ways and at different moments from the start to the end of our project. We faced the cumbersome injunction for international comparison, which we strived to get rid of in our proposal to the EU call. We fixed our methodological and conceptual approach to comparison and did the work accordingly. When the time came to write and revise our articles, we were overwhelmed by questions we thought we had mastered: what to do with national contexts? How to pull ourselves out of the traps of picturing the situations we examined as elements of a typology, or models of broader phenomena, or exceptions to well-established social theories? How to make sense of singularities which emerged out of our comparative approach without giving the impression of being too descriptive and lacking analytical depth? Those were the challenges which the evil spirit of comparison asked us to take up, and which led us to entirely rewrite the articles we submitted. Having gone through that process, we now feel (a bit) more comfortable with the questions Madeleine's colleague raised in the beginning of this paper.

CONCLUSION

Recall that our colleague asked Madeleine about the general lessons we could draw on for our comparative research project. Comparison was indeed long considered as a surrogate experimental device for either revealing the general character of certain social phenomena, or for producing a model of the structure and functioning of society and its elements. The respective merits of quantitative and qualitative methods were fiercely debated: those who followed a positivist approach to society *à la* Durkheim embraced statistical methods, whereas those after Lévi-Strauss viewed society as a mechanics to be dissected and favoured case studies.[8] Those debates on 'variable-based' versus 'case-based' comparison (Ragin 1981) have certainly evolved, but they have left two legacies: (1) that social sciences should overcome the singularity attached to case studies; and (2) that comparison is the methodology par excellence for elaborating and testing general causal explanations in social sciences.

The conception of comparison as a set of methods for generalising observations and research findings still looms large in many discourses, most notably in ones about EU research proposals. Explaining differences between national case studies by national contexts is the alpha and omega of EU comparative projects. For reasons related to our political agenda and our actor-network theory background, we did not go with this causal explanatory framework. Our contention was that whatever national contexts are, patients' organisations display strikingly similar epistemic capacities for shaping health issues they deem relevant, transforming their environment for these issues to be considered at an individual and collective level. We were simultaneously very sensitive to the irreducible character of each organisation, and argued that patients' organisations cannot be compared using a predefined exogenous metrics. This sounds like a catch-22: how to maintain that patients' organisations are similar and yet irreducible? How to work out the 'same but different', as Deville et al. (this volume) nicely put it?

The methodology we staged aimed to handle this puzzle and propose an alternative approach to classic international comparisons. We progressively forged our consortium as a comparator: as a collective of individual researchers, case studies and concepts whose work was to make the situations we selected commensurable, i.e. searchable through the same set of research questions and procedures for data collection, and to augment contrasts within each situation in light of cross-examination and cross-interpretation of our observations. This way of comparing came with a radically different conception of generalisation: that is, generalisation in our research project was not a matter of 'montée en généralité' (Boltanski and Thévenot 1987), where case studies are abstracted from their idiosyncratic character. Rather, it was a matter of singularisation, which entailed shedding light on and making sense of how each patients' organisation construed its cause and its context (Asdal and Moser 2012) in light of how other organisations do it. Our approach towards 'how to compare' and 'what for', attempts to put an end to the prevarications between sociology and history (Wievorka 1992; Passeron and Revel 2005). We neither built a social theory of patients' organisations out of case-based comparison, nor did we celebrate the uniqueness of events which punctuate the history of each organisation. What we did instead was to highlight the existence of common practices amongst patients' organisations, and to examine each organisation through the lenses of these practices. This eventually enabled us to pick out each organisation's specificities, and to deepen understandings on their singular and original way of dealing with their own problems.

There are two additional issues which we would like to conclude with. One is the issue of how to measure patients' organisations' successes/failures in order to change policies. As it stands, this question does not resonate with our preoccupations, not because it is of no interest to us, but because it supposes the existence of a standard against which to evaluate successes/failures. Yet, we cannot compare *ceteris paribus* what happened before and what occurred after one patients' organisation engaged in a condition-area, for patients' intervention transformed the network of issues, problems, and actors at stake. It is the scope of these transformations and their effects that we should examine closely if we are to grasp the meaning of patients' activism. Moreover, we suspect that this question of success and failure conveys another supposition, that certain national contexts are more conducive to patients' and health activism than others. One commonplace thinking, for instance, is that within the EU certain countries are 'advanced' whereas others are 'backward' in respect to patients' participation in health policies.[9] Though tempting, such a supposition does not do justice to patients' organisations' transformative effects, including in the production of ideas on which countries are moving forward, and which ones are lagging behind in the condition areas they are concerned with. Our project also supported a more dynamic view on the ongoing construction of the EU by offering an alternative understanding of differences and similarities between its member states.

The last issue we would like to conclude with is the effect of our own comparative research project. From the outset, we were willing to act politically (i.e. to contribute something to the recognition of patients' organisations as genuine actors in the domain of health and medicine), and not just as auxiliaries to traditional stakeholders (i.e. researchers, health institutions, political authorities, the industry), or as social movement organisations opposing traditional stakeholders. Our project certainly strengthened our political agenda: our data and analysis provided evidence on patients' organisations' active involvement in 'collective enquiries' which give shape to 'publics and their problems' (to borrow from Dewey [1927]), and helped us to argue that these POs' practices are core to their activism. To convey the idea that patients' organisations are legitimate experts on issues they raise, we organised a participative conference with social scientists, patients' organisations, and stakeholders in the condition areas we studied. This conference took place in Lancaster in September 2011, and gathered about sixty participants. The epistemic-political message we transmitted over the conference was that whatever their specificities, all patients' organisations have epistemic capacities: that is, they do not consider knowledge as mere resources for defending their causes, but as 'things' they are able to work around inventively and reflexively for transforming the politics and polity in their condition areas. This is what we actually meant by our notion of 'evidence-based activism', and this was diversely appreciated. Some patients feared that it echoed evidence-based policy and evidence-based medicine (EBM) too much, and may well have adverse effects in picturing patients' organisations as insiders into research and political milieu. Others warmly welcomed our notion, arguing that it indeed offers a positive view on patients' organisations as 'knowledge-able' (Felt 2013) and responsible actors who contribute something to society. So, one effect of our comparative project was to have extended dialogue (including with patients' organisations) around the fact that despite their heterogeneity, they must be considered, and consider themselves, as full-fledged epistemic actors able to question the relevance and legitimacy of evidence onto which collective decisions are made. No doubt, we will continue to dig around this message, for it is what our comparative project enabled us to articulate.

ACKNOWLEDGEMENTS

The EPOKS project that we discuss in this article was funded by the European Commission FP7 (more information on the project is available on http://www.csi.ensmp.fr/WebCSI/EPOKSWebSite). We owe a lot to our research partners who contributed a creative and friendly atmosphere over the three-year duration of the project. We warmly thank the participants of the workshop organised by Joe Deville and Michael Guggenheim on this edited book, and who offered inspiring suggestions on a previous version of our article. We are particularly grateful to Joe Deville and Roland Bal for their thoughtful remarks. Our final thanks go to the members of Centre de sociologie de l'innovation of MINES ParisTech for their comments on the first draft of our article.

NOTES

1 European legislation defines rare diseases as conditions that affect less than 1 out of every 2,000 people, or 5 out of every 10,000 people in a given area.
2 The EU call was funded by the 'Science in Society' initiative of the European Commission FP7.
3 There were notable exceptions such as Steven Epstein (1996), who studied HIV-Aids activism in the US, and Janine Barbot (2002) and Nicolas Dodier (2003), who studied HIV-Aids activism in France.
4 We warmly thank Joe Deville for suggesting this idea of an 'agency of comparison'.
5 In her piece, Marilyn Strathern opposes 'perspectivalism' and 'perspectivism': 'To be perspectivalist acts out Euro-American pluralism, ontologically grounded in one world and many viewpoints; whereas perspectivism implies an ontology of many worlds and one capacity to take a viewpoint'(2011: 92).
6 This grid is taken from Akrich and Rabeharisoa's PowerPoint presentation at the EPOKS Kick-off Meeting, 24 February 2009.
7 We suggest adopting Isabelle Baszanger and Nicolas Dodier's (1996) term 'ethnographie combinatoire' (combinatory ethnography), described as a process of selective collection of data/events which aims to account for situated activities that cannot be interpreted in terms of a unified set of normative references.
8 On those early debates about what comparison entails, see for instance the introduction to the special issue of *Common Knowledge* (2001) provocatively titled: 'Comparative Relativism. Symposium on an Impossibility'. See also Niewöhner and Scheffer (2008) and Krause (this volume).
9 On these 'development rankings' of EU Member States, see also Teresa Stöckelova's paper in this volume.

BIBLIOGRAPHY

Akrich, M., et al., *The Dynamics of Patient Organizations in Europe* (Paris: Presses de l'Ecole des Mines, 2008)
Akrich, M., C., Méadel, and V. Rabeharisoa, *Se mobiliser pour la santé. Des associations de patients témoignent* (Paris: Presses de l'Ecole des Mines, 2009)
Akrich, M., and C. Méadel, 'Prendre ses médicaments/prendre la parole: Les usages des médicaments par les patients dans les listes de discussion électroniques', *Sciences Sociales & Santé*, 20.1 (2002), 89–116
——'De l'interaction à l'engagement: Les collectifs électroniques, nouveaux militants de la santé', *Hermès*, 47 (2007), 145–53
Akrich, M., and V. Rabeharisoa, 'EPOKS Kick-off Meeting', PowerPoint presentation at EPOKS kick-off meeting, 2009

Asdal, K., and I. Moser, 'Experiments in Context and Contexting', *Science, Technology, & Human Values*, 37.4 (2012), 291–306

Barbot, J., *Les malades en mouvements: La médecine et la science à l'épreuve du sida* (Paris: Balland, 2002)

Boltanski, L., and L. Thévenot, *De la justification: les economies de la grandeur* (Paris: Gallimard, 1991)

Collins, H. M., 'The TEA Set: Tacit Knowledge and Scientific Networks', *Science Studies*, 4 (1974), 165–86

Deville, J., M. Guggenheim, and Z. Hrdličková, 'Same, Same but Different: Provoking Relations, Assembling the Comparator', Working Paper 1 for *Centre for the Study of Invention & Social Process* (CSISP), Goldsmiths, University of London, 2013

——'Same, Same but Different: Provoking Relations, Assembling the Comparator', this volume

Dewey, J., *The Public and Problems* (New York: Holt, 1927)

Dodier, N., *Leçons politiques de l'épidémie de sida* (Paris: EHESS, 2003)

Dodier, N., and I. Baszanger, 'Totalisation et altérité dans l'enquête ethnographique', *Revue Française de Sociologie*, XXXVIII (1997), 37–66

Epstein, S., 'The Construction of Lay Expertise: AIDS Activism and the Forging of Credibility in the Reform of Clinical Trials', *Science, Technology, & Human Values*, 20 (1995), 408–37

——*Impure Science: AIDS, Activism, and the Politics of Knowledge* (Berkeley: University Press of California, 1996)

Felt, U., 'Innovation-driven Futures and Knowledge-able Citizens', Lecture given at *Science and Society – Meet with Excellence* series, Department of Science and Technology Studies, Vienna, 2013

Glaser, B. G., and A. L. Strauss, *The Discovery of Grounded Theory: Strategies for Qualitative Research* (New York: Aldine de Gruyter, 1967)

Haraway, D., 'Situated Knowledges: The Science Question in Feminism and the Privilege of Partial Perspective', *Feminist Studies*, 14.3 (1988), 575–99

Hassenteufel, P., 'De la comparaison internationale à la comparaison transnationale: Les déplacements de la construction d'objets comparatifs en matière de politiques publiques', *Revue Française de Science Politique*, 55.1 (2005), 113–32

Huyard, C., 'Who Rules Rare Diseases Associations? A Framework to Understand their Action', *Sociology of Health and Illness*, 31.7 (2009), 979–93

Jasanoff, S., *Designs on Nature: Science and Democracy in Europe and the United States* (New Jersey: Princeton University Press, 2005)

Jensen, C., 'Comparative Relativism: A Symposium on an Impossibility', *Common Knowledge*, 17.1 (2011), 1–12

Klawiter, M., 'Breast Cancer in Two Regimes: The Impact of Social Movements on Illness Experience', *Sociology of Health and Illness*, 26 (2004), 845–74

Knorr-Cetina, K., *The Manufacture of Knowledge – An Essay on the Constructivist and*

Contextual Nature of Science (Oxford: Pergamon Press, 1981)

Krause, M., 'Comparative Research: Beyond Linear-causal Explanation', this volume

Langstrup, H., and B. Ross Winthereik, 'The Making of Self-monitoring Asthma Patients: Mending a Split Reality with Comparative Ethnography', *Comparative Sociology*, 7.3 (2008), 362–86

Lévi-Strauss, C., *Anthropologie Structurale* (Paris: Plon, 1958)

Löfgren, H., E. de Leeuw, and M. Leahy, eds., *Democratizing Health: Consumer Groups in the Policy Process* (Northampton: Edward Elgar, 2011)

Marcus, G. E., 'Ethnography in/of the World System: The Emergence of Multi-Sited Ethnography', *Annual Review of Anthropology*, 24 (1995), 95–117

Niewöhner, J., and T. Scheffer, 'Comparative Sociology: Introduction', *Comparative Sociology*, 7.3 (2008), 273–85

Passeron, J. C., and J. Revel, eds., *Penser par cas* (Paris: Éditions de l'EHESS, 2005)

Rabeharisoa, V., and M. Callon, *Le pouvoir des malades: L'association française contre les myopathies & la recherche* (Paris: Presses de l'École des mines, 1999)

Ragin, C. C., 'Comparative Sociology and the Comparative Method', *Comparative Sociology*, 22.1 (1981), 102–20

——'Introduction: Cases of "What is a case?"', in C. C. Ragin and H. S. Becker, eds., *What is a Case? Exploring the Foundations of Social Inquiry* (Cambridge: Cambridge University Press, 1992), pp. 1–18

Stengers, I., 'Comparison as a Matter of Concern', *Common Knowledge*, 17.1 (2011), 48–63

Strathern, M., 'Binary License', *Common Knowledge*, 17.1 (2011), 87–103

Stöckelová, T., 'Frame against the Grain: Asymmetries, Interference and the Politics of EU Comparison', this volume

Wievorka, M., 'Cases Studies: History or Sociology', in C. C. Ragin & H. S. Becker, eds., *What is a Case? Exploring the Foundations of Social Inquiry* (Cambridge: Cambridge University Press, 1992), pp. 1–18

6

FRAME AGAINST THE GRAIN: ASYMMETRIES, INTERFERENCE, AND THE POLITICS OF EU COMPARISON

Tereza Stöckelová

> Since it is only worth comparing the incommensurable, comparing the commensurable is a task for accountants, not anthropologists (Viveiros de Castro 2004: 14).

EDUARDO VIVEIROS DE CASTRO MAY HAVE BEEN TOO NARROW-MINDED about accountants (since 2008, we have learnt the hard way that their practice is much more creative than previously imagined), but he surely was right about anthropologists. Comparing the apparently commensurable not only offers very little insight beyond confirming what has been assumed already, but it also politically aligns social science analysis with the dominant orderings of reality. (In)comparability is not a perpetual, given feature of the phenomena we investigate, but a result of *framing(s)* enacted by various actors – researchers included. To paraphrase Bruno Latour's principle of (ir)reducibility (1988: 158), nothing is, by itself, either comparable or incomparable to anything else. It has to be made so.

Since (in)comparability is not 'out there', a framing that makes reasonable specific comparisons and excludes others is by no means politically and epistemologically innocent. Implicated in power relations, it is a practice that can stabilise, strengthen, or subvert. And, as we will see, it (re)shapes the realities concerned. It is in this sense that I use here the notion of frame and framing, freely inspired by a variety of social scientists (e.g. Goffman 1974; Callon 1998). These scholars have deployed it to analyse the apparent paradox between the (often hidden) constructed-ness of things, persons, and issues (which in one regard are not given by nature, but are socially, materially, and discursively enacted) and their relative stability and effectuality. Surely quantification is today's favoured strategy for imposing frames of comparison as if they were natural, thus rendering them effectively invisible (Porter 1995). The vivid social life of university rankings, which apparently make all institutions across the globe easily comparable at a single glance, is just one example (for evidence from the Netherlands, see de Rijcke et al., this volume). Such framing and comparative efforts – serving as a tool with which to govern academia in managerial and bureaucratic modes – have been elaborately analysed and criticised by social scientists (e.g. Strathern 2000; Shore 2008). There are, however, other practices implicated in enacting frames and units of comparison in which academics (including social scientists) massively partake. Among these are the entrenched geopolitical orderings that I will attend to closely in this chapter.

This chapter is certainly not an argument against comparing or comparative research. Rather, it is a call to pay attention to hidden framings and asymmetries of comparison, and for a reflexive, or diffractive (Haraway 1992) discussion on the effects of 'making (in)comparable', in which our social science research practices prominently participate.

From this perspective, I reflect on two interrelated research projects I was involved in between 2006 and 2010. Focused on changing academic cultures and practices, both of these projects had strong comparative elements. The first project, Knowledge, Institutions and Gender: An East-West Comparative Study (KNOWING) (2006–2008), was funded by the EU's Sixth Framework Programme (FP6), and involved five research teams from Austria, the Czech Republic, Finland, Slovakia, and the UK. Each team carried out qualitative research including interviews, focus group discussions, and participant observation in two academic institutions in the social sciences (most often but not solely sociology), and in the biosciences (molecular biology, biochemistry, organic chemistry). The primary aim of the project was to 'examine the production of knowledge contexts and cultures, including the role of gender, from an "East-West" perspective and identify structural and institutionalised practices and procedures, including standards of excellence, that hinder and/or promote the equal participation of women in science' (KNOWING Proposal, Annex I 2005: 4).

The second project, Articulations of Science Policies in Research Practice and the Academic Path (2009–2010), funded by the Grant Agency of the Academy of Sciences of the Czech Republic (GAAV), was a follow-up to KNOWING in the Czech Republic and focused on two selected topics (academic paths, and assessment and accountability). It drew upon KNOWING data and group interviews conducted with researchers in different disciplines and types of academic institutions. Alongside our interest in investigating the topics in more detail, we also saw potential to follow the ongoing changes in Czech science policy and their 'translations' into variable institutional and regional contexts. Our study was carried out amidst the most intense academic protests in Czech history against cuts in the research budget for the Academy of Sciences, the increased public funding for industrial research and innovation, and the introduction of a research evaluation framework that ties public funding to strictly quantitative criteria for assessing research performance. This is important, as it introduced a special dynamic into the relationship between research participants and us as researchers, something that I will discuss further on in the text.

Both projects thus intended to make multiple comparisons between European countries, between 'East and West', selected academic disciplines, and different types of research institutions. At the same time, the investigated realities already involved a number of framings such as assessment exercises comparing the 'research performance' of teams (in an institute) or researcher organisations (in a country). Here I look into how and with what (collateral) effects we as researchers practised comparisons in these two projects: what was taken as the frame of comparison? How did researchers' framings interfere with those of research participants? How were the frames reflected, taken into account, or made an object of enquiry *sui generis*? What epistemic and geopolitical asymmetries were embedded in our practices of comparison, and how may they have become destabilised over the course of the two projects? While we cannot stop framing, I will argue in the conclusion that there are alternatives to how we compare, and we should try to frame (in the EU projects) 'against the grain'. I suggest that we should be more courageous and challenging in relation to epistemologically and politically established framings.

MAKING UNITS

Comprised of research teams from different countries, the consortia of EU-funded projects addressing societal challenges imply comparisons between EU member states. This corresponds to the European idea of 'identity in diversity' (of cultures, people, policies, and so on) that has to be investigated, understood, and constantly managed and harmonised.[1] These comparisons do not simply represent realities 'out there' – they contribute to their enactment. In an analysis of the performative effects of the Eurobarometers, John Law observed that

> these statistical methods are creating a *homogeneous* European *collective space* containing isomorphic individuals which is then *re-stratified* into sub-spaces or sub-populations (for instance, 27 country distributions of opinion) and, so, in re-creating the nation state in a particular mode' (2009: 248).

What are the assumptions and effects of multi-member-state EU projects (including qualitative ones), and how do they shape the realities they study?

Let us look closely at the KNOWING project. Although we were interested in the disciplinary differences between the social sciences and the biosciences (and in comparisons along gender lines), what moved strongly to the forefront during the project were comparisons between 'each country's distinct epistemological culture and practice' (KNOWING Proposal, Annex I 2005: 13). As in many other social science projects carried out in the European Commission (EC) framework (Godfroy 2010), each team in this project investigated the research landscape and institutions in its own member state and in its native language (except for one German researcher in the Czech team who had been living in Prague for many years and who investigated – mostly in English – Czech and foreign researchers at the bioscience institute). When we met for a consortium-wide workshop, members of each team spoke mainly about (and from) the perspective of their own 'national' data. While discussions among the Czech team back in Prague contained differences and similarities between investigated domestic fieldwork sites, 'national reality' tended to come to the forefront in the consortium debates and become *homogeneous*. Most of the time, it was 'national reports' that were mainly and solely elaborated through work packages, and which we exchanged before consortium meetings. In essence, they became the basic elements of our collective debates.[2] They were the durable and mobile inscriptions that we could always easily refer to during the whole project.

In each country, there are surely distinct evaluation systems as well as funding schemes, agencies, and specific (language) audiences (particularly in the social sciences) that call for national comparisons and the identification of similarities and differences between nation-states. However, the strong comparative logic of EU member states – as projected into the format of 'national' research teams and funding for domestic fieldwork – tends to make certain kinds of phenomena less visible and researchable. In quantitative surveys such as the Eurobarometer in Law's (2009) example, nation-states are in most cases enacted as internally homogeneous units of comparison. In qualitative studies such as KNOWING, epistemic asymmetries (and possibly huge heterogeneities inside a member state) may be made invisible, as researchers – due to the constraints in project budget and researchers' capacity influenced by multiple project obligations – tend to carry out their fieldwork in the area where they live and work. That is also where research institutions able to successfully apply for EU funding are situated.[3] However, in consortium debates and international publications, the results are then often taken as representative of the country or national culture as such.

At that point, the assumption of the research process was that EU member states are relatively stable entities with distinct research cultures which can be reasonably compared, and which are faced with (and need to) negotiate the 'European discourse' of excellence. And by means of our own research, we contributed to strengthening the stabilisation of these entities. Here is an illustrative quotation from a collective monograph published from the KNOWING project:

> Already a first analysis of our material shows that the excellence discourse has reached all the countries investigated and that national and European discourses are closely intertwined (although in the UK, national excellence discourses are perhaps less explicitly entangled with European ones). Yet the way this concept becomes operationalised, filled with meaning and transformed into practice differs in interesting ways. These variations might be seen as linked to the different histories of national research systems, to the imagined place a country/institution holds on a more global research map and in particular to when and how research assessment exercises have started to be integrated (Felt and Stöckelová 2008: 76).

How, then, are such comparative conclusions arrived at, and backed up?

JUGGLING COMPARABILITY

In our research practice, the actual material for comparison did not involve primary data. These we did not share – due to language barriers, privacy protection, and the potential epistemological and ethical difficulties of working with ethnographic data generated by someone else in a different fieldwork. We felt this could not be seriously tackled in a three-year project with a limited budget (there were, for example, no resources for translation). Additionally, the proposition that at least some non-ethnographic data could be generated and exchanged for a comparative analysis was strongly resisted by some teams in the consortium. There was a proposal in the first work package of the project to distribute a 'life course questionnaire' (LCQ) as a standardised tool with supposedly 'identical' questions to researchers in the academic institutions under study. These would be processed statistically across the five countries prior to the participant observation phase of the fieldwork, and a sort of comparative baseline between them would be established. The ultimate point of disagreement was over the obligatory use of a Lickert scale in the questionnaire. This caused a major conflict within the consortium. Some of us were wary of creating an impression of easy and objective comparability packaged in statistics, and argued, for example, that

> [a]lthough we seem to be quite aware of contingencies, contexts or cultural specificities in the construction and structuring of epistemic communities that we study we do not assume these same contingencies when constructing our methodology [...] [There are] different cultures of expressing discontent or dissatisfaction. How are we then going to interpret the measurements: Are people in institutions in one country more critical/satisfied/hesitating or are the conditions in the institutions more/less satisfactory? (Internal consortium communication 2006)

Others believed that

> it is necessary for all teams to have a common basis to work on. We do not share the idea that quantitative analysis of Lickert-scaled questions only makes sense if all conditions are equal. We rather think it can be quite interesting when keeping in mind these unequal conditions. We also do not want to risk giving up the original idea of the project to have it commonly conducted, and fear this could happen if we now start using different methods. We are aware of the fact, that there is a need to consider nationally differing and distorting variables in interpreting the LCQ [...] [W]e think that comparisons of raw data and first analyses can be possible – or should not be made impossible right from the beginning at least. We think it would be a pity if we did away with possible ways of comparison this early, especially as it does not seem too time-consuming or extensive to add such questions (Internal consortium communication 2006).

Though all the teams were determined to generate the LCQ data, the conflict over the questionnaire's content and form of its actual implementation (e.g.

by personal interview vs. by post) was so polarising within the consortium that it could only be resolved through the voting procedure stipulated in the official contract, and not by negotiation. The margin of the vote on the question of whether 'it is obligatory for each partner in the consortium carrying out the research to use the Lickert-scale item questions' was very narrow – 4:3 in favour of each partner being free to include, or not, the Lickert-scale items. What is interesting about the whole controversy is that all the different positions of comparability and incomparability were argued with reference to *nation-state specifics*. The nation-state teams were reassembled as sites of epistemic autonomy in the consortium – they voted and expressed positions.[4] Moreover, at the same time, the nation-states were reinforced as the units of in/comparability.

The failed attempt at comparing 'raw data' did not, however, prevent us from making any comparisons at all. In the later stages of the project, what was compared most often were the 'claims' made about national research practices, as well as cultures and policies based on our fieldwork (but often also other experiences of ours as academics, committee board members, and so on). These were either formulated in national work package reports, during consortium discussions when commenting on each other's chapter drafts (Felt 2009: 35), or through various informal conversations and cross-cutting relations established throughout the project.

Comparability (and the limits to it) was gradually built up through a series of exchanges in the consortium during the lifespan of the project. At the same time, certain ambivalence remained about the nature of our comparative efforts across the team. In our collective monograph, we say that '[p]erhaps comparison, then, may reside not in the comparing of data, or results or findings, but in consideration of what questions it even made sense to ask in the first place' (Molyneux-Hodgson 2009: iii). Equally, we suggest it resides in 'the capturing of important similarities and differences among the countries participating in the study' (Felt 2009: 35). The key point for my argument is that in the first place, during the process of (hopefully) making sense and travelling well beyond the consortium, our claims re-enact the very existence of the countries as substantially homogeneous units that can later be compared.

Sian Lazar distinguishes between the 'representative form of comparison' (comparing samples in more or less strict statistical terms), and 'disjunctive comparison', which involves setting 'two groups (or cultures, societies) alongside one another and see[ing] what comes out of an examination of their similarities and differences' (2012: 352). What happens in qualitative EU projects is surely not a representative statistical comparison. But it is not simply a disjunctive comparison either, as it is not arbitrary but speaks to the (pre-)existing EU political realities and the image of a 'harmonised Europe'. Though applicants might deny subscribing to this agenda, they know very well how the application has to be phrased in order to get funding. This is what we promised as an 'EU added value', a category required in the application:

> The added value of this project lies in its comparative design. By pairing new member states with established EU member states, the project will benefit from both prior experience and new outlooks. Further, this comparative collaborative framework maximises the usefulness of the project results on a European scale by incorporating varied contexts. The recommendations produced from the project will serve to better harmonise standards of scientific excellence throughout Europe, thus contributing to existing debates on scientific excellence (KNOWING Proposal, Annex I 2005: 20).

The uses and effects of knowledge codetermined by such 'harmonised' coordinates are only partly in the hands of researchers.

REWRITING ASYMMETRIES

The above quote points to the fact that the frame of comparison used in the research project corresponds to a specific EU political imagination, and it also suggests that the units compared are not equal. The proposal distinguished between 'new' member states and the 'established' ones, and this had implications for our comparative practice. Even though we reflected in our collective monograph that '[t]he original intent to somehow bring "East" and "West" into a form of relation – by anticipating difference between the contexts and cultures implied by these geopolitically influenced words – was found in the end to offer little that was meaningful' (Molyneux-Hodgson 2009: ii), the position of one of the countries counted among the established in the original proposal (namely the UK) remained distinctive in many respects. In essence, it was the most established amongst the established. First, the science policies introduced in different times across Europe were the most 'advanced' in the UK (e.g. the nationwide Research Assessment Exercise). Second, the UK (as well as Germany and the United States) was often referred to by our research participants as a comparative benchmark in terms of research quality and a desired mobility destination. Third, a great deal of the Science and Technology Studies (STS) literature that we worked with was concerned with the UK, was written by UK researchers, and was, obviously, in English. And last, but not least, consortium meetings took place in English, which, in principle, gave an advantage to native speakers who were able to express themselves more easily and in a more nuanced way. Anglo-Saxon realities were thus omnipresent.

This had at least two interrelated effects on the comparisons that were made. On the one hand, the UK – the research team as well as researchers under study – compared itself less to other European countries, and if they referred to other countries it was most often the US. The UK played out as a rather self-contained case. On the other hand, it was difficult for other research teams to avoid direct or indirect, and explicit or implicit, comparisons to the UK.[5]

Susan Meriläinen et al. (2008) analysed a similar dynamic when they traced the peer review process of a paper they submitted to the journal *Organization*, which today declares itself to be 'theory-driven, international in scope and vision, open, reflective, imaginative and critical, interdisciplinary, facilitating exchange amongst scholars from a wide range of current disciplinary bases and perspective' (Organization 2013). Meriläinen et al. interpreted their experience of this process to be an example of 'hegemonic academic practice', as the journal's reviewers called on them to use UK data as a benchmark for Finnish data, and the data on male managers as a benchmark for female managers (2008:591). They also stated that '[w]hile Britishness became the norm, Finnishness was reduced to a deviation from the norm' (Ibid. 591).

Although I have not experienced any explicit pressure from journals such as that described by Meriläinen and her colleagues, negotiating Anglo-Saxon realities has been a near-constant process, as most of the (STS) literature we worked with in the project drew upon research, and technical, cultural, and natural references from those geopolitical parts of the world. Furthermore, it must be emphasised that most of the time I actively and happily participated in re-enacting these comparative asymmetries, even if I tried to make some difference to (and with) them. To give an example from a policymaking context, our team made use of the asymmetry between the Czech Republic and the UK when we invited our UK colleague in the project consortium to speak at a conference (on science policy) that we organised in the Senate of the Parliament. We did not present the UK simply as an advanced case to be followed and 'caught up with'; instead we tried to 'problematize the idea that Western European countries have found an ideal science policy that can be mechanically transferred to the Czech Republic' (quote from the Science Policy and Science in Action Conference Invitation). However, as far as we understood them, all the questions that were asked after our UK colleague's presentation in the Senate seemed to proceed from the assumption that she must be trying to justify the UK Research Assessment Exercise (RAE)/Research Excellence Framework (REF) system as a positive model that would help the local academic community argue against the current version of research assessment in the Czech Republic.

Academics on the 'periphery' do not often subvert; on the contrary, they try to capitalise on the hegemonic configuration. As Meriläinen et al. observed,

> [i]n general, scholars from peripheral countries such as Finland are seduced to marginalize themselves in international fora so that they may gain benefits domestically (getting articles accepted in high impact journals improves their position at home, e.g. in applying for academic jobs). They are forced to opt in core-periphery relations if they want to stay in the "game" in the periphery' (2008: 594; for a similar argument see also Aalbers 2004: 320–321).

I was, of course, interested in publishing in English in UK-based journals, and in packaging my arguments for the Anglophone 'model reader'. As well as my interest in reaching the wider STS community, I also knew that doing so would count in the institutional assessment of my work. Somewhat paradoxically, a key argument of one of my articles was a critique of the understanding (largely shared by science policies and science studies) of scientific knowledge and objects as 'immutable mobiles' (Latour 1987) and the problematic consequences this has for the social sciences in non-Anglophone countries – as well as for the local relevance of the knowledge they produce, and for their contribution to the performance of globally converging societies (Stöckelová 2012). And to round out the paradox, I later got a special financial bonus from my research institute for having published in a journal with such a high impact factor, as it increased the public funding of the institute – calculated according to a research assessment methodology that I critically analyse in the same article. The attempt to disturb the asymmetry in evaluating and valuing knowledge was at the same time incorporated in its operation.

The special and repeated efforts needed to displace and diffract asymmetries can hardly be overestimated. As noted above, in the KNOWING project we investigated two research institutions in each country – one in the biosciences, and one in the social sciences. The epistemic and policy landscape in which our study was conducted was strongly unbalanced in favour of the biosciences. On the one hand, a great majority of STS concepts (such as the notion of 'lab ethnography') were developed on the basis of empirical material drawn from the field of natural and biosciences (Garforth 2012). And it is also these disciplines and types of research that serve as a more or less explicit model of and for policy (Garforth and Stöckelová 2012). It almost took permanent effort and reflection in order for us to overcome this uneven condition when we were developing our understanding of studied research practices, cultures, and policies, and to avoid talking about the social sciences as an exception or deviation from a 'standard'. Paradoxically, the fact that we all came from the social sciences did not help much. On the contrary; it may have created a feeling that we all understood our field already, and that we did not need to spend as much time discussing our social science data. The political and epistemic economy worked in favour of the asymmetries embedded in the comparison. I will note in the conclusion below that going against these asymmetries can be an effective methodological strategy.

INTERFERING WITH THE RESEARCHED

The complexities of comparing data generated in the context of different disciplines made themselves very apparent in the follow-up to KNOWING. This was carried out in the Czech Republic from 2009–2010. In the project, 'Articulations of Science Policies in Research Practice and Academic Path', we carried out additional group interviews with researchers in different disciplines and institutional contexts. What was extraordinary about the project was its timing in that it coincided with the introduction of major changes in the research assessment system in the country. Experiments with a new assessment system began in 2004 when basic measures were introduced to quantitatively evaluate research outputs. They did not draw much attention from ordinary researchers as they had no immediate consequence. However, in 2009, institutional funding for research and university organisations began to be closely tied to evaluation scores at the same time as overall cuts were being made in the public budget for research. To make a long story short, this resulted in substantial cuts in the budget for the Academy of Sciences (which, unlike universities, gets public money solely for doing research) and a consequent increase in tension between the institutions and disciplines inside the Academy which have to compete with each other for diminishing resources. In this atmosphere, there were heated debates (in public as well as in academic spaces) about the adequacy of the evaluation procedure and its criteria. Some of the questions often raised were what types of output (academic, extra academic), and what types of institutions (research institutes, universities) and disciplines (social sciences and humanities, natural sciences, technical disciplines) are comparable or commensurable, and what the appropriate levels are on which to make comparisons and rankings (on the level of disciplines, institutions, research teams, and individuals).

We set out to study how, and with what effects, the unprecedented quantitative comparisons of the entities characterised by these multiple differences were constructed.[6] We were interested in the processes of commensuration and 'making things comparable'. In our analysis, we showed how the national evaluation was originally an initiative of a group of bioscientists who strove to establish their superiority in the research system in terms of professional accountability, but who later started to lose control over the whole process as industrial lobbies, the bureaucratic logic, and managerial accountability asserted themselves (Linková and Stöckelová 2012). During the fieldwork, our study was perceived by the research participants as interfering rather directly in the controversy. Most researchers that we approached with a request for an interview had a strong opinion on these issues, and they wanted to share and make their opinions heard through our research. While the national evaluation tried to impose universal commensurability and ranking, its opponents denounced the hidden asymmetries in the seemingly impartial evaluation criteria, and argued either for a different frame of comparison (one more favourable to them and their institutions and disciplines), or for acknowledging the incommensurability of the compared entities – for instance, noting the incommensurable nature of the output of different disciplines, their epistemic genres, and societal roles. Those in the latter group actually saw our 'comparative research' project as a possible means of showing these entities to be incomparable – and making them so.

The situation of the public and policy controversy might be specific to an extent, but it illuminates an important issue concerning comparative studies. Research never starts on un(infra)structured grounds, and it inevitably interferes with the existing frames of comparison and the (in)commensurabilities practised by various actors in the field (not least by Viveiros de Castro's accountants). These interferences may remain invisible if the frames of comparison and their asymmetries are settled and practised more or less consensually in the studied field, and if the researcher does not set out to deliberately unsettle the framings but instead goes along with them. In this case, she *interferes* by effectively strengthening them. I argue that an empiricist approach to comparison – which prescribes that only what is 'objectively' comparable can be legitimately compared – does exactly this. It strengthens the dominant frames of comparison by respecting them – as in the case of anthropological 'cross-cultural comparisons' – when practised as a comparison of 'the others' (solely) among themselves, thereby re-enacting the West as coherent, unique, and indeed incomparable.[7]

COMPARING AGAINST THE GRAIN

Comparing boxing and computer programming, Robert Schmidt (2008) makes a case against a kind of comparison which 'simply emphasizes the links and commonalities between the objects of comparison' (2008: 340), and argues for an experimental approach to comparison. He insists it is the latter that can bring about a desirable epistemological rupture and unexpected insight. In a similar vein, I argued in this chapter against the epistemological naïveté of comparability dwelling 'out there' as a limit to what we can and should compare as researchers.

My point is, however, more political. The trap of the notion of comparability awaiting the researcher 'out there' is not only epistemological. It concerns what reality is, and how it will change and develop. Indeed, there exist recognised units and frames of comparison and in/comparabilities in the reality we investigate. However, they are not given but practised by various actors and inscribed into infrastructures, architectures, and imaginations. Social research can, and should, study these comparative practices and arrangements, while it cannot itself avoid engaging in and with them (be it in a critical or affirmative mode). With researchers' contributions, they can be practised differently, or not. I do not argue that as researchers, we should always stand in a subversive relationship to the framings practised by the actors we study. There might be minor or subaltern frames of comparison we decide to reinforce and make visible. Also, strategically sharing a dominant frame may help to make certain points that it would otherwise be hard to hear. But it seems crucial to remain aware of the performativity of our comparative undertakings. What would the elements of cultivating such awareness be?

The first issue is *timing*. Awareness should influence the ways we design our research projects. What are the key frames and units of comparison present in the field we are about to enter? Do we want to strengthen or question them? Are there lateral ways of formulating and researching our themes that would not only open new intellectual horizons, but would also deploy new or hitherto marginal realities? And in the context of (qualitative) multinational EU projects, an explicit quest should be to examine how we can unsettle the entrenched research design where national teams study the (homogenised) reality of their nation/member state. Certainly, there are things that cannot be planned and avoided in advance. We can only learn about them from the responses, requests, and traces we leave in the field. Nevertheless, we *should* learn.

It is remarkable that the KNOWING project was an explicitly feminist one, but it still generated rather limited reflection within (and after) the project on asymmetries and inequalities. While the proposal stated that

> [r]esearch conducted from a feminist perspective is characterized by a critique of social inequalities (including but not limited to gender), a research design that provides space for the exploration of women's everyday experiences and knowledges, is sensitive to and tries to minimise the power differentials between researcher and research participant, and is motivated by the desire to create positive social change' (KNOWING Proposal, Annex I 2005: 22),

we were little prepared or equipped to handle the power differentials within the project consortium, particularly in the researched reality. If we were pushed to reflection at one point, it was only due to a conflict (which is not a bad thing in principle). However, severe conflicts may threaten a project as a whole, erode mutual trust, and needlessly use up a lot of energy. Thinking in the terms of the EC newspeak of 'work packages', it would be useful to include 'reflection' alongside 'management' for the duration of a project. In the busy schedule of other work package meetings, milestones, and deliverables, there is indeed very limited time-space and energy for such reflection – even when the willingness and interest are there.

The second issue concerns *scale*. In the social sciences, the gravity of the performativity issue will rarely be linked to a single project. Rather, it is the multiple, recurring execution of projects that creates powerful machinery for the reproduction of specific frames, units, and asymmetries. This raises questions not only for a single project, but for research and disciplinary communities. In this chapter, I sketched contours of what we create (intentionally or not) by engaging in projects and reproducing the arrangement where national/member state research teams investigate their national/member state realities. Is this what our disciplines wish to (and should) contribute to Europe?

I would argue that one of the key intellectual missions and socio-political roles of the social sciences has historically been to open established black boxes. However, the black boxes of the nation/member states are reproduced rather than opened up by the usual arrangements of the 'societal challenges pillar' of EU-funded research. Such arrangements not only re-enact black boxes, but they also deaden empirical research sensibility for complex realities escaping established categories. I am neither arguing for any easy cosmopolitism, as if Europe is – or should necessarily be – a smoothly shared, common socio-material-discursive space, nor for switching to an alternative standard for European social research. On the contrary, I insist that as much as the European *cosmopolitics* of composing a shared world (Latour 1999) needs to be experimental, the social research contributing to it also needs to be so. In my view, more space and resources should be dedicated to unexpected comparisons and experimental research designs.

Such research could seemingly not drive the 'fast lane' of academic production (Vostal 2015) and be slower and stumbling, thus coming into conflict with the current standards and measures of 'excellence' in ever-growth-oriented academia. As STS has numerously shown (especially in relation to (non-social) sciences), the epistemic content and organisational process of research cannot be separated (e.g. Latour 1987). Thus, it can hardly be underestimated that 'research design' issues are not simply methodological, but they simultaneously concern multiple facets of politics, including the academic one.

As a research community (always incoherent and multi-vocal, of course), we also have to find a way to translate these debates into messages regarding implications and limits of current research arrangements to sponsors and funders (such as the European Commission). The reason is that the actual funded projects are responses to – explicit or implicit – expectations inscribed in calls and evaluation criteria. However, in the context of Europe, the wording of the Vilnius Declaration – a recent, and so far rather unique, message from the social sciences and humanities to policymakers – conceals the performativity of social research. It talks about the social sciences and humanities as 'indispensable [*sic*] in generating *knowledge about* the dynamic changes in human values, identities and citizenship that transform our societies', and about '*realigning science with ongoing changes in the ways in which society operates*' (Horizons for Social Sciences and Humanities 2013; my emphasis). Here, science is supposed to catch up with (a single) pre-existing (though changing) society, and it asks for the resources to do so.

I believe we need a more reciprocal understanding of the relation between the social sciences and the realities they study, and a more performative take on knowledge and knowing. For the sake of what there is, and what can be, social research should strive to create investigative frictions and make comparisons that go 'against the grain' of prevailing notions, rather than polish (however inadvertently) existing dominant realities. I am sure this would not be to the detriment of intellectual creativity.

ACKNOWLEDGEMENTS

This chapter has been inspired and shaped by many debates with many people. I would specifically like to thank Lisa Garforth, Marcela Linkova, Katja Mayer, Morgan Meyer, Iris Wallenburg, and the editors of this volume for their invaluable comments on earlier versions of this chapter. Robin Cassling and Jennifer Tomomitsu helped me greatly with fine-tuning my English. The writing of the paper has been supported by grant no. P404/11/0127 of the Czech Science Foundation.

NOTES

1 This idea may be undergoing change now (in the 'crisis') with differences between the 'North' and 'South' of Europe appearing unbridgeable and escalating into conflicts. We have yet to see if and how this change will translate from economic policies to research ones.

2 Thanks to Lisa Garforth for drawing my attention to the significance of 'national reports' in this context.

3 Across the KNOWING consortium, there was indeed only one case study carried out outside the area of a researcher's residence.

4 In fact, the consultant to the project based in the UK voted differently from the UK partner team carrying out the research, while the consultant based in the Czech Republic abstained from voting.

5 Lisa Garforth (a UK colleague from KNOWING) provided an interesting complementary perspective on the issue of asymmetry when she commented on a draft of this chapter. While she agreed that the UK context kept asserting itself as a particularly vivid reality and standard for comparison in the project, she also pointed to another side of this privileged position. She noted that 'UK teams have no "private" research findings (in principle everything is available in its first language to the whole team) or non-common language at meetings which occasionally we found a bit problematic; there can be no "asides" in a native language just for colleagues, for example; everything is potentially hearable by everybody' (2014). And she added that 'we were also constantly aware of being the least "European" team with the least experience of EC funding systems, reporting systems, even Euro-English language (e.g. the comfortable use of "scientific" to mean what we would call "academic" in EC speak, which I think was also familiar and comfortable to most of the researchers but we never internalised it). For us, this meant that some version of "Europe" or "European research" was being encountered as a relative novelty, especially via the EC's language and systems' (written feedback on the draft of the chapter, 2014).

6 Different comparative 'remarks' concerning the value and quality of different academic disciplines and intuitions in the Czech Republic had been in the air for several years, but were never translated into an official and quantitative evaluation system.

7 For an analysis of practices of the modern/non-modern incommensurability, see Latour (1993); for a nuanced critique of comparative approaches in anthropology, see Gingrich and Fox (2000).

BIBLIOGRAPHY

Aalbers, M. B., 'Creative Destruction through the Anglo-American Hegemony: a Non-Anglo-American View on Publications, Referees and Language', *Area*, 36.3 (2004), 319–322

Callon, M., 'An Essay on Framing and Overflowing: Economic Externalities Revisited by Sociology' in M. Callon, ed., *The Laws of the Markets* (Oxford: Blackwell, 1998), pp. 244–269

De Rijcke, et al., 'Comparing Comparisons: On Rankings and Accounting in Hospitals and Universities', this volume

Felt, U., 'Introduction: Knowing and Living in Academic Research', in U. Felt, ed., *Knowing and Living in Academic Research: Convergence and Heterogeneity in Research Cultures in the European Context* (Prague: Institute of Sociology of the Academy of Sciences of the Czech Republic, 2009), pp. 17–40

Felt, U., and T. Stöckelová, 'Modes of Ordering and Boundaries that Matter in Academic Knowledge Production', in U. Felt, ed., *Knowing and Living in Academic Research: Convergence and Heterogeneity in Research Cultures in the European Context* (Prague: Institute of Sociology of the Academy of Sciences of the Czech Republic, 2009), pp. 41–124

Garforth, L., 'In/Visibilities of Research: Seeing and Knowing in STS', *Science, Technology, & Human Values*, 37 (2012), 264–285

Garforth, L., and T. Stöckelová, 'Science Policy and STS from Other Epistemic Places', *Science, Technology, & Human Values*, 37 (2012), 226–240

Gingrich, A., R. G. Fox, eds., *Anthropology, by Comparison* (London and New York: Routledge, 2000)

Godfroy, A. -S., 'International Comparisons in Science Studies: What and Why do we Compare?', *Innovation: The European Journal of Social Science Research*, 23 (2010), 37–48

Goffman, E., *Frame Analysis: An Essay on the Organization of Experience* (New York: Harper and Row, 1974)

Haraway, D., 'The Promises of Monsters: A Regenerative Politics for Inappropriate/d Others', in L. Grossberg, C. Nelson, and P. A. Treichler, eds., *Cultural Studies* (New York: Routledge, 1992), pp. 295–337

Latour, B., *Science in Action: How to Follow Scientists and Engineers through Society* (Milton Keynes: Open University Press, 1987)

—— *The Pasteurization of France* (Cambridge, MA: Harvard University Press, 1988)

—— *We have Never been Modern* (Cambridge, MA: Harvard University Press, 1993)

—— *Politiques de la nature: comment faire entrer les sciences en démocratie* (Paris: La Découverte, 1999)

Law, J., 'Seeing like a Survey', *Cultural Sociology*, 3 (2009), 239–56

Lazar, S., 'Disjunctive Comparison: Citizenship and Trade Unionism in Bolivia and Argentina', *Journal of the Royal Anthropological Institute (N.S.)*, 18 (2012), 349–368

Linková, M., and T. Stöckelová, 'Public Accountability and the Politicization of Science: The Peculiar Journey of Czech Research Assessment', *Science & Public Policy*, 39 (2012), 618–629

Meriläinen, S., J. Tienari, R. Thomas, and A. Davies, 'Hegemonic Academic Practices: Experiences of Publishing from the Periphery', *Organization*, 15 (2008), 584–97

Molyneux-Hodgson, S., 'Preface: The Contexts of Knowing', in U. Felt, ed., *Knowing and Living in Academic Research: Convergence and Heterogeneity in Research Cultures in the European Context* (Prague: Institute of Sociology of the Academy of Sciences of the Czech Republic, 2009), pp. i–iii

Organization Journal, < http://org.sagepub.com/ > [accessed September 2014]

Porter, T., *Trust in Numbers: The Pursuit of Objectivity in Science and Public Life* (Princeton, NJ: Princeton University Press, 1995)

Shore, C., 'Audit Culture and Illiberal Governance: Universities and the Politics of Accountability', *Anthropological Theory*, 8 (2008), 278–98

Schmidt, R., 'Gaining Insight from Incomparability: Exploratory Comparison in Studies of Social Practices', *Comparative Sociology*, 7 (2008), 338–61

Stöckelová, T., 'Immutable Mobiles Derailed: STS and the Epistemic Geopolitics of Research Assessment', *Science, Technology, & Human Values*, 37 (2012), 286–311

Strathern, M., ed., *Audit Cultures: Anthropological Studies in Accountability, Ethics and the Academy* (London and New York: Routledge, 2000)

Vilnius Declaration – Horizons for Social Sciences and Humanities (2013), <http://horizons.mruni.eu/> [accessed 18 January 2014]

Viveiros de Castro, E., 'Perspectival Anthropology and the Method of Controlled Equivocation', *Tipití: Journal of the Society for the Anthropology of Lowland South America*, 2 (2004), article 1 <http://digitalcommons.trinity.edu/tipiti/vol2/iss1/1> [accessed 18 January 2014]

Vostal, F., 'Academic Life in the Fast Lane: The Experience of Time and Speed in British Academia', *Time & Society* (2015), 71–95

SECTION THREE

RELATIONS

7

LATERAL COMPARISONS

Christopher Gad and Casper Bruun Jensen

INTRODUCTION

COMPARISON HAS BEEN AN IMPORTANT, PERHAPS EVEN DEFINING, METHodological and conceptual preoccupation in fields ranging from anthropology and history to linguistics. However, to the extent that comparison has been important in science and technology studies (STS) – our 'home field' – it has largely functioned implicitly and rarely programmatically (but see Barnes 1973; Jasanoff 2007: 13–42; Knorr-Cetina 1999). Considered genealogically, the disinclination towards comparative studies per se can be related to the generic constructivism of most STS and its attendant scepticism towards stable yardsticks capable of grounding comparative analysis. Indeed, it does not seem likely that a long-lasting agreement on the relevant units of comparison will ever be reached, or even that it would be desirable: for what might be the units guiding comparative study? The cultures of national science policy (Jasanoff 2007)? Organisational forms (Scott 1981)? Types of technology relations (Ihde 1990)? Epistemic cultures (Knorr-Cetina 1999)? Modes of existence (Latour 2013)? Held under a constructivist microscope, each of these units seems equally prone to disperse as units.

A similar dispersal has fuelled the growing scepticism towards comparison (in the classical 'grand style') in anthropology. Indeed, whereas comparison used to be something of a 'gold standard' in anthropology, it is noteworthy that the comparative endeavour has increasingly fallen by the wayside. Like STS, this decline can be related to vigorous postmodern and reflexive critiques of representation, universalism, and holism. Not least, these critiques were directed at an earlier evolutionism premised on the large-scale comparison of different 'cultures'. Even so, certain modes of comparison have recently regained vigour (e.g. Otto and Bubandt 2010). This paper aims to further that trajectory by examining some potentials of comparison at the intersection of STS and anthropology.

The notion of 'lateral reason' comes from anthropologist Bill Maurer's (2005) work on Islamic banking and alternative currencies in the US. Laterality centres on the observation that it is not the prerogative of social scientists to conceptualise and compare, for ethnographic fields are rife with such efforts. Informants are thus 'fellow travellers along the routes of social abstraction and analysis' (Maurer 2005: xv). As a consequence, social science comparisons are located 'alongside' the worlds of those they compare; they offer no general overview or meta-perspective on them. And, as a result, the traffic of comparisons and their effects run in multiple directions. It follows that although social science comparisons are often viewed as *elucidating* aspects of a found social reality, social science might also *learn from* indigenous comparisons about how to rethink its own analytical strategies.

At one level, this is to do with extracting and transforming modes of understanding found in the field. At another, it is a matter of recognising that comparison takes material-technological forms as often as linguistic-discursive ones. And yet another laterality points to the fundamental open-endedness of the relation between academic analysis and (other) worldly practices. Comparisons of the kinds we describe below might therefore give rise to further comparisons that extend into other academic, practice, or policy domains – as testified by several contributions to this volume. The lateral point is that no rulebook can predict how this may happen, nor can it dictate how it ought to happen.

The present analysis focuses specifically on *comparative technologies*; those used on board a Danish fishery inspection vessel for assorted purposes (including the navigation of the sea and Danish and EU bureaucracies). Exploring assemblages of comparison on the ship's bridge (and in the broader ecologies of bureaucracy), we elicit acts of comparison as parts of variably configured and emergent practices that move across a series of standard divisions of social science. These comparisons include description and conceptualisation (Jensen 2011; Maurer 2011, 2012; Ratner 2012; Riles 2000), informant and researcher (Hansen 2011; Maurer 2005), and indeed, humans and technology (Gad 2012; Walford 2013).

The comparisons at hand are diverse. Some are built into machines. Some are deployed by informants to make sense of the sea environment, and yet others are put to use by researchers to address social scientific questions. This diversity suggests the difficulty of localising comparison at any particular empirical or analytical level. Our attempt to take into account the coexistence and movement of multiple forms of comparison is thus lateral in a double sense. Its premise is based on a refusal to circumscribe what counts as comparative material. Moreover, it centres on the variability, hybridity, and extendibility of comparison.

As an analytical propensity, lateral comparison is relentlessly non-hierarchical. It refuses to assume the privilege of any particular kind of comparator, including the researcher. Instead, the motor of lateral comparison is that the most heterogeneous actors unceasingly compare the most unpredictable things in the most surprising ways (see Meyer, this volume). Indeed, this point is exemplified by Deville, Guggenheim, and Hrdličková's appropriation of the very notion of the comparator (this volume). While they tell us the term generically refers to a standard against which an object is compared, their usage is drawn from the capacities of a *microchip* (also called a comparator) which both compares and regulates fixed and variable voltages. Offering this lateral comparison *of comparison* enables Deville et al. to conduct their analysis in a novel register, emphasising description and intervention in the same analytical movement.

Aside from enriching description, one of the benefits of such a move is that it steers clear of the always-lurking representationalism in anthropology and STS which tends to belittle the value of inventive conceptualisation in the name of getting descriptions right (see Holbraad 2012). Instead, Deville et al. emphasise that it is premised on the recognition that representation is both intervention (see Hacking 1983; Haraway 1994) and invention (see Wagner 1975). It highlights the notion that who compares, what is invented by comparing, how such inventions may come to matter, and in which ways, is undecided from the get-go.

The premise does not suggest that everything *is* always compared, or that everything necessarily *should be* compared. Rather, the point is that everything *may* be rendered comparable (Latour 1988: 161–62; see Stöckelová, this volume). We might then say that our own comparisons should also be allowed to intermingle with those of others. Yet this formulation is slightly misleading insofar as it suggests that the researcher retains the capacity to make the decision. More precisely, we know that social scientific comparisons often *come to mingle* with those conducted by informants in unforeseeable ways. Lateral comparison takes this contingent possibility seriously, but just for that reason it contains no normative prescription – for enforced comparative mingling is not what is at stake.

To locate the distinctiveness of lateral comparisons, we begin by turning back the clock to the mid-to-late 1980s (a time when the comparative methods of anthropology had begun to show some serious cracks).

FORMS OF COMPARISON: A SHORT GENEALOGY
Comparison and Its Discontents

In 1987, the anthropologist Ladislav Holy dedicated his introduction to *Comparative Anthropology*, showing that the anthropological preoccupation with 'cross-cultural comparison as the method for generating and testing hypotheses derives from the positivistic paradigm' (1987: 1). Classical anthropology, Holy wrote, considered itself a branch of Durkheim's comparative sociology; not a 'particular branch of sociology', but rather 'sociology itself insofar as it ceases to be purely descriptive and aspires to account for facts' (Ibid. 2, citing Durkheim 1964: 139). According to this understanding, 'description provided the facts, and comparative method was adopted to account for them; it was seen as a means of formulating and testing hypotheses and generalizations valid not only for one specific society or culture but cross culturally' (Holy 1987: 2; see Kuper 2002: 144–45). For Mark Hobart (writing in the same volume), the special status of comparison in anthropology related to the fact that it underpinned explicitly or implicitly almost all the ways of talking about other cultures. Whether we study agriculture or food, narrative or myth, divinity or witches, we are comparing our popular or technical categories with other peoples. Analysis in terms of economic 'infrastructures' or self-interest assumes the shared reality of production or the utilitarian nature of human action. Discussions concerning 'political systems' presuppose the generality of systems, and makes a suggestion that forms of power are comparable (1987: 22).

Hobart further noted that comparison has been viewed as the 'anthropological equivalent of the controlled experimentation of natural scientists' (Hobart 1987: 23; see Jensen 2011: 3–5).

In tandem with the interpretive, reflexive, and postcolonial turns in anthropology, comparison nevertheless came to be viewed with increasing scepticism. One problem concerned 'the relations between anthropologists' descriptions of particular cultures and societies and their generalisation about human culture and society' (Holy 1987: 1). As Fox and Gingrich argued in *Anthropology, By Comparison*, though comparison from afar seems both fundamental and unproblematic, upon closer inspection it tends to dissolve 'into dozens of other issues, pieces and fragments' (2002: 1). Adam Kuper similarly pinpointed the tendency of comparison to fragment: he argued that the units of anthropological comparison are fundamentally contestable since the boundaries of what is compared are always uncertain:

> Are the South African Bushmen one ethnographic case or several? Second, in what sense are the units that are constructed strictly comparable? Can the Bushmen reasonably be treated as a 'case' alongside 'the Bedouin', let alone Ming China? Much the same difficulties arise when it comes to defining an ethnographic object for purposes of comparison. Is 'sacrifice' among the Nuer really a distinctive, separable thing? And in what sense is it like 'sacrifice' among the ancient Israelites, or in Classical Greece or among the Aztecs? (Kuper 2002: 145).

In 1987, Holy had already argued that 'there is no longer a "comparative method" in anthropology'(1987: 2). If ever there was such a method, it had been 'replaced by varying styles of comparison' (Ibid.), generally used 'to facilitate our understanding of [...] culturally specific meanings, i.e. to identify or bring into focus cultural specificity' (Ibid. 10). In their later edition, Fox and Gingrich argued that

> it is possible to move beyond the ruins of a monopolistic claim to one kind of comparison and beyond the stifling of intellectual competition it visited upon anthropology. Now, a rich *plurality of qualitative comparative methodologies* has emerged – none claiming exclusive rights, each offering its insights and evidence (2002: 12).

In a special issue on 'Thick Comparison', Jörg Niewöhner and Thomas Scheffer likewise observed that 'the standard *mode of comparison* has been criticised as mechanistic, technical, and naïve (vis-à-vis hegemonic concepts and categories)' (2008: 274). They strengthened the argument for a plurality of comparisons by emphasising that 'the rising demand for cross-cultural and comparative research has proved productive for ethnographers (as cultural translators)' (Ibid.).

However, the pluralisation of comparison identified by Holy, promoted by Fox and Gingrich, and enhanced by Niewöhner and Scheffer, has also been considered analytically costly. Specifically, it has undermined what some view as one of the central virtues of comparison in the 'grand style' – namely its attempt to generalise. This effort has been replaced by a plethora of specific studies that generally have limited comparative aspiration (see Beaulieu et al. 2007; Jensen 2013).[1] As rich and diverse as such ethnographies may be, they often rely on a descriptivist ethos, opening their flanks to Edmund Leach's classical swipe at an ethnographic 'butterfly collection' (1961: 25) where the harvesting of descriptions and facts serves no overarching analytical or comparative purpose.

Forty years after Leach's complaint, Kuper offered an amplified version of the same critique:

> Ethnography is now the core business of social anthropology [...] and long-term immersion in ethnographic research is increasingly common. [...] The

challenge is to add value to the dauntingly large body of ethnographic and historical reports available on almost any region (2002: 144).

Yet, Kuper lamented, some refuse 'to move beyond the handful of people they have studied intensively at first hand, though it is difficult to see why we should take an interest in an arbitrary little network of friends or informants unless we can learn something of more general relevance' (Ibid. 148). Quoting Maurice Bloch's denouncement of ethnographies consisting of 'assemblages of anecdotes of this and that' (Holbraad 2012: 32, citing Bloch 2005: 9), Martin Holbraad similarly points to 'the strong tendency in recent years to refrain from comparative theoretical generalisations and to favor accounts of particular ethnographic instances' (2012: 31).

One way forward is found in Niewöhner and Scheffer's argument that 'thick comparison' implies a focus on the production of comparability itself (2008: 275). They ask ethnographers to pay close attention to how ethnographic comparisons interact with comparative endeavours already occurring in the field, and how this *produces* comparability and 'objects of comparison' (Ibid. 280). They urge engagement with such emergent objects of comparison 'in their performative force, meaning the ways they make new links and relations and explicate novel qualities and dynamics (both within the ethnographic field and in ethnographers' social scientific discipline)' (Ibid.). In a related vein, Helen Verran (2001) has turned the empirical study of forms of generalisation into a comparative project in its own right. Thus, she has compared the ways in which Western educators and Nigerian maths teachers do mathematical generalisation, and the forms of understanding that undergird Australian aboriginals' and eco-scientists' forms of land management.

Some of our own recent work similarly advocates for an agenda of 'comparative relativism' (e.g. Jensen 2011; Strathern 2011; Viveiros de Castro 2011), emphasising the importance of conducting 'comparison of comparisons' in order to open up and relativise understandings of what different people 'compare for'. This latter aspect ties in directly with the lateral comparisons we pick up on in this paper. What laterality adds is a sense of the unforeseeable movements of such diverse, relativised comparisons.

Comparison with a Difference

Though STS by no means embraces comparative relativism, some scholars in this field have also grappled with the question of how to do comparison differently. In his contribution to the aforementioned special issue on thick comparison, Robert Schmidt draws on Max Weber to consider what comparison might mean if detached from a positivist agenda. Schmidt argues that Weber's perspective offers a distinct vantage point from which to redefine comparativism. For Weber, he reminds us that

> comparing critically (*kritische Vergleichung*) does not serve a search for analogies and parallels but rather should be deployed to shed light on the peculiarity (*Herausarbeitung der Eigenart*) of the cases and objects (1999: 7).

Quite contrary to the frequent scepticism about comparative analysis in ethnography and qualitative research, Weber depicts comparative perspectives not as abstracting from or overriding the uniqueness of social phenomena, but rather as uncovering them (Schmidt 2008: 357). Accordingly, Weber's comparative project does not presuppose 'shared properties of objects' and should not be seen as 'equating objects and cases to each other' (Ibid. 358). Instead, Schmidt's reading of Weber suggests that the focal interest is 'to make use of contrasts and differences, to gain insights from incomparability and inadequacy' (Ibid.).

In STS, one of the best examples is Karin Knorr-Cetina's studies of epistemic cultures. Her interest is in charting the different contours of 'expert systems' (1999: 1) such as the different modes of making knowledge that characterise molecular biology and physics. Rather than strive to identify 'shared properties', Knorr-Cetina calls attention to the fragmentation and disunity of science (see Galison and Stump 1996). Her aim is to display 'different architectures of empirical approaches, specific constructions of the referent, particular ontologies of instruments, and different social machineries' (Knorr-Cetina 1999: 3). 'A comparative optics', she argues, 'brings out not the essential features of each field but differences between the fields' (Ibid. 4) such as 'the communitarian science of physics', and 'the individual, bodily, lab-bench science of molecular biology' (Ibid. 4). Whereas physics aims to go beyond 'anthropocentric and culture-centric scales of time and space in its organization and work, the other (molecular biology) holds on to them and exploits them' (Ibid.). While physics 'is characterized by a relative loss of the empirical', molecular biology is 'heavily experiential' (Ibid.). Furthermore, whereas physics 'transforms machines into physiological beings' (Ibid.), the reverse is the case for molecular biology.

In the context of science policy studies, another prominent STS scholar, Sheila Jasanoff, has likewise proposed a novel comparative agenda. In the chapter 'Why Compare?', Jasanoff (2005) notes the general decline of universalism and objectivism and the rise of poststructuralist and constructivist approaches in much of social science. She suggests it is increasingly recognised that science, technology, and policy are mutually embedded and co-produced.

Whereas comparison of science policies used to seem unnecessary (since science, assumed universal, was not supposed to be influenced by politics or culture), a first wave of comparative studies came to focus on the 'national styles of policy', aiming to identify the 'styles' most conducive to supporting scientific progress. Advocating a second wave, Jasanoff states that such research needs

> a different justification than simply propagation of improved managerial techniques. Rather than prescribing decontextualized best practices for an imagined global administrative elite, comparison should be seen as a means for investigating the interactions between science and politics, with far-reaching implications for governance in advanced industrialized democracies (2005: 15).

In agreement with Weber's injunction, her proposal centres on the exploration of political culture – defined dynamically. Thus, her comparisons both rely on, and challenge, such 'quasi-holistic' notions as 'the state' and 'political culture'. Aiming to elucidate topographies of comparison inhabited by national and scientific cultures, Jasanoff's comparative agenda is explicit about its own ontological and epistemological commitments.

Knorr-Cetina and Jasanoff offer some of the most explicit illustrations within the STS corpus of what comparison after positivism might look like. Neither 'equates' cases with one another, but uses comparison to highlight distinctive features of phenomena. In some ways, however, both also retain a rather classical vision of comparison.

First, while their comparisons work by the extraction of certain 'traits' from practices, they do not generally extend their interest to acts of comparison within practices. Thus, they exhibit limited interest in how and why the actors themselves compare. In that sense, they fall short of Niewöhner and Scheffers' call for 'thick comparisons'. This is probably due to the fact that both Knorr-Cetina and Jasanoff maintain a rather strict separation between empirical practices (which are compared) and academic analyses (where researchers use theoretical frameworks to compare). It is therefore little surprise that neither pays much attention to the lateral comparisons that informants themselves use to relate and distinguish their practices from one another. Furthermore, these authors show little concern for how their own comparisons establish lateral linkages.

In contrast, our ambition is to push the comparative envelope by focusing on such linkages. We find inspiration to do so in a series of recent studies located at the intersection of STS and anthropology.

Lateral Inspirations

One inspiration for the interest in lateral comparison arises from the now generally observed complexity of the relationship between 'observer' and 'observed'. If this complexity has diverse sources, one of them is the experience of meeting informants whose projects and ways of thinking are not radically different from (or indeed sometimes very similar to) and certainly comparable to those of the researcher (Riles 2000). This is prominently (but by no means exclusively) the case when anthropology and STS study 'modern' knowledge practices.

This increasingly common situation challenges the implicit, if not basic, 'social scientific contract', according to which the relationship between researcher and informant implies a division of labour such that the latter 'offer' to the former their practices and thoughts for analysis and explanation. Presently (whether in science or business), expert informants with significant cultural capital are fully able to read and comment on social science texts, and they are quite likely to disagree and offer alternative perspectives.

Annelise Riles has argued that the collapsing distance between 'our' and 'their' knowledges calls for a new anthropological response, one that is capable of drawing, in more sustained ways, upon the ways in which informants themselves theorise their activities. Her argument aligns with actor-network theory's insistence that informants' theories are often more relevant for 'our' understanding of 'their' practices than social scientific ones. Insofar, however, as actor-network theory (at least sometimes) claims to eschew theory in favour of elucidating actors' perspectives, the solutions diverge. For Riles, the pressing question is how to respond to the threat of collapsing distance, without unwittingly accelerating that collapse through efforts to mimic our informants. In *The Network Inside Out*, for example, she compares the making of Fijian mats to the making of policy documents by a Fijian NGO working on gender issues (2000: 70ff).

Bill Maurer has also pinpointed the undercurrent of representationalism lurking underneath actor-network theory (and much other STS thinking). In Maurer's view,

> Latour's realism is problematic for the same reason that it is so useful: refusing the separation of epistemology from ontology opens up the innumerable black boxes that warrant 'reality', but it does so in terms of that refusal's own agnosticism (Maurer 2005: 14).

Even so, actor-network theory has considerably more on offer than an inclination to realism. For one thing, it has attuned us to the notion that acts of comparison are not carried out exclusively by human actors (e.g. Hutchins 1995; Latour 1988). Instead, it offers a view of comparison as a distributed activity, a hybrid achievement involving heterogeneous actors that only retrospectively tends to be condensed and attributed to (individual) human actors, rather than networks *in toto*. Anthropologist Atsuro Morita (2014) has also recently deployed this argument to inventive effect: comparisons, he argues, occur not only in the human domain, but also 'within' machines that contain their own contexts and scales. Morita accepts anthropologist Marilyn Strathern's premise that the study of others cannot avoid entailing the study of our own practices and knowledges. This mutual implication is invariably brought out in the discrepancy between our own presuppositions and the surprises arising from ethnography.[2]

Describing the work of Thai mechanics to make a Japanese cultivator operate efficiently in the environment of north-eastern Thailand, Morita argues that the breakdown of the cultivator led not only to comparisons of the expertise or skill levels of Thai and Japanese engineers, but also to the elicitation *from within* the machine of comparisons between the ecological conditions of Thai and Japanese fields. In a lateral extension, Morita continues to compare the operations of the cultivator to ethnography, a move that allows him to envision the anthropological enterprise as itself a 'machine' for articulating 'strange connections'.

Now, if the separation between human and technology is a modern preoccupation, so is the maintenance of boundaries between analysis and description, and theory and practice. However, Morita's analysis shows that lateral comparison enables a cross-cutting analytical movement, whereby the 'theories' embedded in machines can inspire the practice of anthropological analysis. In our view, the principal interest of this study lies in its demonstration of the inventive potentials of tracing comparisons ethnographically, only to subsequently utilise them for other analytical or practical purposes.

As a final example, Bill Maurer aims to reinvigorate comparison by explicit deployment of lateral comparisons. In his exploration of alternative currency experiments in the US, Maurer refrains from comparing these cases using theoretically derived categories. Instead, he traces lateral connections between them:

> Islamic banking and Ithaca HOURS [an alternative currency] became necessary to one another in my own efforts to restage what I saw them doing. They do not 'represent' each other or 'shed light' on each other so much as they draw on each other – but only sometimes, contingently and laterally. They metastasize into one another, but that metastasis is not essential to either of them, nor is it causal. For each overlaps and interconnects with other things, too (2005: 10).

Maurer insists this does not mean that the two cases 'automatically suggest each other, either' (Ibid.). Instead, he writes, 'at every step my effort to "compare" got interrupted by the form of that which I was "comparing"' (Ibid.). These movements, at once empirical and conceptual, 'revealed the tropes of Islamic banking, alternative currencies, and my inquiry as open and unsteady' (Ibid. 11).

It is precisely this sense of the 'open and unsteady' course of comparisons that guides us as we turn to a study of comparative technologies in fisheries inspection.

ON THE WEST COAST[3]

The *West Coast* is a 49.9-metre-long vessel used for fisheries inspection on the Danish sea.[4] A crew of nine men (including a captain), one or two mates, two marine engineers, a cook, and one to three ship assistants, operates the ship. Contemporary fishing is a highly regulated arena, involving a range of regulatory issues including (but not limited to) quotas, equipment, catch landing, registration, and licensing issues. The inspection work carried out by the *West Coast* aims to ensure that fishermen comply with these regulations. Presently, inspection accounts for about 95% of the work hours, though the ship is also a key actor in the Danish National Rescue Service. Equally crucial is the fact that work on the *West Coast* relies on technologically mediated information of many sorts. Not least, technologies provide updated knowledge about the environment of the ship and its location. As we discuss in the following, the production of reliable information is integrally related to a series of comparisons.

On the Bridge: Local Assemblages and Immanent Comparisons

In her study of Dutch drug users under rehabilitation, Emilie Gomart (2004) found comparison to be an important preoccupation among doctors and patients. These comparisons were consequential: 'drugs were alternatives, they were the very possibility to negotiate, to adjust and to change slightly' (2004: 98). As we shall see, the need 'to adjust and change slightly' is also an important aspect of the navigational requirements on the bridge of the *West Coast*. It, too, is facilitated by comparison. Contrary to Gomart's study of human comparisons, however, these comparisons are embedded in technological assemblages.

Upon boarding the *West Coast*, one is immediately struck by the density of the technological environment. This is especially the case on the ship's bridge. Throughout Gad's fieldwork, one of the most prominent tasks of inspectors consisted of engagement with multiple navigational technologies. It would not be unreasonable to suspect that these technologies embody a division of labour in which each fulfils its own specific and specialised role. Certainly, this was Gad's assumption when, ignorant to their purposes, he first encountered these technological black boxes. However, it gradually became clear that many of these different technologies had similar functions.

Today, navigation is primarily done using the electronic sea chart. This chart was introduced on the *West Coast* around the mid-2000s. However, even as this chart (on which the position of the ship is continuously updated by a geographical positioning system (GPS)) is now the primary means for navigation, the striking fact is that none of the older technologies have been discarded. Thus, in principle (and occasionally in practice) navigation can be done in several ways – namely using radar, compass, or landmarks. Danish law requires the ship to maintain paper maps and even a sextant. Somewhat absurdly, a positioning system that used to receive FM waves from land towers filled an entire panel on the bridge, although it had not been used for a long while.

Perhaps the apparent irrationality of this (more or less) obsolete technological arrangement diminishes if one thinks in economic terms. If the space is not urgently needed, there is little incentive to refurbish the whole bridge simply because one technology no longer serves a current purpose. However, the overwhelming sense of redundancy (extending to compasses and sextants) which few have the skills to use any more, points to a more general aspect of the technological environment: technologies tend not to replace one another on the *West Coast*. Instead, new ones are simply added to the existing assemblage of technologies and tasks on board the ship. The sense of redundancy or replication is intensified once it is realised that some technologies come in pairs. For example, on the bridge there are four steering gears and two radars.

What might account for such functional overlaps? The most obvious reason is safety and risk management. A variety of technologies, similar and different, new and old, are available as backups in case others fail. If, as Marilyn Strathern observed about the comparative enterprise of anthropology, that 'a distinct challenge [...] is how to pace oneself for a future that is not ashamed of finding 'old' as well as 'new' resources' (2002: xiv), then this might be equally said of navigation (whether 'old' anthropological resources might be seen as a 'backup' in case newer ones fail need not detain us at this point). Even so, figuring out just what these diverse technologies are good for, and in which situations, is not simple. This is not only the case for the ignorant ethnographer, but also for the members of the crew. Moreover, these complications are precisely the starting points for acts of comparison.

For example, whether the new electronic sea chart is more 'trustworthy' than the older radar is contingent upon various considerations. The similarity of these technologies is easily understood, since both display the position of the ship relative to land and other vessels. However, when queried about their differences, crew members stated that the radar shows reality as it 'really' is. Over the years, stand-alone radars have proven their capacity to reliably represent the position of the ship. In contrast, the more advanced representation made available on the sea chart is mediated by software running on a PC, which makes it vulnerable to assorted errors and breakdowns.

At the same time, the radar was not considered sufficiently trustworthy and the ship regularly used two radars at once. Furthermore, the information collected via radar could also be challenged by comparison with other positioning technologies, including the sea chart. Thus, while the radar can be tuned to filter out high waves in bad weather, this comes with the risk of missing small boats. For the sailors, as for Isabelle Stengers' scientists, 'objectivity is not the name for a method but for an achievement, for the creation of a rapport authorizing the definition of an object' (2011: 50). Comparison, that is, facilitates the making of situated but authoritative definitions of which information is reliable and safe – i.e. what is 'real'. This is not a question of using a fail-safe method, but of learning to 'pay due attention' (2011: 62) to relevant differences.

Reliability and safety varies with the constantly changing sea environment. This sets in motion another series of comparative acts. For example, it might be assumed that looking out of the window is the best way to observe 'reality'. Why bother then with all these technologies? For one thing, the radar can 'see' far in all directions and it will sound an alarm if other ships or obstacles approach. Second, 'unmediated' observation using eyesight is only feasible in situations where the sky is clear and the sea is calm. If there is heavy rain, a gusting storm, or if waves splash against the window, it is hardly possible to see anything. Since the radar can ignore most deflections due to bad weather, it offers a far better 'window' onto the realities of sea under such conditions (one captain explained – not without pride – that he had once docked in harbour using *only* the radar). Again, the trustworthiness and reliability of technologies are comparatively established and relative.

However, there is more to this variability than technological properties, for the addition of new technologies to the bridge also affects crew members' skills and knowledge. Not least, the introduction of advanced technologies means that sailors must exert themselves to learn their use. Invariably, the ability to use old technologies begins to fade. Though many technologies are available, not every crew member is able to use them. Today, few can position using the sextant or fully master the mandatory paper charts.

The question of how to maintain 'good old' seafaring skills, in a context where new technologies are continuously added, was indeed a matter of concern aboard the ship. After all, as one crew member said, technologies are only good 'as long as they work'. Thus, the fading ability to use older technologies – intimately bound up with the traditional skills and identities of sailors – was linked to a common worry about 'deskilling'. In the parlance of actor-network theory, this process can be described in less nostalgic terms as the ongoing (and invariable) redistribution of technical and social competencies, and the attending (again invariable) transformations of what it means to be a sailor. The important point, however, is that establishing what counts as deskilling in this context (saturated by technology), can *only* be done comparatively.

Surprisingly, concerns about the use of technology were brought to light not only in consideration of technologies that, although available, may in fact no longer be usable, but also about technologies that seem to *work too well*. Insofar as technologies appear to operate with smooth efficiency, sailors are prone to rely too much on them, and this can be dangerous. Stories circulated about captains who had trusted their equipment so much that they had failed to look out the window and wrecked their ships. Whether apocryphal or not, these stories highlight the life and death importance of relevant and timely navigational comparisons. Certainly, the GPS system is not infallible. Thus, paradoxically, in an inherently unstable sea environment, any technology that appears to be *too* trustworthy risks losing trust.[5]

Similarly, the autopilot and other technologies of automation were seen to carry the risk of rendering sailors inattentive at the precise moment when their skills would be most needed. To fight the threat to vigilance posed by automation, the crew adopted innovative, if somewhat banal, routines. Rather than removing sailors from the bridge, the autopilot gave rise to the new demand that *two* persons must always be present. A motion detector linked to an alarm ensured that the crew would be alerted if the bridge had become too quiet for comfort.

By looking into immanent comparisons on the bridge, this section has aimed to show that reliability and safety are effects of ongoing practices of comparison at sea. Technologies, new or old, become trustworthy only insofar as they are confirmed by other technologies. In rare cases where the technologies on the bridge produce realities that refuse to align, the entire assemblage ceases to resonate and becomes unreliable and unstable. Under such circumstances, crew members initiate investigative 'repair work'. Reparation, however, does not move us outside the orbit of comparison. Instead, it entails even more detailed and intensive comparative efforts, such as recalibrating the radars, and using one radar to check the reliability of another display.

On the *West Coast*, reliable navigational information is thus constructed through a series of interlinked comparative practices. Comparisons are elicited through relationships between technologies on the bridge. They are neither human centred, nor strictly technology driven. Instead, the whole technological set-up on the bridge can be seen as *an assemblage for comparison*. What it generates is temporary and partial trust in information, which allows the *West Coast* to navigate safely.

Techno-bureaucratic Practices: Within a Comparative Ecology

If the previous section focused on immanent comparisons on the bridge, the present discussion highlights the web into which a single one of these technologies (i.e. the Vessel Monitoring System (VMS)), is spun. Rather than narrowing analysis, this exploration requires extension.

Brit Ross Winthereik and Henriette Langstrup Nielsen have argued 'in favor of comparing sites [...] by juxtaposing analyses' of contexts (2008: 364). Similarly, Timothy Choy's work on *Ecologies of Comparison* urges attention to 'techniques and politics of specification, exemplification, and comparison' (2011: 5). Choy offers these as 'trigger words inviting reflection' on how 'practices draw and conceptualize connections' between an array of concerns and things such as 'forms of life and their environs [...] what is considered big and [...] small, between particulars and universals, between particular cases of a common rule, between specificities and generalisations' (Ibid. 5–6). The VMS, too, is part of an ecology that stretches far beyond the *West Coast* and invites consideration of how sites are comparatively juxtaposed.

The VMS, as other technologies we have encountered, enables inspectors to position the *West Coast* and it helps them make decisions about how to move around at sea. As a navigational device, the VMS is also part of the assemblage of comparisons on the bridge. At the same time, it is tied into a broader, distributed ecology of comparisons that extend far beyond the physical confines of the ship. As part of this ecology, it relates to other techno-bureaucratic practices. It is therefore interwoven with different 'scales and levels of obligation' (Povinelli 2000: 509).

The VMS was introduced in 1999 in response to an EU initiative which committed member states to adopt information technologies for the inspection of their fishing fleets. By 2005, all Danish fishing vessels longer than fifteen metres were subject to this requirement. Technically, the VMS consists of a transceiver and an aerial installed on board each fishing vessel, and the transceiver is connected to GPS. It sends information about position, course, and speed to a satellite controlled by the International Maritime Satellite Organisation (INMARSAT). The satellite passes on this information to a communication centre located in the Netherlands, which in turn passes it on to the fisheries directorates of the member states. The VMS on the *West Coast* receives this information from the Danish directorate. The *West Coast* retrieves information about vessels registered in Denmark and located in any maritime territory in Europe, as well as foreign vessels operating in Danish territory. The frequency of the signals can be set individually for each boat.

Aboard the *West Coast*, this information is accessible on a PC sitting on the bridge. An application called vTrack allows for visualisation of the whereabouts, speed, and course of each vessel. In order to decide where to head next, inspectors open vTrack several times each day. To enable efficient boarding of many vessels, they usually look for clusters of ships.

In addition to information about the location of ships, inspectors can use vTrack to trace the movements of a vessel over time. They can also gather information about the state of the transceiver on any vessel. For example, if the transceiver has been turned off, this information is automatically stored in the VMS. The importance of this hinges on the fact that a boat that emits no signals; in fact it signals possible misconduct, since the transceiver signal may well have been intentionally shut off.

Furthermore, inspectors can access information about previous sightings of a vessel, whether registered by the *West Coast*, by other inspection ships, or by land-based inspection. Information about any previous illegalities, quotas, and licenses is also available. The monitoring system is thus quite comprehensive.

Yet, the inspection system does not rely exclusively on the VMS. Indeed, multiple forms of data are necessary to make inspection decisions. Thus, the ship has internet access via satellite connection, enabling the crew to send and receive messages about inspection plans, new legislation, and other relevant data. This 'Fisheries System' complements the VMS by providing information about vessels, records of catches, personal details about fishermen, information about licenses, observed vessels, lawbreakers, and more. The combined set of information is used by inspectors to prioritise their efforts, and determine what to search for on a vessel boarded for inspection.

In principle then, the VMS makes available to inspectors knowledge of the whereabouts of each vessel, and they have a range of supplementary information at their fingertips. However, because this information is continuously updated, they struggle to keep abreast and maintain an overview. The abundance of information both expands and limits their practical knowledge (see Jensen and Winthereik 2013: 159–63). The result is new forms of specialisation, whereby one inspector may become an expert in regulations about cod, while another may be knowledgeable about the allowed sizes of nets, and so on. To enable comparison of specific fishing vessels with the most updated regulations, inspectors increasingly rely on one another as information brokers.

Even if information is turned into knowledge, it is by no means certain that it can be made relevant and useful for inspection purposes. The problem of creating operational knowledge out of a sea of information is most clearly seen in relation to the phenomenon of 'quota jumping'. Suspicions of quota jumping are likely to emerge when a ship is observed crossing back and forth over the border between two fisheries zones. The zigzagging movement suggests that the vessel is catching fish in one zone, and registering it in another, thus jumping the quota. However, in order to establish a legal case for quota jumping, the pattern of movement seen on the computer screen provides insufficient evidence, for it is not illegal merely to sail in this pattern. Conclusive evidence requires the *West Coast* to be co-present with the offending vessel and observe the act of illegal fishing directly.

The trouble is that if the *West Coast* sails even remotely close to the zigzagging boat, the latter is highly unlikely to continue to do anything illegal. Hence, the legally required comparison is almost impossible to effect in practice. The consequence is that even when inspectors using the VMS observe what they take to be unequivocal signs of quota jumping, they often decide *not to investigate*. Since the *West Coast* has no way of sneaking up on an offending vessel, the effort would at best be only temporarily preventive, and most likely futile.

Delving into the comparative ecology of the VMS, we can identify in another guise a 'problem of representation' to which acts of comparison on the bridge were also the solution. On the bridge, we showed acts of comparison deployed to establish trustworthy information about the sea environment. The question was how to know that technologies reliably represent the world. Focusing on the sociotechnical ecology of vTrack, the problem is in some sense the reverse:

inspectors do 'know' that the technologies are reliable, but they cannot reliably link that knowledge with action as required by law. In principle, inspectors are convinced of the commensurability between sign and reality. In practice, the 'sign' displayed by vTrack remains incommensurable with this reality, since the time and movement required to verify illegality would disrupt the verification process. The problem of comparison here is not about knowledge's validity, but about how to make the world respond to reliable knowledge.

Our discussions have highlighted that at sea no technology is an island. On the bridge, the efficacy of each technology is established within a localised assemblage of comparison, but technologies like the VMS are also part of more extended ecologies, stretching into legal systems, Danish bureaucracies, Dutch databases, and into the EU. Indeed, the very existence of the VMS is partly the result of the EU's own comparisons of the monitoring capacities of its member states (Ministry of Food, Agriculture and Fisheries of Denmark 2006: 52–57). Whether we focus on local assemblages or broader ecologies, the general fact thus remains that in all cases, technologies are used comparatively to deal with the 'fields of embodied obligation' (Povinelli 2000: 510) of inspection work.

There is no room within this mode of analysis for the assumption that any form of comparison is more *inherent* to work on the *West Coast* than any other. We can neither define navigational comparisons as primary and legal comparisons as derivative, nor vice versa. No aspect of comparative activity ultimately indexes the 'real stuff' (Ibid.) of fisheries inspection more authentically than any other. Laterally speaking, the form comparisons take (as well as the implications they may have) are always in principle open-ended (see Krause, this volume).

LATERAL COMPARISONS

On the *West Coast*, we encountered an assemblage of comparison. Upon further inspection, technologies also turn out to operate as comparative devices in a much broader bureaucratic ecology. But wait – did we really 'encounter' such an assemblage? Did the technologies simply 'turn out' to operate comparatively? The lateral answer is both 'yes' and 'no', for whereas our characterisation is supported by ethnography, it is not *determined* by it. Rather, the analysis is actualised simultaneously by our concern with comparison, as a social scientific tool *and* as empirical finding. It thus moves between the two, in both directions.

The intrinsic relationship between comparisons unfolding ethnographically and comparisons activated analytically can be elucidated by means of a contrast between two approaches that, at first glance, appear radically opposed. On the one hand, anthropologists like Riles and Maurer insist on the inventiveness of ethnographic re-description, a form of creativity they consider stifled by actor-network theory's purported 'realism'. As Maurer insists, '[t]he point is not to identify entanglements and name them when you see them, but to obviate that very move as the analysis proceeds and to remain very much within that procession' (2005: 14).

On the other hand, philosopher of science Stengers argues that the central question is whether 'we impose comparison or we [are] authorised to compare by the subjects we address?' (2011: 48). Stengers argues that this question is 'very demanding' because it implies that 'no comparison is legitimate if the parties compared cannot each present his own version of what the comparison is about; and each must be able to resist the imposition of irrelevant criteria' (2011: 56). No comparison is legitimate, she argues, if it is unilateral – and most social scientific comparisons are. If Riles takes the liberty of comparing Fijian mats with policy documents, or Maurer compares Chinese characters with offshore banking (Martin and Maurer 2012), are we not witness to the imposition of irrelevant criteria? Similarly, when we describe the bridge on the *West Coast* as an assemblage of comparison, does this not introduce an extant analytical apparatus? This worry begins to dissipate with the realisation that comparisons are at once omnipresent and multiple, immanent and cross-cutting, both among our informants and ourselves.

For one thing, much that happens on board the *West Coast* is in response to things that are *as foreign* to the crew as our characterisation of their work: things like international law, EU regulations, and regimes of natural resource management. However, while the demands these regimes impose are in some sense 'unilateral', the ongoing comparisons on the ship work to 'indigenise' these impositions. Local comparisons make them amenable to particular forms of manipulation and re-inflection. Through comparative work, the impositions gradually become *part of the local assemblages*. In other words, the clear-cut distinction between external and internal blurs.

Even so, it can surely be said that the terminology of assemblage and ecology that we use to describe these situations is foreign to the field. This is certainly the case, for it comes out of reading works by scholars like Latour, Deleuze, Strathern, and Maurer as part of our disciplinary education, and in response to our own emergent research interests. Obviously, and unavoidably, those interests shape our sense of what an interesting comparative project might look like. Hence, the particular comparisons on which we have focused are elicited in a dynamic interplay between our intellectual preoccupations *and* what we encountered on the *West Coast*. These comparisons are neither 'imposed' nor simply found there. Exemplifying the lateral point, they operate in the uncertain space in-between. At the end of the day, these are nevertheless our comparisons. After all, Christopher's informants have other things to do than write for this volume. However, that these comparisons are ours *in that sense* does not imply that we were ever in a position to fully control them, even if we wanted to. But then, we explicitly did not.

Explaining her analytical interest in Dutch doctors and drug addicts, Gomart wrote that

> I would not assume they were *like* me; but I would allow that others pose questions *with* me. My aim became to describe [...] the experimentations they were able to deploy in such settings (2004: 86).

Gomart insisted that '[t]o learn something from these actors', she would have to discipline herself to be 'surprised' by their experiments (Ibid.). For Gomart, as for us, such disciplining is not simply an act of will. It is a learning process that draws not only on ethnographic experience, but also on a set of emergent intellectual dispositions. Such dispositions are shaped by a corpus of readings and discussions that train us to be attentive to *empirical* and *conceptual* surprises, as well as to the surprises of their interacting effects, *all at once*.

Undoubtedly, this creates a vantage point from which social science comparisons are *imposed* in that they are not those of informants – but also one in which the imposition is not unilateral – since the comparisons conducted by informants turn into surprises for research. Those surprises, in turn, generate the comparisons made by the social researcher *for other purposes*. Intentionally or not, some of those comparisons may fold back upon, and affect, the practices of informants. One of the surprises generated by the study of fisheries inspection on board the *West Coast* is that, in a certain sense, their reasons for deploying comparisons are analogous to the reasons for social scientific comparison. In both cases, comparisons are about tuning and attuning to reality in order to make it amenable to both analysis and action. Nevertheless, of course, *the kinds of analysis and action* that the comparisons enable are *radically different*. It is this interplay between similarity and difference that subsequently facilitates lateral deployments of others' comparisons.

The work of fisheries inspectors unfolds in a world only partially known. This uncertainty guides their comparative efforts to maintain navigational safety. Each technology within the assemblage on the bridge offers a 'generous constraint' (Gomart 2004: 105), contingently taken into account in producing a trustworthy picture. As part of inspectors' practical ontological work, then (Gad, Jensen, and Winthereik 2015), acts of comparison function as tools for creating reliability. Comparison helps them calibrate a reality experienced as potentially disorderly.

In the social sciences, the 'problem of representation' continues to recur in a range of situations and debates. How can we know what the world *is*? How can we know that we are representing it *correctly*? As we have argued, on board the *West Coast* this problem is routinely dealt with in a form far more pressing than the one encountered by most social scientists: at sea, failure to know the world adequately can lead to shipwreck. We cannot say whether the inspectors are realists or constructivists with respect to this world, for though they come up with what we might refer to as realist or constructivist responses as part of their comparative practices, they never named such positions. Even so, *the way in which this question is handled* bears little resemblance to the demands of social scientists or philosophers keen on accurate representation. Inspectors maintain a pragmatic attitude, premised on the precautionary refusal to ascribe trust in any single version of reality offered by any technology.

Though fisheries inspectors need accuracy to navigate safely, they have little need for the idea of a static reality. More akin to Maurer's depiction of anthropology as 'open and unsteady', the fluctuating reality of fisheries inspection is temporarily stabilised through ongoing efforts to make timely comparisons. The technological assemblage and wider ecology of comparison into which fisheries inspection is spun, enables inspectors to hold the dynamic sea environment sufficiently in check to continue their work.

Stefan Helmreich (2011) has observed that over the decades, social scientists have mined the sea for metaphors and concepts. Indeed, he suggests, the sea functions akin to a 'theory-machine' from which widespread theories and frameworks centring on flows, fluidity, and circulations have emerged. Helmreich draws the conclusion that

> [t]heory (and for that matter seawater) is at once abstraction as well as thing in the world; theories constantly cut across and complicate our paths as we navigate the 'real' world (2011: 5).

Rather than engage with the sea as an entity on its own, we have followed the work of fisheries inspectors who are constantly preoccupied with its unpredictable behaviour. Their attempts to maintain a sense of control in this fluid environment rely on a technological assemblage of comparisons. Even their much-cherished idea of the 'free life at sea' (Gad 2012) is deeply entangled with the management of uncertainty enabled by this assemblage.

COMPARATIVE IMAGINATIONS

In her preface to *Anthropology, By Comparison*, Marilyn Strathern expressed concern that an abiding sense of connectedness generates epistemic laziness among its proponents (2002: xv). She suggested the metaphor of extended networks 'gobbles up all the spaces between' and depicts 'a continentalizing empire, leaving nothing that is not potentially connectable to everything else' (Ibid.). Although our comparative endeavour can hardly be said to refute 'twenty-first century imaginings', the *West Coast*'s ecology of comparisons might give us pause.

There is no doubt that fishery inspection is entangled in an extended web. Indeed, was it to be detached from this wider ecology, there would be little chance that the work could continue. Yet it is not clear whether this ecology adds up to an 'empire': certainly all the spaces in between have not yet been 'gobbled up'. Indeed, even though fishery inspectors worry about their increasing dependence on wider networks of regulations and technologies, their concern is not with a general 'continentalisation' of their work. It is rather with retaining room for specific kinds of manoeuvre within their ecologies of comparison. Thus, while fishery inspectors are unceasingly critical about the bureaucratic regimes of which they are part, they also manage to find ways to 'operate in the gaps' in order to do 'good' inspection. Distancing themselves from governmental demands made by the Danish state and the EU, they often emphasise their similarity with the fishermen whose job it is to inspect.

This particular comparative alignment elicits the paradox (from the point of view of the inspectors) that it is their task to control other sailors, who, like themselves, ought to be 'free'. An important aspect of inspection is the navigation of this troubling contradiction, both in terms of the 'identity crisis' it generates for the inspectors, and in relation to the question of how to respectfully enter the private homes (i.e. the ships) of fishermen in order to control their behaviour. A similar carefulness might, in turn, be said to describe the relationship between the crew members, their own ship, and its different technologies. Reciprocally, the technological assemblage on the ship could of course also be seen as taking care of the inspectors. Indeed, inspectors quite often referred to the ship as their 'second home'.

It is impossible to say how long this comparative chain could be expanded. However, this is precisely the point of lateral comparison. For in the cases we have characterised, the location and boundaries of comparisons are invariably somewhat loose and indeterminate. They stretch across inspectors and their machines; bureaucracies and tracking systems; felt moral obligations and legal requirements; and also ethnographers' observational capacities and their conceptual inclinations. Thus, lateral comparisons are likely to occur anywhere and everywhere (Jensen and Gad 2009; Gad and Jensen 2010), but the ways in which they are conducted, assembled, and brought together across domains are altogether variable. This is the basis for our initial refusal to delimit what may count as comparative material.

Even so, in a book chapter there are clear practical limitations on extendibility, and therefore there are always choices to be made about description and exposition. Here, we have articulated *just this* lateral comparative chain for a very specific purpose: not primarily to give deep insight into the working lives or technologised practices of fisheries inspectors, but precisely to make visible some potentials that lateral comparison might hold for STS, anthropology, and social science.

In our view, a reinvigoration of the comparative imaginations of the social sciences is both timely and promising, but its promise does not lie in the specification of a new comparative agenda *tout court*. One of the major problems with such an agenda is that it offers few possibilities for 'inventing around'. Its rigour comes in the way of noticing and playing with the lateral comparisons that invisibly sustain it. As Strathern wrote about the now deceased project of grand-style anthropological comparison,

> it was hard to see how it could be added to, qualified, introduced into other contexts or travel, like Latour's mutable mobiles – in short, how it could become interesting. It only produced knowledge like itself (2002: xv).

However, whereas a return to comparative studies in the grand style is thus not only epistemologically and methodologically unfeasible, but also delimiting and uninteresting, it seems equally clear that acts of comparison – both ethnographic and analytic – still matter. Indeed, as our cases have suggested, acts of comparison are both practically crucial and conceptually magnetic, not only to social scientists, but also to their informants, who deploy them in the most diverse ways. As Stengers wrote, we are indeed, 'all comparativists' (2011: 48).

Here we have argued that one way to heighten our comparative imagination, and keep the surprises and effects of comparisons in full view, is to focus on their lateral movements and to experiment with new ways of inventing around them.

NOTES

1 Holy noted that '[t]he possibility of generalizing from a single case was of course not ruled out, but the merits and deficiencies of this type of generalizing in contrast to generalization on the basis of systematic comparison of several cases, were addressed as a methodological problem (Köbben 1970, cited in Holy 1987: 2). This intriguing possibility has been reintroduced under the rubric of 'comparative relativism' (Jensen 2011).
2 For example, Strathern has used Melanesian ethnography to elucidate English kinship (1992) and Western audit cultures (2000).
3 Gad did fieldwork on the *West Coast* from 2008–2009, mostly on the ship's bridge.
4 The ship *might* as well have been just a bit over fifty metres long, Gad was told, but in that case the law would have required the ship to have an additional crew member. In this sense, the length of the *West Coast* was 'determined' by a comparison between the ship and security standards.
5 Situations in which too much trust turns out to be dangerous and may cause subsequent breakdowns of trust, are also prevalent elsewhere. For instance, uncritical reliance on mapping and positioning devices is also problematic for drivers (see e.g. ranker.com 2014). These cases illustrate that trust in technology without a comparative basis is common, but also that it is often risky. This is an insight of which fisheries inspectors were well aware.

BIBLIOGRAPHY

Barnes, B., 'The Comparison of Belief-Systems: Anomaly versus Falsehood', in R. Horton, and R. Finnegan, eds., *Modes of Thought: Essays on Thinking in Western and Non-Western Societies* (London: Faber, 1973), pp. 182–198

Beaulieu, A., A. Scharnhorst, and P. Wouters, 'Not Another Case Study: A Middle-range Interrogation of Ethnographic Case Studies in the Exploration of e-science', *Science, Technology, & Human Values*, 32.6 (2007), 672–693

Bloch, M., 'Where did Anthropology go? Or the Need for "Human Nature"', in M. Bloch, ed., *Essays on Cultural Transmission* (Oxford: Berg, 2005), pp. 1–20

Choy, T., *Ecologies of Comparison: An Ethnography of Endangerment in Hong Kong* (Durham, NC, and London: Duke University Press, 2011)

Deville, J., M. Guggenheim, and Z. Hrdličková, 'Same, Same but Different: Provoking Relations, Assembling the Comparator', this volume

Durkheim, É., *The Rules of Sociological Method* (New York: Free Press, 1964)

Gad, C., 'What we Talk About When we Talk about Sailor Culture: Understanding Danish Fisheries Inspection through a Cult Movie', *Culture Unbound*, 4 (2012), 367–392

Gad, C., and C. B. Jensen, 'On the Consequences of Post-ANT', *Science, Technology, & Human Values*, 35.1 (2010), 55–80

Gad, C., C. B. Jensen, and B. R. Winthereik, 'Practical Ontologies: Worlds in Anthropology and STS', *NatureCultures*, 3 (2014), 67–86

Galison, P., and D. J. Stump, eds., *The Disunity of Science: Boundaries, Contexts, and Power* (Stanford, CA: Stanford University Press, 1996)

Gingrich, A., and R. G Fox, eds., *Anthropology, By Comparison* (London and New York: Routledge, 2002)

Gomart, E., 'Surprised by Methadone: In Praise of Drug Substitution Treatment in a French Clinic', *Body and Society*, 10 (2004), 85–110

Hacking, I., *Representing and Intervening: Introductory Topics in the Philosophy of the Natural Sciences* (Cambridge: Cambridge University Press, 1983)

Hansen, B. G., 'Adapting in the Knowledge Economy: Lateral Strategies for Scientists and Those who Study them', PhD Thesis, Copenhagen Business School, Department of Management, Politics and Philosophy, 2011

Haraway, D., 'A Game of Cat's Cradle: Science Studies, Feminist Theory, Cultural Studies', *Configurations*, 2.1 (1994), 59–71

Helmreich, S., 'Nature/Culture/Seawater', *American Anthropologist*, 113.1 (2011), 132–144

Hobart, M., 'Summer's Days and Salad Days: The Coming of Age of Anthropology?', in L. Holy, ed., *Comparative Anthropology* (Oxford: Blackwell, 1987), pp. 22–51

Holbraad, M., *Truth in Motion: The Recursive Anthropology of Human Divination* (Chicago and London: University of Chicago Press, 2012)

Holy, L., 'Introduction: Description, Generalization and Comparison: Two Paradigms', in L. Holy, ed., *Comparative Anthropology* (Oxford: Blackwell, 1987), pp. 1–21

Hutchins, E., *Cognition in the Wild* (Cambridge, MA, and London: MIT Press, 1995)

Ihde, D., *Technology and the Lifeworld: From Garden to Earth* (Indiana: Indiana University Press, 1990)

Jasanoff, S., *Designs on Nature: Science and Democracy in Europe and the United States* (Princeton, NJ: Princeton University Press, 2007)

Jensen, C. B., 'Introduction: Contexts for a Comparative Relativism', *Common Knowledge*, 17.1 (2011), 1–12

——'Continuous Variations: the Conceptual and the Empirical in STS', *Science, Technology and Human Values*, 39.2 (2014), 192–213

Jensen, C. B., and C. Gad, 'Philosophy of Technology as Empirical Philosophy: Comparing Scales in Practice', in J. K. Berg Olsen, E. Selinger, and S. Riis, eds., *New Waves in Philosophy of Technology* (New York: Palgrave, 2009), pp. 292–315

Jensen, C. B., and B. R. Winthereik, *Monitoring Movements in Development Aid: Recursive Infrastructures and Partnerships* (Cambridge, MA, and London: MIT Press, 2013)

Knorr-Cetina, K., *Epistemic Cultures: How the Sciences Make Knowledge* (Cambridge, MA, and London: Harvard University Press, 1999)

Krause, M., 'Comparative Research: Beyond Linear-causal Explanation', this volume

Kuper, A., 'Comparison and Contextualization: Reflections on South Africa', in A. Gingrich, and R. J. Fox, eds., *Anthropology, By Comparison* (London and New York: Routledge, 2002), pp. 143–166

Latour, B., *The Pasteurization of France* (Cambridge, MA, and London: Harvard University

Press, 1988)

——— *An Inquiry into Modes of Existence: An Anthropology of the Moderns* (Cambridge, MA, and London: Harvard University Press, 2013)

Leach, E., *Rethinking Anthropology* (London: Athlone, 1961)

Maurer, B., *Mutual Life, Limited: Islamic Banking, Alternative Currencies, Lateral Reason* (Princeton, NJ: Princeton University Press, 2005)

——— 'Money Nutters', *Economic Sociology: The European Electronic Newsletter*, 12.3 (2011), 5–12

Maurer, B., and S. Martin, 'Accidents of Equity and the Aesthetics of Chinese Offshore Incorporation', *American Ethnologist*, 39.3 (2012), 527–544

Meyer, M., 'Steve Jobs, Terrorists, Gentlemen, and Punks: Tracing Strange Comparisons of Biohackers', this volume

Ministry of Food, Agriculture and Fisheries of Denmark, *Fiskeridirektoratets kontrolstrategi – Erhversfiskeriet* (Copenhagen, 2006)

Morita, A., 'The Ethnographic Machine: Experimenting with Context and Comparison in Strathernian Ethnography', *Science, Technology and Human Values*, 39.2 (2014), 214–35

Niewöhner, J., and T. Scheffer, 'Introduction', *Comparative Sociology*, 7.3 (2008), 273–285

Otto, T., and N. Bubandt, eds., *Experiments in Holism: Theory and Practice in Contemporary Anthropology* (Malden and Oxford: Wiley-Blackwell, 2010)

Povinelli, E., 'Consuming Geist: Popontology and the Spirit of Capital in Indigenous Australia', *Public Culture*, 12.2 (2000), 501–528

Ranker.com, 'Car Accidents Caused by Google Maps and GPS', <http://www.ranker.com/list/9-car-accidents-caused-by-google-maps-and-gps/robert-wabash/> [accessed 4 April 2014]

Ratner, H., 'Promises of Reflexivity: Managing and Researching Inclusive Schools, PhD Thesis, Copenhagen Business School, Department of Management, Politics and Philosophy, 2012

Riles, A., *The Network Inside Out* (Michigan: University of Michigan Press, 2000)

Schmidt, R., 'Gaining Insight from Incomparability: Exploratory Comparison in Studies of Social Practices', *Comparative Sociology*, 7.3 (2008), 338–361

Scott, W. R., *Organizations: Rational, Natural, and Open Systems* (New Jersey: Prentice-Hall, 1981)

Serres, M., *Detachment* (Athens: Ohio University Press, 1989)

Stengers, I., 'Comparison as a Matter of Concern', *Common Knowledge*, 17.1 (2011), 48–63

Stöckelová, T., 'Frame Against the Grain: Asymmetries, Interference, and the Politics of EU Comparison', this volume

Strathern, M., *After Nature: English Kinship in the Late Twentieth Century* (Cambridge: Cambridge University Press, 1992)

——— ed., *Audit Cultures: Anthropological Studies in Accountability, Ethics and the Academy* (London and New York: Routledge, 2000)

——'Foreword: Not Giving the Game Away', in A. Gingrich, and R. J. Fox, eds., *Anthropology, By Comparison* (London and New York: Routledge, 2002), pp. xiii–xvii
——'Binary License', *Common Knowledge*, 17.1 (2011), 87–103
Verran, H., *Science and an African Logic* (Chicago and London: University of Chicago Press, 2001)
Viveiros de Castro, E., 'Zeno and the Art of Anthropology: Of Lies, Beliefs, Paradoxes, and other Truths', *Common Knowledge*, 17.1 (2011), 128–145
Wagner, R., *The Invention of Culture* (New Jersey: Prentice-Hall, 1975)
Walford, A. C., *Transforming Data: An Ethnography of Scientific Data from the Brazilian Amazon*, PhD Thesis, IT University of Copenhagen, 2013
Winthereik, B. R., and H. L. Nielsen, 'The Making of Self-monitoring Asthma Patients: Mending a Split Reality with Comparative Ethnography', *Comparative Sociology*, 7.3 (2008), 362–386

8

COMPARATIVE TINKERING WITH CARE MOVES

Peter A. Lutz

INTRODUCTION

THIS CHAPTER STEMS FROM MY ETHNOGRAPHIC STUDY OF SENIOR HOME CARE in the United States and Sweden. In this study, I trace relations between people and technology as they come together in gatherings or 'collectives' (Moreira 2010) for care. Specifically, I am interested in how care *moves* with these collectives and generates interrelated consequences for the human and nonhuman actors concerned. However, these relational moves of care are rarely smooth. Instead, they comprise ongoing tensions or 'frictions' (Tsing 2005) which situate multiple acts of negotiation and 'tinkering' (Mol 2008; Mol et al. 2010). As such, 'care moves' offers a conceptual-empirical figure for fine-tuning ethnographic attention to care as a rough and tinkered process. It denotes an analytical emphasis on care as a mediating phenomenon interwoven with collective relations on the move, empirically and conceptually – entailing both effects and affects.

At the same time, I have not sought after a standardised social scientific comparison of two national healthcare systems, even though I worked in two different countries. Rather than rely on established categories, I remain interested in how to ethnographically tinker together – and thus *care with* – transnational comparisons in a more fluid or flexible manner. As such, I seek an experimental and ethnographic approach sensitive to the specific ways care moves with its collective relations.

Nevertheless, in my efforts, I have met numerous and unexpected hurdles. In this chapter, I revisit some of these challenges. They interrelate with informant or 'emic' comparisons about care and how it should move. These range from how to attend to mobility in and around the home, to future concerns including when to transfer into assisted living. My ethnographic travels between these different care moves led to perspectives that resist straightforward comparison. For instance, some seniors have family members nearby who help with home care, while others do not. Some have sufficient health coverage, while others struggle to find affordable good care. Some face serious health challenges that impede mobility and increase isolation, while others retain relatively good health. More importantly, care situations change dramatically in a single instant, and from one day to the next. If an older person falls, for example, it may dramatically alter the senior home care arrangements.

In this diverse field of care, certain comparisons suddenly seem unwieldy, while others become irrelevant or mundane. I find getting stuck in these comparative complexities akin to Donna Haraway's (2008) notion of 'staying with the trouble'. In other words, my efforts to compare became tightly connected with the troubles and rough moves of care that I encountered. Here, I have in mind a different breed of comparison, untethered from modes of comparison that solely adopt the standardised categories of a scientific repertoire. In this chapter, I set out to develop this approach as 'comparative tinkering'.

Ethnography is central to this approach because it generates 'passages' to tinker with different comparisons of care moves. As such, ethnographic passages help ground comparative tinkering as a tool for mobilising social scientific insights. Like senior home care moves, comparative tinkering with ethnographic passages equates to rough, zigzagging, analytical moves. Michel Serres' (1980) 'northwest passages' is a good analogy here.[1] The difference is that my ethnographic passages entangle reflexive comparisons between careful doing and thinking. More generally, my comparative efforts relate to an experimental turn in social scientific methodology (Otto and Bubandt 2010; Lury and Wakeford 2012) and the interest in ethnographic transnational comparison.

Through my ethnographic passages – consisting of 'field-desk relations' (Strathern 1999) or 'conceptual-empirical mixtures' (see Gad and Ribes

2014) – a series of questions emerge that ground this chapter. How, for instance, do complex care moves compare in senior home care? Similarly, how do the subtle tinkering moves of care compare in a transnational analysis? How might social scientists make careful comparisons of others' comparisons without losing sight of the messy work and moves of care itself? Moreover, how do such questions challenge what we deem to be 'noteworthy' comparisons – namely comparisons worth taking notes on in the field and tracing as valuable insights in scientific discussions? With these questions, I focus attention on how noteworthy comparison can entail *travel* worthiness, whereby comparisons with care move both empirically and conceptually.

The assertion that comparison resides in motion is relevant here, and relates to recent ideas in anthropology and science and technology studies (STS) about how to blend different kinds of scientific-informant, or etic-emic, knowledge relations. Work by Gergely Mohácsi and Atsuro Morita is exemplary. They focus on the interrelations between travel and transnational comparison and proffer the notion of 'travelling comparisons' (2013) as an experimental analytical approach. With this notion, they draw attention to the importance of mundane human and nonhuman movements that make and unmake similarities and differences in practice. For instance, in one account, Morita (2013a) traces how Thai workers compare Japanese-made cultivator blades that become tangled with Thai weeds when tilling the land. He shows how these machine-weed tangles situate Thai farmers' and mechanics' comparisons between their local work practices, their environments, and the Japanese-made machines, which the Thai import, modify, and copy. Morita explains:

> In this context, the specific parts of the machine that caused the trouble – the blades entangled with weeds – generated a sort of comparative vision. The mechanics and farmers saw the weeds wrapped around the blades as a difference between the Japanese environment that the machine embodied and the actual environment in the farmers' fields. In other words, the blades entangled with the weeds produced a double vision in which the Thai and the Japanese environments were seen at once through their difference (2013a: 235–6).

Thus, Morita argues that the coming together of heterogeneous entities – farmers, mechanics, engineers, blades, weeds, and so on – offers an opportunity to locate social scientific comparison in practice. Key in Morita's analysis is the attention to others' use of technology, and how machines present workers with the opportunity to generate transnational comparisons. For inspiration, Mohácsi and Morita also turn to Marilyn Strathern and others who argue for analytical experimentation in the relationship between emic and etic comparisons, and what some consider 'lateral' moves (Maurer 2005; Gad and Jensen, this volume).

Similarly, I hope to contribute to this way of rethinking the agency of social scientific comparison in relation to movement and transnational research, and between emic and etic concerns. Two of my previously published articles provide material for my deliberation. One article focuses on the movement of household clutter and technology in US senior home care (Lutz 2010). In the other, I centre on how healthcare technology helps generate different spatiotemporal 'surfacing' moves in Swedish senior home care (Lutz 2013). It is important to stress, however, that I sidestep transnational comparison in these publications. At the time of writing, I simply did not find what seemed like traversable ethnographic passages for a transnational comparison. As I indicate above, senior home care in both countries, and in its different situations, appeared undeserving of comparative travel.

With the idea of comparative tinkering in hand, here I retrace the potentials of comparison in these passages. This includes a search for links between my own comparisons and those of my informants. Drawing on ideas in anthropology and STS about comparison and human-nonhuman care, I tinker carefully with how care moves might inspire social scientific comparison in an ethnographic and transnational mode. As an experimental concept, comparative tinkering denotes the rough and uncertain process of mediating categorical differences to generate new comparisons, which link to how care moves in practice. Although this does not align with the usual notion of scientific comparison, I propose that it situates a significant comparative approach.

The literature on care in practice (Mol 2008; Mol et al. 2010) influences my thinking about careful comparisons as relational tinkering.[2] Others have suggested similar terms. For instance, Jeanette Pols (2012) emphasises 'fitting', while Myriam Winance (2006) proffers 'adjustment'. In Mol's view, the aim is to find ways to study care 'in and on its own terms' to open up different ways of knowing what care is and evoke 'what it is to hang together' (2010: 265). I suggest that this also pertains to making scientific comparison work and move with care, and this entails accounting for the comparative practices of informants.

A team of Swedish care workers provide an apt example. One morning, over coffee, they explained their approach. With the increasing number of senior clients in their care, they decided to alternate their client rounds each week so that every worker could gain fresh knowledge about every senior's changing situation. This approach made their work less monotonous. More importantly, it supported the collective decision-making about necessary adjustments to an individual's care routine. 'Otherwise', they remark, 'we have no real perspective'.

These multiple tinkering care moves – with its adjustments and ongoing comparisons – relates closely to my own reflexive efforts to comparatively tinker with ethnographic passages. In this way, I suggest that tinkering comparisons opens up possibilities to blur the distinction between emic and etic. Yet, the scientific literature often takes a different path by fixing its comparative categories. To exemplify this, next I review how the gerontological literature treats the transnational comparison of senior care in the US and Sweden. This will help to further orient the analytical challenges I found in my own work and motivate the notion of comparative tinkering, which I develop in the rest of the chapter.

COMPARISONS OF CARE

> We should not compare US and Swedish geriatric services [...] The cultures and healthcare systems are just too different to support meaningful comparisons.
>
> – John Rowe (2011)[3]

There are many comparative studies of healthcare systems in the scientific literature. However, I only found a handful that explicitly compare the situation for older people who require home care in the US and Sweden. Why do some scholars apparently sidestep this transnational comparison? In the quotation above, Rowe indicates the issue of cultural and healthcare differences. Marti Parker echoes this point when she suggests that such a comparison risks absurdity, given the vast population differences in each country (2001: 86). Sweden is a country of more than 9.5 million, while the US population has reached 320 million (World Population Review 2014).[4] In addition, some US seniors face extreme poverty, while there has been a lack of poverty among Swedish seniors since World War II (Parker 2001: 26). Parker also argues that these two countries historically represent ideological opposites in terms of welfare policies and services. For instance, Sweden traditionally has universal public healthcare, while the US typically adopts a market-driven model.

On the other hand, Parker considers how this comparison also makes sense. Both countries face welfare challenges linked to the changing demographics – so-called 'population ageing'. Currently, people over the age of 65 make up 19% of the Swedish population and 14% of the US population (World Bank 2014). In addition, Parker argues that both countries increasingly adopt similar healthcare strategies. For example, in Sweden, there is a growing emphasis on decentralisation and privatisation, while initiatives like the Affordable Care Act – also known as ObamaCare – have increased the national regulation of healthcare in the US. In addition, there is a growing emphasis on targeted healthcare needs and evaluation, although each country has developed a different version (Parker 2001: 73). Parker concludes that this increasing 'convergence' of healthcare for seniors offers opportunities to learn from the successes and failures in each country (Ibid. 88).

Additional studies that follow this comparison include Adam Davey et al. (2005), Dennis Shea et al. (2003), and Dominique Wang and Christian Aspalter (2007). Both Davey et al. and Shea et al. compare 'formal' or paid home care – provided by professional care workers – and 'informal' or voluntary home care provided by family members or friends in each country. Here the label 'Activities of Daily Living' (ADLs) groups together a diverse and complex range of needs into a single category.[5] These articles, based on statistical analysis, conclude that while there is some convergence between the two countries, Swedish seniors are more likely to find ADL support. This conclusion confirmed the authors' initial assumptions that the Swedish system offers several advantages for seniors in comparison to the US.

In their article, Wang and Aspalter (2007) survey healthcare systems in several countries, including the US and Sweden. To achieve their comparison, they focus on a series of 'healthcare indicators' consisting of statistical economic data on national healthcare expenditures. Their article does not distinguish senior home care per se, but it does offer implications for its broader socioeconomic conditions. The authors conclude that market forces largely shape the inequalities of healthcare in the US, while the tradition of universal public healthcare (based on solidarity and a strong public sector) still plays a dominant role in Sweden. In other words, while these studies acknowledge the convergence to which Parker refers, they also agree that Swedish seniors typically enjoy better care.

What additional insights might we gather from this handful of studies in terms of social scientific comparison? For instance, at first glance, this lack of US-Sweden comparison might appear to suggest a knowledge gap. However, this is not so. Extensive scientific knowledge about the healthcare in each of these countries does exist. Instead, I venture that many healthcare studies bypass transnational comparison to focus on an individual national healthcare system and its policies. The assumption here seems to be that each national healthcare system operates within its own specific set of contextual arrangements, where practices in other countries are less relevant. Such an assumption echoes Rowe's relativistic statement regarding how healthcare differences between these two countries still create the risk of an incommensurable – or 'apples and oranges' – comparison. One might also surmise that transnational comparison simply does not present the most fruitful or easiest path of study. However, institutions like the World Health Organisation (WHO), concerned with global health and research agendas, continue to engage with transnational comparisons to inform their recommendations. Perhaps the issue does not simply concern the possibility or absence of transnational comparison, but whether it produces noteworthy scientific knowledge towards a specific purpose. Yet, how is this achieved in practice?

This question relates to another important point about the use of standardised analytical categories for comparison. For instance, in the above studies, transnational comparisons of healthcare often stem from economic typologies such as 'welfare' versus 'market' systems.[6] These combine medical terminologies to stake out the conceptual ground for transnational comparison. Examples here include: 'convergence' (Parker 2011), 'ADL support' (Davey et al. 2005; Shea et al. 2003), and 'economic healthcare indicators' (Wang and Aspalter 2007). This use of analytical categories for comparison is akin to the notion of a standard 'comparator' – a device for measuring the properties or performance of a system with comparison to an established standard. In other words, standard categories as comparators help generate links between the different national healthcare systems for transnational comparison. However, I wager that such standard comparators also sidestep the empirical complexities of how care moves. We might think of this as regionalising or 'domaining' comparison without magnification (Strathern 2004), especially in terms of how senior home care transforms with its movements in practice.

From one point of view, the notion of ADL support presents an exception in the sense that it supposedly relates more specifically to the practice of care itself. ADL is shorthand for bathing, dressing, mobility, toileting, and eating – basic activities that concern senior home care in practice. However, I suggest that grouping these different practices together under the term ADL support glosses over the important and ongoing situational challenges that emerge with care moves. For instance, in Davey and Shea, we do not learn how any one ADL plays out in practice, nor what challenges it surfaces. Instead, they emphasise percentile differences between formal and informal support in both countries, based essentially on an abstraction. Thus, I propose that even a term like ADL support can generate conceptual-empirical gaps that miss the pervasive, ongoing specificities of care and its comparisons. Senior home care remains rich with comparative variations that weave incontinence, disease, disabilities, local healthcare infrastructures, family members, and volunteers (or their absence). Perhaps comparisons of care can also include attempts to resonate with such complexities on the move.

To summarise, I have argued that perspectives akin to Rowe's tend to consider the differences between senior healthcare services in the US and Sweden as too vast for transnational comparison. On the other hand, the studies I outline in this section challenge this perspective. Yet, to pursue their transnational comparison they establish comparative categories – or standardised comparators – that bypass the endless stream of generative frictions produced as care moves in practice. For instance, ADL support, as a standard comparator, does not necessarily bring the analysis any closer to the multiple complexities found in care, in or on its own terms (Mol 2008, 2010). This critique echoes other observations about how comparisons of healthcare tend to sidestep or ignore the complex tensions of comparison in practice (Langstrup and Winthereik 2010). Related arguments also stress the need to weave social scientific comparison with comparisons made in care, including particular and ongoing decisions about the doing of 'good enough' care (Mol 2002). My intention is not to dismiss the above comparative literature. Indeed, I agree with Parker that senior home care in the US and Sweden can offer valuable comparisons. However, might such comparisons do more, such as challenge the conceptual assumptions built into the standard comparators? Moreover, how might we pursue transnational comparisons that initially seem unworthy? What if we rethink the value of comparison as hedged in the uncovering of incommensurable gaps rather than trying to fill them? What kind of *tertium comparationis* – or comparative thirdness – might we need?

Such questions relate to Deville et al.'s (this volume) alternative notion of the 'comparator assemblage' that temporally surfaces as a hybrid mixture of people and things, including the researcher(s) in the doing of comparison. Likewise, Christopher Gad and Casper Jensen (this volume) propose the idea of 'lateral' comparisons that embrace non-hierarchical relations that reside in conceptual-empirical mixtures. These approaches set out to reject predetermined or standardised comparative categories, and instead accommodate comparison as a mutually transformative practice that runs in multiple directions.

Similarly, I revisit connections between my own comparisons and the comparisons I found other care workers making. By revisiting two of my earlier articles that sidestep transnational comparison, I aim to experiment with how ethnographic passages might open up new avenues for comparison that initially appeared jammed. In the same turn, I also expose not only my own social scientific authority, but also my earlier hesitations about comparison.

This retrospective turn to tinker with comparative views equates to what Strathern (2011) has termed a 'binary license' – the privilege to anthropologically compare, through textual contrasts and bifurcations, the relative comparisons of different others. As such, my comparative tinkering relates to concerns about social scientific method as well as what counts as scientific knowledge. To preface this move, I next introduce the practical conditions of my study. This will help to further situate comparative tinkering as a generative and experimental approach.

COMPARISONS IN CARE

My fieldwork on senior home care in the US and Sweden grew from a larger European research project. The wider objective of this project was to inform the future design and development of 'ambient intelligent telecare' for senior home care. Ambient intelligence is a term that references the artificial capacity to sense and respond to environmental cues and human expectations, while telecare is a general term for technology that supports home care. This initial research sought to contribute ethnographic knowledge that could intervene with design assumptions about senior home care, and thereby support the robust design of such technology. As noted, I focused on the question of how care moves and the relational frictions that such moves generate in these two countries. Given the underlying concern with the social scientific comparison in this chapter, below I overview how the conditions of this research entangled my own comparative efforts.

Various interests in the project influenced the decision to pursue fieldwork in the US and Sweden. In part, these stemmed from the project's organisation. The Dutch multinational hi-tech conglomerate, Philips Research, led the project, while the European Commission financed it.[7] Both actors were interested in the development of technology to meet the challenge of population ageing. In addition, Philips had recently acquired a North American telecare business (Lifeline), which offers a popular emergency response service based on wearable wireless technology. The project's assumption was that a comparative ethnographic study of senior home care in practice could inform the design of new healthcare technologies in North America and Europe. In addition, we assumed that my personal knowledge of Sweden and the US, based on previous time spent in each country, could ease the challenge of fieldwork access. Thus, practical considerations influenced the direction of my comparative efforts with senior home care.[8]

Yet, as my travels and collected materials accumulated, my certainty about a standard transnational comparison weakened. In the previous section, I outlined reasons why a transnational comparison appeared questionable. These include differences in how these two countries finance and manage senior home care. In my fieldwork, personal dynamics also played a role, such as the informants' willingness to share their 'moving' stories about care. This mixed with my capacity to establish trust and rapport. At the same time, with each new situation, my uncertainties increased. There were endless complexities stemming from the shifting concerns about ageing bodies, relations to household clutter, and the different spatial-timings of senior home care.[9] Emergencies like falling could introduce urgent comparisons between ideas about stable and unstable bodies. Other comparisons concerned seniors' past and present conditions, as well as the direction that future care moves should take. Despite the project's initial comparative ambitions, it was clear that a standard transnational comparison would face difficulty.

The actual routes of my fieldwork, interlinked with the wider national healthcare contexts, also influenced my ability to compare. For example, in the US, telecare users were my primary pool of informants. After a series of initial telephone screenings from a randomly compiled list of one hundred telecare customers living in Washington State, I selected seniors willing and interested to meet for face-to-face home interviews. After retracted interest and scheduling conflicts, I eventually met with approximately twenty seniors. These first-time meetings were usually one-on-one engagements with a senior informant. When available, a family member also joined. With six of these people, I carried out more extensive fieldwork engagements, including participant-observation in their home care activities. To complement these meetings and broaden the picture of senior home care, I also added interviews with home care administrators, nurses, and local senior healthcare advocates.

In Sweden, my fieldwork routes proceeded along different lines. Although private home care organisations are on the increase in Sweden, I felt I could reduce conflicts of interest by only recruiting in public home care organisations, rather than in privately owned home care businesses. In addition, with the absence of a customer database, I recruited my senior informants in person, in three municipal home care service organisations. After briefing the managers and their staff about my project, they agreed to identify senior clients whom they felt could best participate. Overall, health and mental alertness were among the factors the staff took into account.[10] Once the seniors had confirmed their interest and availability, I proceeded in one of two ways. Either I contacted seniors myself for the initial interview, or I joined the care staff on their rounds to meet the interested seniors in person. The different needs each senior required, as well as the relations between seniors and their care workers, also influenced my ability to recruit. Seniors who had good relations with the care workers were generally more eager to participate. I observed well over forty home care situations and interviewed many of the seniors in these situations. Approximately half a dozen of these seniors I then met on repeated occasions. As in the US, these follow-up visits often provided opportunities for participant-observation.

The US fieldwork generally produced more individual accounts based on one-on-one interactions, while the Swedish ethnography favoured group interactions consisting of one-on-three (or more) encounters – namely a senior client, one or more care worker(s), and myself. These variations also linked with the differences in how these two countries organise senior home care. Thus, in the absence of Lifeline customers in Sweden, or public home care workers in the US, my ethnographic passages increasingly prompted the problem of incongruent comparisons. In turn, these tinkered with my own empirical-conceptual moves. This included the rethinking of key terms such as 'senior', 'home', 'care', as well as 'technology' – all of which enfolded vastly different heterogeneities.

This knotting together of ethnographic passages, including my scribbled field notes on how care moves, spurred numerous questions about which factors to compare, as well as how to compare, without losing sight of their complexities. Increasingly, I felt it necessary to sidestep my initial comparative ambitions. In retrospect, akin to Rowe's view above, I had detoured around the challenge of transnational comparison in my analysis. The two published articles I discuss below, each focused on a different country, evidence this avoidance. In what follows, I revisit these articles and their ethnographic passages to reconsider ways to tinker with new comparisons. My ambition is not to smooth over the comparative frictions, but rather to experiment with how these might generate additional opportunities for social-scientific comparison.

Comparative Tinkering with Spatial-Timings

In 'Surfacing Moves: Spatial-Timings of Senior Home Care' (Lutz 2013), I argue for spatiotemporal differences in Swedish senior home care and develop the term 'surfacing' for this purpose. My article was an attempt to work through the distinction between subjective and objective time, which is pervasive in the social scientific literature. Inspired in part by Janelle Taylor (2005), and especially Bruno Latour's (1997) ideas on spatial-timing, I consider how humans and nonhumans come together in care moves to generate multiple surfacings that challenge the subjective-objective distinction of time. I also consider the policies of time management in Swedish public senior home care. These policies set out to economise and standardise senior home care. However, I show how such policies add to the complexity of care and its spatiotemporal surfacing, which actors must tinker with to sustain good care.

Ethnographic passages, entailing the use of technologies for scheduling Swedish senior home care, ground this particular article. One example is how a scheduler interacted with her software using the finger-mouse to orient multi-coloured blocks on the computer screen. These blocks represent different spatiotemporal entities that she neatly ordered into rows and columns on the screen to determine the weekly home care schedule. This spatiotemporal surfacing connected care workers with different seniors and their needs. The scheduler translated these needs from several standardised entries, including ADL codes that index ageing body needs with the necessary days and hours of the week for care. Simultaneously, this same move triggered the programme to automatically calculate the necessary times and routes for each senior client.

However, this formalisation of space-time was impossible without first transforming people and things into what Latour calls 'intermediaries' – entities that move other entities with little or no mediation or transformation.

This was no simple task, and required the scheduler's comparative tinkering to make the different spatial-timings fit and travel. In part, the scheduler must select and compare several different resources. These comprised archive documents of past care schedules and consultations with the other care workers, as well as with the managers overseeing the care services. Of course, she also drew from her previous employment experience as a care worker. Sticky notes left by her colleagues, stuck to the edge of her desk and keyboard, were also of central importance. These notes concerned updates in the clients' care routines. On any particular day, senior care needs could conflict with the planned home care routines. This might entail a rescheduled doctor's appointment or emergency hospitalisation. Thus, when it came to the actual hands-on doing of care, workers must again tinker with the timing and spacing of care. For instance, I witnessed how care workers concealed their paper schedule, out of sight in a pocket or the car, when working directly with seniors. When I asked the care workers about this habit, they expressed concern that the schedule would distract the quality of attention they tried to give their senior clients.[11]

During the preparation of that article, I did not find what I felt was a comparable example in my US material. Organisational time management procedures were not clearly present in the relatively informal US senior home care I had witnessed. With more foresight, I speculate that I may have better aligned my ethnographic passages to enable such a comparison. For instance, had I worked with US home care organisations initially, rather than Lifeline customers, perhaps I could have discovered richer comparative opportunities between the US and Sweden. I also consoled myself with the knowledge that at its core, ethnographic fieldwork is often serendipitous and full of uncertainty.

It is clear to me now that I had adopted a relativist stance, akin to Rowe's sidestepping of transnational comparison, when writing the article. Yet, I was never satisfied with this stance. I had the distinct sense that I had missed a comparative opportunity. Perhaps I had thrown out the baby with the bathwater and given the game of comparison away (Strathern 2002).

With the notion of comparative tinkering in hand, I want to now retrace my ethnographic passages to consider how my US informants also tinkered comparatively with the scheduling of home care. Several US seniors struggled to have their care needs met. John's care situation offers one example.[12] John was a ninety-four-year-old widower, former university adjunct, community leader, war veteran, and farmer. His wife had died several years earlier, but he still lived in the same house he designed and built in the 1950s. He had four children. His oldest daughter Julie was in her sixties, and the most active with his care. When I first met John, he was in the process of hiring a new care worker to help with domestic tasks and some personal care. His previous paid care worker, Anita, had been excellent. Anita had been on time, made good food, paid attention to detail, and enjoyed intelligent conversation. However, Anita was a student and found an opportunity to study abroad. Suddenly, John needed to find a replacement.

On a whim, without consulting Julie, he hired Candice from an ad in the local paper. Unfortunately, Candice was often late. Her cooking was bland. She was unorganised and uninterested in conversation. Candice also had the habit of bringing her four-year-old son with her. John allowed this, but he felt it interfered with his own care. John and Julie agreed that Candice was not working out. She could not compare with the standards Anita had established. However, they were stuck with Candice until they could find her replacement. In an effort to improve Candice's performance and accountability, Julie created a weekly schedule which she charted on paper and posted on the refrigerator door in the kitchen. This schedule listed the meals and basic routine duties. While this device temporarily improved Candice's performance, her care remained unsatisfactory. John and Julie therefore replaced Candice with Debbie.

Debbie was timely, meticulous, a good cook, and enjoyed conversation. Thus, she compared more favourably to Anita. In light of these improvements, John and Julie considered removing the refrigerator schedule. However, Debbie suggested that they upgrade it with an erasable whiteboard planner, which they did. This schedule-*cum*-planner eventually helped the three of them better coordinate important changes in John's care. With Debbie's input, this care technology now accommodated phone messages and other reminders about upcoming appointments that shifted the spatial-timings of John's care. However, Debbie now incorporated the basic tasks into her daily work without reminders. This eliminated the need for the display Julie had first created for Candice. In this way, the scheduling of John's care was made less visible, or what Latour would call a shift from mediator to intermediary.

What comparative insights emerge here? For one, Anita helped establish a rough standard of care, which John and Julie implicitly used to compare Candice and Debbie's performance. While this was not a formalised procedure, it did ease comparative decisions about movements in care. Here too, the schedule-cum-planner played a decisive, comparative role. John and Julie had first implemented the schedule to better align Candice's care moves with Anita's version. Then, when Debbie offered John and Julie another point of comparison, their inclination was to remove the technology. Instead, Debbie proposed a modification to allow collaborative adjustments to John's care. In this way, the relatively inflexible schedule became a more flexible and collaborative care technology, transformed with changing collective of care. Here too, I find a comparative link with how Swedish care workers hid the schedule from their client's view to generate more attentive hands-on care. Thus, tinkering with the visibility of more formalised care scheduling procedures in both cases connects to the doing of attentive, if not good, care.

My intention here is to show how comparative tinkering with care moves in ethnographic passages can produce important transnational comparisons. These comparisons do not stem from pre-established standardised categories but rather from the effects of care moves with technology. Starting with a curiosity about how spatiotemporal differences surface in Sweden, I employ a binary license to comparatively tinker with the possibility of similar effects in the US. More than the surfacing of different spatial-timings, I also show how care technology itself can shift and transform, namely from a disciplining device to one that flexibly and more implicitly coordinates collective decisions about care and how it should move. This insight echoes the notion of care as a human-nonhuman collective, which accompanies my zigzagging ethnographic passages. Thus, comparative tinkering has produced a heterogeneous comparator akin to Deville et al.'s formulation of a heterogeneous 'comparator assemblage'. Next, to further articulate the potentials of comparative tinkering, I turn to the issue of clutter in care and how it can generate additional opportunities to compare.

Comparative Tinkering with Clutter

In 'Clutter Moves in Old Age Homecare' (Lutz 2010), I consider the relation between domestic clutter and how it moves in US senior home care. This article starts with the observation that many US seniors live with household clutter. The gerontological literature often classifies this clutter as a hazard that can lead to problems with mobility, especially falling. However, I found that some US seniors used clutter in ways that challenge the conception of risky clutter. In my article, I unpack the category of clutter and highlight its positive implications for US senior home care. This includes rethinking the category of clutter as 'care technology'. For instance, some of my informants created cluttered 'nests' around their favourite chair or bed to reduce the need for physical movement around the house. These cluttered nesting relations could comprise many things – from reading materials to personal healthcare items such as pillboxes, eyeglasses, mobile phones, and remote controls. Other more 'sentimental' collections suggest another type of clutter care technology, which mix with concerns about ageing identity. Examples here include love letters, family photographs, and favourite antique heirlooms. A few US seniors also had relatively elaborate systems of organisation. For instance, I relate how one informant kept a series of shoeboxes for each of his children. Every time he found an item concerning one of his children, he put it in the corresponding box for later distribution. Based on such findings, my article proposes the notion of 'clutter technology' to think through the productive and beneficial aspects of clutter in US senior home care. As such, the article tinkers with the category of care technology.

Household clutter was present in some of the Swedish situations I encountered, and I also found examples of nesting and distribution. Hence, this comparison suggests that clutter moves with care in similar ways, in both countries. However, I found clutter more often and in greater quantities in my US fieldwork. For instance, in some US homes, papers, clothing, food, and other objects littered the floor to such an extent that I could not easily walk in a clear path. Given this stark contrast between the US and Sweden, a transnational comparison of clutter seemed lopsided, uninteresting, and not worth noting.[13] Nevertheless, as with the previous article, I had the sense that I had missed a comparative opportunity.

Next, I revisit a different set of ethnographic passages to tinker with the potentials of this transnational comparison, unpacking further the notion of clutter as a kind of 'technology' for care. In my Swedish fieldwork, I met Anna-Lisa, eighty-one years old. She had arthritic pain that made walking difficult. Her doctor had prescribed medication, but the side effects made her feel tired and weak. Eventually she decided to take her care into her own hands. Despite her pain, she stopped taking several of her medications, improved her diet, and increased her exercise. When she started feeling better, and grew weary of the public home care visits, she discontinued this service too, including help with cleaning and physical therapy.

Anna-Lisa lived with some domestic clutter. Compared with the US, however, it was not extreme. Even more remarkable was her cluttered assortment of pets. Anna-Lisa had grown up on a farm. Upon retirement, she decided that she wanted the experience of living with animals again. When I met her, she had six cats, two dogs, a parakeet, and several pet mice. This, I proffer, introduces a different form of nonhuman clutter – what Haraway (2008) might call 'multispecied' clutter.

The care for these animals presented some practical challenges, especially with her painful arthritis. For instance, she was unable to walk the dogs or clean the litter boxes as frequently as needed. Apparently, a neighbour had caught wind of her difficulties. One day, based on an anonymous tip, the *Länsstyrelsens Djurskyddsinspektion* (Swedish Animal Protection Authorities) paid her an unannounced visit. They found her home too cluttered and unhealthy for the animals. A few weeks later, she received a letter that proclaimed her unfit to care for the animals and banned her from keeping them. The authorities also billed her for their legal process. Upset and angry, she appealed the decision. However, she lost and the authorities forced her to give the animals away. After this, she struggled with a bout of depression. She explained that she perceived her pets as part of her well-being and self-care and that they had helped keep her active:

> The animals gave me life. They cared for me in their own way. They gave me the company I needed and physical attention. Now, without them, I get filled up with silence and loneliness. So I have that instead. I am filled up with the loneliness and try to find ways to empty some of it out but it's not easy.

This ethnographic passage highlights how different categories of care and clutter can generate comparative frictions in practice. A key example here is the way the Swedish authorities attended to pet care, but ignored the importance that multispecied clutter played for Anna-Lisa. Here, the comparison of an actual care situation to an inflexible standard of 'pet care' produced an unfortunate outcome – namely a senior who lost her care companions. This also suggests how a standardised comparison can deny the opportunity to tinker with a mutually beneficial arrangement.[14] In other words, although the categories of senior home care or domestic clutter do not typically include animals, here the categorical shift is clear. More importantly, this tinkered comparison suggests an ethnographic passage back to my US material.

In the US, I worked with Beth, who was in her in her mid-nineties, and her granddaughter, Mary, in her mid-fifties. Mary's mother had died fifteen years earlier. On her deathbed, Mary had promised her mother that she would take care of Beth. For the past fifteen years, Mary drove once a week to visit her grandmother, a two-hour round trip, to the house she had lived in for more than sixty-five years. Until recently, Mary had enjoyed these visits. She had taken Beth out for lunch, or just sat and talked. Gradually, though, Beth's health declined. Her ailments included glaucoma and blindness in the right eye, severe osteoporosis, acute neck pain, congestive heart failure, hearing loss, and difficulties linked with mobility – for example, walking, balancing, and climbing the stairs. Mary had started to notice more bruises on Beth's body, but Beth denied falling and insisted that her guardian angel had caught her. Mary joked that he must have been missing her more these days. Mary also suspected that Beth had developed Alzheimer's disease because Beth increasingly mistook Mary for her mother, and found it difficult to recall recent conversations.

With Beth's decline, her home became cluttered and disarrayed. Mary added housework to her weekly visits. This included cleaning up and caring for Beth's nine feral cats that she had adopted from the neighbourhood. Cat hair was everywhere. Their litter boxes went unchanged and their food bowls were often left empty. Like the architectural space itself, the house was seeped in their stench. The cats and their material relations had become synonymous with Beth's home. In fact, her sentiments of home were so strong that Beth claimed she would die if she had to move away and leave her cats. Mary, on the other hand, felt she could no longer care for Beth or her cats without extra help. Mary had raised the topic of paid home care, but Beth quickly dismissed the idea, exclaiming, 'I don't want a stranger in my house!'

Mary discussed the possibility of assisted living with Uncle John, Beth's only remaining son and legal guardian, but he refused. He was determined to respect his mother's wishes. Mary felt, however, that he did not understand the situation. John lived several hours away and was extremely allergic to cats, so when he did visit he did not stay long. Mary also reasoned that John was in denial about his mother's decline. He avoided discussing her condition and what to do about it in conversation. Mary felt stuck. Then, one day, John showed up to take Beth to her dentist appointment. When he arrived, he found his mother on the floor, unable to get up. Apparently, she had tripped over one of her cats. Mary partly joked that this had joggled John's perspective: 'It was the straw that broke the cat's back'. John had finally realised that Beth needed constant care and it should be him. For nearly a month, he gave Beth regular meals and saw that she took her medications. Yet, due to his cat allergies he could not stay in the house for more than a few minutes at a time. Instead, he lived in his camper truck parked in Beth's driveway. He quickly grew tired of this arrangement, however. He finally agreed to take Beth for a medical check-up, which confirmed her poor condition. John finally accepted that Beth now needed more intensive home care.

In the meantime, it was difficult to find someone Beth liked enough, and who was also willing to put up with her cats. For instance, one woman had all the necessary qualifications, but during the interview Beth protested that the she had hit one of the cats. The woman explained that she had only reached out to pet it. Mary explained that it was unlikely the applicant had hit the cat, and attributed Beth's reaction to her Alzheimer's and increasing anxiety. Another applicant, Charlene, had shown extra affection for the cats, and Beth took an immediate liking to her. Charlene explained later that she sensed that the cats were the key to Beth's trust. 'Beth's cats are her everything, and you must respect that. She watches the cats to see how they react and she observes that they trust me'. Beth added, 'You spoil them like I do. You really do care'. Mary later confirmed, 'Charlene earned Grandma's trust by taking care of her cats [...] They're still Grandma's cats, but now there's somebody else who cares for them too'.

Like Anna-Lisa's care, Beth's cluttered assemblage of humans and felines emerges as a kind of care technology, with specific effects. This human-nonhuman care collective played a decisive role in the tinkering of comparisons in Beth's home care – especially decisions about present and future care arrangements. Beth's cats mattered in her ability to care for herself and her home. They also impacted how others adjusted and tinkered care with her. This included discussions with the doctor and the hiring of additional home care work.

Here, then, as with the example of spatial-timings in care, an opportunity for transnational comparison emerges. Where a comparison once seemed undeserving, now the notion of multispecied clutter as care technology offers a way to move comparatively between two different entities, namely senior home care in the US and Sweden. Rather than using standardised scientific categories which stem from etic or scientific terminologies alone, my comparisons tinker with care relations as they move in ethnographic passages. Admittedly, I am implicated in this work. It also requires analytical care to tinker these ethnographic passages together into a suitable comparator. As a social scientist, I have an interpretive hand in directing the results. However, it is not my ambition to expose these comparisons to further analysis at this juncture, as doing so would exceed the scope of this chapter. Instead, my aim has been to outline the potentials of careful comparative tinkering and how it can unlock new avenues for social scientific comparison. It requires a retrospective and open disposition towards the multiple and empirical-conceptual relations as they come together in ethnographic passages.

DISCUSSION

Compare, v.

[…] To mark or point out the similarities and differences of (two or more things); to bring or place together (actually or mentally) for the purpose of noting the similarities and differences. […] [Construction] *with* (or *to*) another; *together*. […] to vie *with*, rival.
— Oxford English Dictionary [OED], 2nd edition.

This definition echoes several points I have made in this chapter. First, it mentions the movement of bringing together two or more entities. Thus, to compare implies the gathering and assembling of different comparative elements, similar to Deville et al.'s proposal of a heterogeneous comparator. I have developed this as the gathering together of care moves in ethnographic passages. These entail the noting down of similarities and differences. Hence, to compare relates to the making of noteworthy observations and descriptions, travelled and written in ethnographic passages between field and desk. Moreover, comparative collections do not contain exclusively similar elements. Rather, they entail inherent frictions stemming from their relational combinations. This dimension is clearly present in the etymological roots of the Latin term *comparare* (*com-* 'with' + *parare* 'prepare'), which the OED states as the bringing together to form pairs for a contest or match. This last aspect brings home the significance of comparative tinkering with care moves and their frictional relations, as in to vie with, or rival. Comparison is anything but smooth.

Regarding the implications for social science, my argument is that comparative tinkering offers a means to stay with the trouble of comparison. It focuses on comparisons that emerge with the movements of care in practice. From a conventional view, such frictions easily render comparison unworthy of pursuit. In this chapter, I develop comparative tinkering as a means to transform such frictions into productive potentials for knowledge, which 'dance' in retrospective zigzags with ethnographic passages. This is akin to Gad and Jensen's proposal of 'lateral comparisons', which open up new comparative travels. It also resonates with Strathern and others who propose the comparison of others' comparisons. These concern how care workers negotiate and compare their own care moves. In addition, there is an affinity here between comparative tinkering and Mohácsi and Morita's notion of travelling comparisons.

Although my ethnographic passages do not evidence people's comparisons with care in other countries, they do relate to how technology helps to trace the tinkering comparisons of others in their moves with care. Thus, I argue that tracing the use of technology in ethnographic passages can locate additional opportunities for social scientific comparison. I would also add the importance of remaining attentive to how transformative frictions in practice can ontologically shift the comparative categories themselves. For instance, in my examples I experiment with how care technology transforms with the tensions found in the scheduling and cluttering of home care.

The above ideas point to the analytical treatment of comparative tinkering as a transformative heterogeneous comparator which integrates ethnographic passages. This focus on ethnography resonates with another point Morita makes about the mutual entanglement of ethnography and technology as a comparative 'machine'. For instance, he writes, '[w]e have here a sort of ethnography that works as an evocative machine and a sort of machine that evokes an ethnographic [comparative] effect' (2013b: 16). This way of seeing the interrelations between description and analysis has inspired my use of ethnographic passages as a fundamental component of comparative tinkering. Such ideas echo other scholars who view the importance of ethnographic writing as a social scientific intervention (Michael 2012; Vikkelsø 2007; Winthereik and Verran 2012). Mike Michael, for one, proposes a move from the notion of written stories – or anecdotes – to 'anecdotalization' for interrogating the social scientific research process itself:

> As a form of telling that gathers into itself previous tellings and performs critical reflections upon the mutualities of such tellings and retellings and the analytic resources that made such tellings tellable, anecdotalization has both a topological and a nomadic flavour. In terms of the topological, it brings together what might once have seemed distant and disconnected: past

episodes that are marginal and trivial illuminate contemporary moments of critical reflection and reorientation, and contemporary concerns render what had long been uninteresting past moments full of relevance. This bringing together of the distant and disconnected is also a marker of the nomadic or the rhizomic, according to Deleuze and Guattari (1998). However, the nomadic serves to emphasise what is processual, iterative, emergent and, crucially, changeable and shifting in anecdotatization (2012: 33).

Michael's anecdotalization thus situates a rhizomic and topological move, akin to the gathering and cutting of ethnographic passages, which crisscross in surprising and often dubious ways. Similarly, I have proposed that ethnographic passages situate avenues for a generative comparative methodology – one that not only records, but also brings together and tinkers with comparisons. Comparative tinkering with care moves in ethnographic passages thus suggests rough travel, reminiscent of Serres' (1980) northwest passages that mediate and intervene as they entangle complex frictions.[15] In a similar way, I have drawn on ethnographic passages that interweave the empirical with the conceptual – travel with text – in the same analytical and careful move.

CONCLUSION

This chapter opened with considerations about the relation between movement and social scientific comparison in anthropology and STS. Inspired by such work, I propose comparative tinkering as a generative approach for gathering together different care moves with ethnographic passages. To background my approach, I turn to how the gerontological literature typically treats the challenge of transnational comparison of senior care in Sweden and the US. Standardised categories linked with economic and medical terminologies emerge as important comparative features in this literature. However, I argue that such categories can also sidestep the more nitty-gritty moves on which senior home care depends. At the same time, the different ways care moves and transforms in practice are what make the transnational comparison of senior home care so challenging.

To explore my own efforts to compare, I revisit two previous publications that sidestep transnational comparison. In the 'Surfacing Moves: Spatial-Timings of Senior Home Care' (Lutz 2013) article, I trace ethnographic passages concerned with how different spatial-timings in Swedish senior home care move. These passages implicate technologies for scheduling care, and the way they mediate comparisons in the pursuit of sustainable care. When writing that article, I did not find an opportunity for a noteworthy comparison in my US material. In retrospect, however, I realise that I allowed the standard practice of formalised scheduling to cloud comparative opportunities, particularly the informal use of mundane care technologies in the US. By opening up the category of scheduling care technology as a more fluid category, I found additional ethnographic passages in which to tinker with my comparison. This move rested on how my informants comparatively tinker with the scheduling of senior home care in the US and Sweden to negotiate the multiple spatial-timings that surface in this practice. In other words, attention to the ways my informants comparatively tinkered with the scheduling of senior home care also partly inspired my own comparative tinkering in and with ethnographic passages.

In my second publication, 'Clutter Moves in Old Age Homecare' (Lutz 2010), I focus on clutter in US senior home care as a kind of care technology. Here too, transnational comparison initially appeared unworthy of pursuit. Although I found similarities in the ways seniors in Sweden and the US interacted with their household clutter, my hesitations stemmed from the degree of clutter I found in several of the US home care situations I had visited. In these situations, the extent of clutter was so extreme that it seemed incomparable to anything I found in Sweden. Nevertheless, by rethinking and re-tinkering with the ethnographic passages, which involved multispecied clutter, I could tinker with a different *tertium comparationis* to open up new insights about clutter as a form of care technology in both countries.

This chapter has sought additional avenues for the pursuit of comparison that go beyond the standard measures of national healthcare systems. My aim has not been to discount comparisons that employ standardised categories or statistical models, but to locate additional reflexive pathways for comparison. I have proposed the notion of comparative tinkering with care moves in ethnographic passages as a topographical and heterogeneous comparator. This resonates with Mol's (2008, 2010) assertion about care on and in its own 'terms' – in other words, those which resonate both conceptually and empirically with how care moves in practice, along with their generative or frictional affects and effects. As such, I suggest that comparative tinkering with care moves offers another route to think through, and with care, in contrast to terms for care that stem from medical ethics or policy jargon.

As such, my proposal entails several interrelated implications for the careful transnational tinkering of social scientific comparison. For instance, one implication concerns the importance of ethnographic passages (and how they entangle text and travel) to establish a heterogeneous comparator. Another point concerns the tangled movements in care and how these can disturb or re-tinker with standardised categories of comparison. In turn, rather than stifle or throw out comparison, I have argued that ethnographic passages offer fodder for the comparative tinkering of care, including its standards and categories. This also raises a point about the careful adjustment of frictions between etic and emic comparisons found in practice.

In a complex world where misunderstandings seem increasingly prevalent, it is important to stress the potentials of comparative tinkering as a method for opening up additional transnational comparative perspectives, which also embrace nitty-gritty moves of specific practices. Senior home care has been both the source and testing ground for this notion. However, I also hope this chapter can inspire readers to pull the notion of comparative tinkering in ways that stay with the trouble of care – in all its forms – which concern humans as well as our worldly others.

ACKNOWLEDGEMENTS

I wish to acknowledge the following individuals and opportunities. Casper Bruun Jensen, Randi Markussen, Tine Tjørnhøj-Thomsen, and Antonia Walford gave me useful feedback on my early ideas about comparison. The 'Comparative Relativism' symposium at the IT University of Copenhagen in 2009, as well as the 'Mega-Seminar' on ethnographic comparison, organised by the Danish School of Anthropology and Ethnography in 2011, were influential occasions. Later, in 2011, I co-organised a round-table event with Heather Swanson on 'Comparative Tinkering' at the University of California, Santa Cruz (UCSC). I found much inspiration from the participants, who included Karen Barad, Alan Christy, James Clifford, Lawrence Cohen, Donna Haraway, Susan Harding, Andrew Matthews, Danilyn Rutherford, Warren Sack, and Anna Tsing. In my final stages of writing, Annika Capelán, Alice Santiago Faria, Tora Holmberg, and Zehorith Mitz gave me invaluable comments. The editors of this volume also helped me sharpen my argument. The European Commission's Marie Curie Actions programme (grants 14360 and 249322) and the IT University of Copenhagen financially supported my research.

NOTES

1 Steven Connor has translated Serres' passages as 'complex, digressive, irregular, unpredictable, encompassing wormholes and back-alleys as well as highways – between the different modes of knowledge' (2009: 2).
2 The term 'tinkering' has earlier roots in scholarly usage. For instance, the French anthropologist Claude Lévi-Strauss (1966) introduced 'bricolage' (the French equivalent) as a form of sociocultural invention for making do in novel ways with the limited resources available. Tinkering also finds traction in debates about evolutionary transformation (Jacob 1977; 2001).
3 John Rowe is Professor of Health Policy and Management at Columbia University. He is also a former professor of medicine and a founding director of the division on Aging at Harvard Medical School.
4 Parker's article, from 2001, references a population of 8.6 million in Sweden and 250 million in the US, which indicates a significant population growth in both countries.
5 These authors differentiate this further as 'Instrumental Activities of Daily Living' (IADLs) and 'Physical Activities of Daily Living' (PADLs).
6 Some authors use Sweden as the exemplar of a welfare state (Wang and Aspalter 2007).
7 *Social Intelligence For Tele-Healthcare* (SIFT) was a European Marie Curie Actions funded research project (2006–2008), hosted by Philips Research. Its interlinking interests between business, technology development, healthcare, and government, although highly influential, are beyond the focus of this chapter.
8 Some might argue that such practical concerns would not influence pure academic research – in other words, without industrial or applied constraints. Nevertheless, I would

argue that any social scientific research project must cope with multiple constraints that demand ongoing negotiation and tinkering. Thus, I maintain that the notion of 'pure' research is misleading.

9 Recursively, I found evidence that these complex care moves situate multiple social dimensions such as class, ethnicity, education, and gender. However, I will not develop these aspects here.

10 For ethical reasons, I did not recruit people with dementia in either country.

11 In my follow-up research, smartphone-based digital schedules had replaced the paper schedule. Yet, the care workers continued to conceal these devices during hands-on care work in a similar way.

12 In my work I use pseudonyms for all informants to protect their identity.

13 However, such comparisons do exist. For a Danish example, see Skov (2012).

14 However, there is supporting evidence from Sweden and the US that pets can positively affect care for seniors (Banks and Banks 2002; Beck-Friis et al. 2007; Hejra 2009; Folkesson 2011; Höök and Höök 2010). For instance, one article (Folkesson 2011) mentions a Swedish study involving dog care at a nursing home for seniors with dementia. After six months, the dog's presence had reduced worry and violent outbreaks as well as the need for medication. Other studies have compared live and robotic dogs for senior care (Banks et al. 2008), while Philips Research (2014) has developed the *iCat* for ambient intelligence research and robotic pet interaction. Such studies resonate with Anna-Lisa's story, and suggest the relevance of comparing different notions of care and its technologies, including relations with 'multispecied' clutter.

15 Michael also draws on Serres' philosophy to develop the concept of anecdotalization.

BIBLIOGRAPHY

Banks, M. R., L. M. Willoughby, and W. A. Banks, 'Animal-Assisted Therapy and Loneliness in Nursing Homes: Use of Robotic versus Living Dogs', *Journal of the American Medical Directors Association*, 9.3 (2008), 173–77

Banks, M. R., and W. A. Banks, 'The Effects of Animal-Assisted Therapy on Loneliness in an Elderly Population in Long-Term Care Facilities', *The Journals of Gerontology Series A: Biological Sciences and Medical Sciences*, 57.7 (2002), M428–M432

Beck-Friis, B., P. Strang, and A. Beck-Friis, *Hundens betydelse i vården* [*The Dog's Role in Health Care*] (Stockholm: Gothia, 2007)

Connor, S., 'Michel Serres: The Hard and the Soft', Lecture given at the Centre for Modern Studies, University of York, 2009

Davey, A., et al., 'Life on the Edge: Patterns of Formal and Informal Help to Older Adults in the United States and Sweden', *The Journals of Gerontology Series B: Psychological Sciences and Social Sciences*, 60.5 (2005), S281–S288

Deville, J., M. Guggenheim, and Z. Hrdličková, 'Same, Same but Different: Provoking

Relations, Assembling the Comparator', this volume

Folkesson, L., 'Nadja och Bosse efterlängtade på äldreboenden [Nadja and Bosse Longed For in Senior Housing]', *Svenskt Demenscentrum*, June 21 (2011) <http://www.demenscentrum.se/Arbeta-med-demens/Metoder-och-arbetssatt/Djur-i-varden/Terapihundar-i-Karlskrona-kommun> accessed 25 May 2014

Gad, C., and C. Bruun Jensen, 'Lateral Comparisons', this volume

Gad, C., and D. Ribes, 'The Conceptual and the Empirical in Science and Technology Studies', *Science, Technology, & Human Values*, 39.2 (2014), 183–91

Haraway, D. J., *When Species Meet* (Minneapolis: University of Minnesota Press, 2008)

Hejra, S., *Vårdpersonalens inställning till och upplevelse av djur på särskilt äldreboende* [Nursing Staff's Attitudes and Experience of Pets in Senior Housing] (Uppsala: Uppsala University, 2009)

Höök, I., and L. Höök, *Hund på recept: den professionella vårdhunden* [Dog Prescribed: The Professional Care Dog] (Stockholm: Gothia, 2010)

Jacob, F., 'Evolution and Tinkering', *Science*, 196.4295 (1977), 1161–66

——'Complexity and Tinkering', *Annals of the New York Academy of Sciences*, 929.1 (2001), 71–73

Jensen, C. B., 'Continuous Variations: The Conceptual and the Empirical in STS', *Science, Technology, & Human Values*, 39.2 (2013), 192–213

Langstrup, H., and B. R. Winthereik, 'Producing Alternative Objects of Comparison in Healthcare: Following a Web-Based Technology for Asthma Treatment through the Lab and the Clinic', in T. Scheffer, and J. Niewöhner, eds., *Thick Comparison: Reviving the Ethnographic Aspiration* (Leiden and Boston, MA: Brill, 2010), pp. 103–28

Latour, B., 'Trains of Thought: Piaget, Formalism and the Fifth Dimension', *Common Knowledge*, 3.6 (1997), 170–91

Lévi-Strauss, C., *The Savage Mind* (Chicago: University of Chicago Press, 1966)

Lury, C., and N. Wakeford, *Inventive Methods: The Happening of the Social* (London and New York: Routledge, 2012)

Lutz, P., 'Clutter Moves in Old Age Homecare', in M. Schillmeier, and M. Domènech, eds., *New Technologies and Emerging Spaces of Care* (Farnham: Ashgate, 2010), pp. 77–94

——'Surfacing Moves: Spatial-Timings of Senior Home Care', *Social Analysis*, 57.1 (2013), 80–94

Maurer, B., *Mutual Life, Limited: Islamic Banking, Alternative Currencies, Lateral Reason* (Princeton, NJ: Princeton University Press, 2005)

Michael, M., 'Anecdote', in C. Lury, and N. Wakeford, eds., *Inventive Methods: The Happening of the Social* (London and New York: Routledge, 2012), pp. 25–35

Mohácsi, G., and A. Morita, 'Traveling Comparisons: Ethnographic Reflections on Science and Technology', *East Asian Science, Technology and Society*, 7.2 (2013), 175–83

Mol, A., 'Cutting Surgeons, Walking Patients: Some Complexities Involved in Comparing', in J. Law, and A. Mol, eds., *Complexities: Social Studies of Knowledge Practices* (New York: Duke University Press, 2002), pp. 218–57

―― *The Logic of Care: Health and the Problem of Patient Choice* (London: Routledge, 2008)
―― 'Actor-Network Theory: Sensitive Terms and Enduring Tensions', *Kölner Zeitschrift Für Soziologie Und Sozialpsychologie*, Sonderheft, 50 (2010), 253–69
Mol, A., I. Moser, and J. Pols, eds., *Care in Practice: On Tinkering in Clinics, Homes and Farms* (Bielefeld and New Jersey: Transcript Verlag, 2010)
Moreira, T., 'Now or Later? Individual Disease and Care Collectives in the Memory Clinic', in A. Mol, I. Moser, and J. Pols, eds., *Care in Practice: On Tinkering in Clinics, Homes and Farms* (Bielefeld and New Jersey: Transcript Verlag, 2010), pp. 119–140
Morita, A., 'Traveling Engineers, Machines, and Comparisons: Intersecting Imaginations and Journeys in the Thai Local Engineering Industry', *East Asian Science, Technology and Society*, 7.2 (2013a), 221–41
―― 'The Ethnographic Machine: Experimenting with Context and Comparison in Strathernian Ethnography', *Science, Technology, & Human Values*, September (2013b), 1–22
Oxford English Dictionary, 2nd edn. (Oxford: Oxford University Press, 1992)
Otto, T., and N. Bubandt, *Experiments in Holism: Theory and Practice in Contemporary Anthropology* (West Sussex and Massachusetts: Wiley-Blackwell, 2010)
Parker, M. G., 'Sweden and the United States: Is the Challenge of an Aging Society Leading to a Convergence of Policy?', *Journal of Aging & Social Policy*, 12.1 (2001), 73–90
Philips Research, 'Robotics' (2014), <http://www.research.philips.com/technologies/robotics> [accessed 25 May 2014]
Pols, J., *Care at a Distance: On the Closeness of Technology* (Amsterdam: Amsterdam University Press, 2012)
Rowe, J., '10 Commandments of Geriatrics', [public lecture given at the Harvard Medical School, via personal communication, 2011]
Serres, M., *Hermès V. Le Passage Du Nord-Ouest* (Paris: Minuit, 1980)
Shea, D., et al., 'Exploring Assistance in Sweden and the United States', *The Gerontologist*, 43.5 (2003), 712–21
Skov, S. M., 'Derfor Har Ældre Så Meget Rod [Why Elderly Have so Many Things] (radio Reportage)', Orientering, Danish Radio, P1 (2012) <http://www.dr.dk/arkivP1/orientering> [accessed 25 May 2014]
Strathern, M., *Property, Substance and Effect* (London and New York: Athlone Press, 1999)
―― 'Foreword: Not Giving the Game Away', in A. Gingrich, and R. Gabriel Fox, eds., *Anthropology, by Comparison* (London: Routledge, 2002), pp. xiii–xvii
―― *Partial Connections* (Oxford: Rowman and Littlefield, 1991; repr. 2004)
―― 'Binary License', *Common Knowledge*, 17.1 (2011), 87–103
Taylor, J. S., 'Surfacing the Body Interior', *Annual Review of Anthropology*, 34.1 (2005), 741–56
Tsing, A. L., *Friction : An Ethnography of Global Connection* (New Jersey: Princeton University Press, 2005)
Vikkelsø, S., 'Description as Intervention: Engagement and Resistance in Actor-Network

Analyses', *Science as Culture*, 16.3 (2007), 297–309

Wang, D., and C. Aspalter, 'The Swedish Health Care System in International Comparison', *Journal of Social and Social Policy*, 6.2 (2007), 63–75

Winance, M., 'Trying Out the Wheelchair: The Mutual Shaping of People and Devices through Adjustment', *Science, Technology, & Human Values*, 31.1 (2006), 52–72

Winthereik, B. R., and H. Verran, 'Ethnographic Stories as Generalizations that Intervene', *Science Studies*, 25.1 (2012), 37–51

World Bank, [World Development Indicators: Population Dynamics, Population Ages 65 and above, 2014] <http://wdi.worldbank.org/table/2.1> [accessed 25 May 2014]

World Population Review [Countries, 2014] <http://worldpopulationreview.com/countries> [accessed 25 May 2014]

9

COMPARING COMPARISONS: ON RANKINGS AND ACCOUNTING IN HOSPITALS AND UNIVERSITIES

Sarah de Rijcke, Iris Wallenburg, Paul Wouters, Roland Bal

INTRODUCTION

COMPARISONS HAVE BECOME UBIQUITOUS IN THE MANAGEMENT OF QUALITY in social domains that were previously governed by professional elites. Often these comparisons are framed as 'transparency instruments' (Hazelkorn 2011b: 41) which come in a variety of forms:

- informative guides for prospective 'clients' (e.g. students or patients);
- accreditation procedures to certify the legitimacy of a particular organisation to act as a university or hospital;
- benchmarking as a way to 'compare like with like' or to check the compliance with formalised norms and standards;
- regular formalised evaluations or assessments of the activity, quality, and impact of the products' analysing and processes;
- classification systems to develop sharper profiles of the institute and its components; and
- rankings of universities and hospitals to see who is 'best' in the comparison according to a particular set of measures.

Driven by the aim of transparency and user empowerment in public and private services, comparisons have become a crucial instrument in contemporary capitalism. Typically, they are supposed to 'enable consumers to choose' between telephone companies, universities, power companies, schools, or hospitals. These types of comparison are characteristically framed in terms of 'improving quality' (both in terms of service organisations and individual service workers) and 'empowering consumers' (in regards to how the visibility of performance enables consumers to make a deliberate choice about what service to choose for and by whom) (Shore and Wright 1999). Otherwise, comparisons are framed for organisations to 'publicly account' for their performance, and regulators take measures based on comparative analyses. Comparing is therefore not only an everyday practice; it is also a highly specialised activity that has become ubiquitous in many contemporary forms of governance.

In this chapter, we focus on one comparative technique: ranking. A key difference between ranking and other comparative techniques is that it presents an ordered list of an entity according to how it scores on a particular (set of) indicator(s), often starting with 'the best'. A ranking is easier to grasp than a more complex comparative technique such as benchmarking or a multi-dimensional classification or assessment system. It is also easier to misunderstand. The indicators used for ranking may not measure the qualities the ranking is supposed to capture. Moreover, the entities they measure may not have similar profiles. In this sense, to what extent are the current rankings of universities and hospitals (which are the focus of this chapter) comparing 'like with like'? These criticisms have not diminished the power of rankings – in fact, it is quite the contrary. Though rankings often start with a heterogeneous set of organisations, they are able to make very different entities comparable. As an instance of a comparative technology, a ranking produces certain realities and identities; it creates that which is compared (see Mol 2002). In this sense, rankings are indeed a member of the family of comparative technologies: comparability is their outcome, as well as their foundation.

Below we examine how rankings came into being, how they are done, and what they do by comparing ranking systems for, and within, universities and hospitals. On top of this, we seek to explore our own ways of comparing ranking practices. As the introduction to this book explains, we wish to question the epistemic position of comparative methodologies in the social sciences. We neither believe that they are inherently superior to the in-depth study of one particular case, nor do we agree with the outright rejection of comparative sociology as reductionist. Rather, we are interested in the kinds of effects that comparisons produce – both the comparative technologies of rankings systems, and our own comparative analysis of the ranking of (and within) universities and hospitals.

This chapter presents our comparative layers in the form of a triple jump. First, we describe the emergence and development of rankings in universities and hospitals. In this part of our chapter, we zoom in on some of the differences made by these rankings after their introduction in the past two decades. We describe rankings as tools for governance that revolve mostly around competition and 'commensuration' – social mechanisms through which highly diverse entities (countries, institutions, people) are rendered measurable and comparable through quantitative means (Espeland and Stevens 1998). Second, by drawing on a comparison between university and hospital ranking practices, we analyse how ranking contributes to making organisations auditable and comparable. We examine some of the differences and similarities of ranking practices in universities and hospitals by focusing on three themes that emerged from our comparative work: 1) the ambivalence of ranking; 2) the performativity of ranking; and 3) coordinating ranking practices. We link these themes to the literature on comparisons. Third, we reflect on how we as analysts have 'practised comparison' by expounding on how we enacted ranking in our comparative work (see Urry and Law 2006), and on some of the costs and benefits involved in our comparative endeavour.

The chapter is based on two distinct research projects in which we analyse contemporary practices of university and hospital ranking in the Netherlands. Our cooperation was triggered by similarities we observed in approach and empirical material. The projects share a theoretical focus in the sense that both projects zoom in on the enactment (or the daily work of 'doing' (see Mol

2002) rankings) in 'real' organisational practices. The modest empirical research done by others thus far mainly focuses on higher management levels, and/or on large institutional infrastructures. Instead, we analyse hospital and university ranking practices from a whole-organisation perspective. Both projects look at how rankings translate, purify, and simplify heterogeneity into ordered lists of comparable units, and the kinds of realities that come into being through these ranking practices. Among other things, we are interested in the constitutive effects of ranking (see Dahler-Larsen 2012) and the kinds of ordering mechanisms (Felt 2009) that ranking brings about on multiple organisational levels – ranging from the managers' office and the offices of coding staff to the lab benches and hospital beds.

Both research designs were comparative, and both projects performed ethnographic work in three places. Sarah de Rijcke (SdR) and Paul Wouters (PW) conducted research with three biomedical research groups (a lab, a group of medical statisticians, and a clinical research group) in a Dutch university medical centre. Their project focused on the implications of research assessment and ranking on biomedical knowledge production. The rationale for having three places of investigation in this project emerged in part from institutionalised distinctions between basic, translational, and clinical research at the centre. These boundaries not only related to differences in epistemic cultures, but they were also quite literally felt in terms of institutional architecture (the laboratories were, for instance, located in a separate building). We took it as part of the ethnographic work to analyse the enactment of these epistemic and material differences in the research practices under study.

For each group, we held interviews with researchers at different career stages – with technicians, group leaders, heads of departments, and quality managers. In addition, we performed observations during work-in-progress meetings, seminars, appraisal meetings, and interactions with companies and other stakeholders. SdR had full-time access for a month at each group. The access was granted by the research groups and the dean of the institute, who is also one of the drivers behind a project on 'systemic failure in medical research' at the Netherlands Organisation for Health Research and Development

(ZonMW) (Groen 2013). This ZonMW project was triggered (among other things) by a perceived increase in publication pressure in biomedicine, a lack of interdisciplinary cooperation, and a responsiveness to the 'societal relevance' of research (Ibid. 1).

In the study on hospital rankings, Iris Wallenburg (IW) and Roland Bal (RB) compared three Dutch hospitals.[1] Hospital selection was done by looking at similar sized hospitals but in different competitive environments, due to an expectation that the level of competition hospitals find themselves in would influence the way rankings affect hospitals. More competitive regions show higher levels of tight coupling, emphasising strong hierarchical coordination between managerial and professional departments (whereas loosely coupled organisations allow for more professional autonomy).

For this project, interviews with a multitude of actors implicated in hospital ranking were held, and observations were performed in meetings of quality of care committees, meetings of hospital managers with outside actors (like insurers and regulators), and during administrative work in the hospital (both in clinical settings and information departments). As rankings are increasingly being used in the governance of Dutch hospitals (and policy actors expect much from them), the aim of this project was to get a better understanding of how ranking affects hospital organisations and care practices.[2]

In most rankings, the work of commensuration and classification is black boxed. The same holds for a lot of comparative research in the social sciences; for example, when it is assumed that comparative research designs by definition provide more robust forms of knowledge. As well as analysing the comparative effects of rankings, our aim for this chapter is to be more open about how we enacted comparison, leaving room for reflections on our own classification work. That is, we mobilise observations in one project to discuss findings in the other, and vice versa. This way of creating 'rapport' (Stengers 2011, in Akrich and Rabeharisoa, this volume) played an important role in drawing conclusions from our respective field notes. As a result, comparison turned out to be far messier – both in ranking practices and in our own work – than is often assumed. We think that this is not a deficit but a consequence of the grounded nature of all comparative practices.

HOP: THE GROWTH OF RANKING IN UNIVERSITIES AND HOSPITALS

How did it come to be that we now inhabit a world in which rankings seem to be inevitable? Sociologists and anthropologists contextualise the popularity of ranking as a broader manifestation of audit processes in an increasingly wide variety of societal sectors and professional fields. Audit processes now range from the online rating of movies, books, and restaurants, to assessing professional performance in sectors such as healthcare and higher education. Today, there are virtually no areas in which professionals are not – in one form or another – invited to respond to regular assessment exercises. The rise of performance-based funding schemes is one of the driving forces behind the increased interest in university and hospital rankings. Some studies suggest that shrinking governmental research funding from the 1980s onwards has resulted in 'academic capitalism' (see Slaughter and Lesly 1997). By now, universities have set up special organisational units and devised specific policy measures in response to ranking systems. Recent studies point to the normalising and disciplining powers associated with ranking and to the response to 'reputational risk' as explanations for organisational change (Burrows 2012; Espeland and Sauder 2007; Power et al. 2009; Sauder and Espeland 2009).

The first university rankings were published at the beginning of this millennium (Hazelkorn 2011), roughly two decades after the first signs of an unprecedented growth of evaluation institutions and procedures emerged in the 1980s. This growth was due to (among other things) the increased economic and social role of science and technology; an increase in the scale of research institutes; a general move towards formal evaluation of professional work; and limitations and costs of peer review procedures. Today, universities routinely monitor the publication of national and international league tables, and promote their position on websites, in newsletters, and in advertisements that target new students and staff. There is a growing emphasis on 'reputation management', and the use of quantitative performance indicators in quality assessment policies is steadily increasing. In short, quantitative indicators of science and technology are applied from the most 'macro' to the most 'micro' by governing bodies and agents across those levels.

In Dutch healthcare, performance measurement was introduced at roughly the same time.[3] Healthcare had routinely been characterised by a 'closed shop model' in which physicians decided upon the processes of healthcare delivery – only being accountable to knowledgeable colleague physicians (Harrison and McDonald 2008). However, since the 1990s, medical professional autonomy has gradually eroded, and professional self-regulating principles have intermingled with principles of performance management (Wallenburg et al. 2012; Waring 2007). Generally, the rise of performance management is a consequence of two intertwining developments. First is a shift in healthcare policy. Due to the introduction of New Public Management policies in the early 1990s, healthcare workers are increasingly being held accountable for the care delivered, and as part of this are obliged to provide insight into their work and performance. In the Netherlands, the shift to this ideal of transparency became even more prominent with the introduction of the system of regulated competition in the mid-2000s (Bal and Zuiderent-Jerak 2011).

The second main development is a shift in the regulation of professional work. The medical profession has been confronted with a sharp decline of public trust in medical expertise and 'medicine's good work' (Freidson 2001; Dixon-Woods et al. 2011). Together with the growing specialisation within medicine, the introduction of information technologies, and the regulation of working hours, medical work has become increasingly 'normalised' and regulated (Nettleton et al. 2008; Wallenburg et al. 2013). The comparison of hospital performance by ranking has been made possible as part of (and due to) these changes in healthcare governance. In the Netherlands, the most well-known are the rankings of the popular newspaper *Algemeen Dagblad*, and the weekly magazine, *Elsevier*. Yet in the past few years, healthcare insurers, patient organisations, and social entrepreneurs have created many more rankings. These rankings are, amongst others, based on patient experiences, and on the organisation and the outcomes of care – for instance, as seen in mortality rates for specific diseases or the percentage of pressure ulcers (Jerak-Zuiderent and Bal 2011).

Though ranking has become increasingly important in public service sectors, not much research has been done as of yet on the ways in which these comparative processes affect these sectors. The little evidence that exists tends to focus on universities. Here, an interest in ranking indeed seems mainly driven by a competition in which universities are being made comparable on the basis of 'quality' and 'impact'. One of the most obvious manifestations of the increased popularity of ranking practices is apparent in the way universities have started to routinely monitor the publication of global league tables, and in how they advertise their position in these tables on websites, in newsletters, and in advertisements that target new students and staff. This responsiveness is telling of the importance ascribed to rankings, though the rationales behind their construction tend to be disregarded. All measurements are of course preceded by decisions pertaining to the object(s) and focus of measurement. Certain factors are labelled as relevant in this categorisation process, and others as less relevant (or even irrelevant). Decisions will be made pertaining to the parameters of the categories that will be taken into account. These decisions fundamentally shape the subsequent measurements.

First of all, every form of ranking is based on data about a limited number of features which are subsequently made measurable. Global university rankings, for example, will focus on the 1,000 or so universities that are visible at the international level while ignoring the other 16,000, because these only play a role at the local level. They also tend to focus on research performance since this can more easily be made comparable at the international level (by way of citation analysis). Hospital rankings, in their turn, are criticised for using quickly changing performance indicators that underlie the rankings, rendering it difficult for hospitals to meet the criteria that are being set. Moreover, they are targeted at easily measurable aspects of care such as mortality, while ignoring other aspects – which are sometimes deemed more important – like diagnostic accuracy or empathy for patients. At the same time, the kinds of parameters that are used fundamentally shape the outcomes. Some rankings strongly favour large universities or ones with long-established reputations, or they give more weight to publications in certain types of journals (e.g. *Nature*, *Science*), thereby implicitly leaning towards the devaluation of certain types of research (e.g.

humanities, social sciences). In addition, composite rankings like the Shanghai University ranking or the Dutch hospital rankings will merge different aspects of university performance (e.g. research, teaching, valorisation, social impact) or hospital performance (e.g. mortality, infection rates) into one number. How this composite number is calculated is rather arbitrary, not always transparent, and changes over time. It is therefore unclear as to what extent a change in position has on an actual change in performance, or if it should be ascribed to an insignificant fluctuation. In addition, even individual outliers can cause seemingly robust improvements of the performance of universities or hospitals.

SKIP: COMPARING UNIVERSITY AND HOSPITAL RANKING PRACTICES

As discussed above, rankings in hospitals and universities show some similar characteristics in that they are embedded in, and form an infrastructure for, competition on a 'market' for public services (in this case, healthcare and research/education). They are also developed against a background of increasing demands for accountability of elite professions, and tap into a neoliberal agenda where auditing is seen as a practice of soft regulation.

One of the goals of our own comparison was to gain more insight into how rankings are enacted in day-to-day university and hospital practices (more than would have been possible without the comparison). We therefore started to compare some of the outcomes of our research projects. In comparing our findings, we developed three themes that we further discuss below: 1) the ambivalence of rankings; 2) the performativity of rankings; and 3) coordinating ranking practices.

The Ambivalence of Ranking

In the ranking literature, the adequacy of indicators or their composites is generally critiqued (see Jacobs et al. 2005; van Dishoeck et al. 2011; Marginson

2012; Rauhvargers 2011, 2013). This literature questions the validity of rankings, and argues that using rankings in regulation and funding decisions should generally be avoided. Similarly, in our case studies, rankings induced ambivalent responses. Regarding hospital rankings, our respondents commonly felt that rankings are not important for the ways in which organisations operate. They stressed the lack of validity and the volatility of rankings, arguing that they are 'lotteries' and are unpredictable. It was argued that rankings do not appear to have any consequences in terms of patient choice or insurer commissioning of care. Other respondents, particularly physicians, pointed out that indicator-based performance measurement directs attention to measurable agendas, while the most difficult agendas with regard to performance in the domain of quality and safety are related to the tacit expertise of professionals (such as diagnostic interpretations).

In our fieldwork in universities, we noticed that an interest in global university rankings and the development of adaptive strategies seemed mainly relevant at the level of deans and other research managers. The researchers who acted as informants seemed mainly involved with their own performance and that of their colleagues. As noted in the dialogue below, their commitment with their institution's ranking scores was rather low:

> SDR: Do you think that university rankings affect trust relations between different academic medical hospitals?
> PROFESSOR [switches to 3rd person plural]: Well, when they go up in the ranking, this leads to a celebratory announcement on our intranet. It is much like what happens when the Dutch national football team wins an important match' (4 November 2012).

Perhaps this lack of commitment to institutional ranking scores makes sense if we take into account how academic careers currently take shape. Job insecurity may trigger researchers (as members of an increasingly flexible 'workforce') to be more committed to pursuing the next step in their career than to the performance of the organisation they are affiliated with. Similarly, in hospitals, medical specialists were usually more interested in their relations to the same speciality in other organisations than to the performance of the hospital in which they work. Yet, at the same time, it was felt that rankings had to be taken seriously, as they were one of the drivers of the increasingly important reputation of hospitals and universities. For example, during an interview, the quality manager from hospital A pointed towards the limited usefulness of rankings, and continued her argument by saying

> [w]e still want to end high. When we dropped from the top 25 to place 60, that wasn't liked much (12 November 2012).

During interviews, informal conversations, and meetings, rankings were often criticised. Yet we noted this did not impede managers and practitioners in actively engaging with ranking practices:

> During one of our [IW and RB] interviews, a hospital administrator criticised current measurement policies that, according to him, did not reflect reality: 'According to the numbers we were a kind of "death hospital", but it all depends on how you measure mortality rates'. According to this administrator, hospitals are heavily disciplined by ranking policies, clearly objecting to the practice and even lecturing us on Foucault's notions of discipline. After having said this, he turns to a pile of papers on his desk, showing us the figures of the performances of the different hospital wards: 'You see, ward Z did an excellent job, they will have cake and a picture with me on the intranet next Monday! [smiling] They love it if we celebrate good performance' (Observation notes, 22 June 2012).

SdR and PW made a somewhat similar observation when they discussed the possibilities for ethnographic research in a large medical research centre:

> The present and future dean, the director of research, and a quality manager hosted the meeting. On the basis of our research proposal, all of us reflected on adverse effects of the increasing use of quantitative performance indicators. Until the quality manager received an e-mail, which he read on his

iPad, containing bibliometric data on the centre's performance (as measured through citation analysis). Compared to the year before, the institute had 'gone up' on all bibliometric indicators, a fact he immediately shared with the present dean by handing him the iPad. The dean was quick to ask whether 'his' institute was now 'first', and began to fantasise about presenting a list of the scores of all competing medical research centres at his farewell party a couple of weeks later (Observation notes, 1 March 2012).

This meeting to establish researchers' access (along with the meeting with the CEO in one of the hospitals) revealed how indicators and rankings were both criticised and embraced, depending on the specific 'partial connections' that were made (Strathern 2000). Although our respondents express their experiences of how rankings may be critiqued in a variety of ways, they cannot escape from rankings. Essentially, rankings are actively used to enhance organisational performance. In the above extract from our fieldwork at the university medical centre, a complex set of bibliometric measures was translated into a 'simple' ranking by one of the deans. This 'responsive' or 'implied' ranking practice affords this dean strategic use of a more intuitive comparison between organisations than would be possible if he were to draw on the entire bibliometric assemblage that was presented to him by the quality manager. The hospital manager, in turn, used the ranking to encourage nursing wards to enhance their performance. Nursing wards that performed well were displayed on the intranet, with the CEO being part of them. Yet in the same 'moment', ranking also induced a deep criticism and a feeling of discomfort, as these managers (both also professionals) were highly sceptical about the practices underlying the rankings.

As researchers, this two-sided picture of resistance and engagement surprised us. Although our ethnographic methodology does not allow for strict causal analysis, we did wonder why this experience was so strong. Rankings seem to perform comparison in ways that tie in with deeply embedded cultural notions of performance and competition (i.e. 'who is the best' is a notion which already starts at pre-school). The tighter coupling between perceived performance and distribution of resources since the 1980s has further strengthened the effects of rankings. In addition, 'to rank' comes naturally for professions that have become highly competitive amongst themselves. Many researchers and medical specialists seem driven by the urge to outperform their colleagues, and the ranking mechanisms we encountered make this quite visible. We suggest that it is this simple visibility of an ordered list that makes rankings stand out compared to more complex forms of comparison.

To us researchers, the excerpts above were exemplars of what Marilyn Strathern has pointed out as 'ethnographic moments' – a relation that joins the understood (i.e. what is analysed at the moment of observation) to the need to understand (i.e. what is observed at the moment of analysis) (Strathern 1980; Mol 2011). In our situations, with more or less overlapping observations in both research projects, these 'moments' acted as points of recognition and of shared surprise and feelings of discomfort. It was stimulating to have long repeated debates about the ambivalence of ranking and about its contesting values and ethics (e.g. 'good practice is much more complex and thus not easily measureable' versus 'we want to be outstanding, and measurement and ranking may help to achieve this') and all other ambivalences involved. It made us realise that criticising ranking is (too) easy, just like understanding ranking as a practice of 'gaming' or creating a well-cut and organised world next to a much more fuzzy world of professional work. Instead, ranking involves both conflicting ideas and ways of acting; it is both order and mess, and these go hand in hand.

Performativity of Ranking

In the sociological literature, university rankings are associated with competition at the level of the entire organisation. We also noticed how rankings were used to police work processes and enhance organisational performance. In one of the hospitals, for instance, the clinical pathway for breast cancer treatment was revised to reduce waiting times for surgery in order to obtain higher scores on the national ranking of best hospitals. However, our comparative approach revealed that rankings enacted organisational practices that went beyond this competitive aspect. Ranking was also used to create or enhance group identity (e.g. by displaying the medical research centre as the best), to reform routine practices, and to encourage individual workers to excel. Within the translation of rankings to everyday work processes, the complex metrics that underlies a ranking were reconfigured to simplified lists of factors that made performance measurable and comparable. The presence of such 'implied' ranking practices points to the performativity of ranking – that is, a reinforcing loop that redefines organisations, individuals, and also projects, in terms of a ranking:

> Professor D is preparing a funding application for Cardiovascular Onderzoek Nederland (CVON) as one of the Principal Investigators (PI) in a larger consortium; his institute is the prospective 'coordinating group'. Funding schemes such as this one explicitly use the 'H-index' as an indicator for the aptness and 'proven track record' of PIs (CVON call 2012, p. 5).[4] The calculation of this index is relatively simple: an H-index of X means that the researcher has published X articles that have each been cited at least X times. Consortia need at least one PI with a high H-index for a proposal to be eligible for funding at all. These PI's can take part in maximum one proposal a year. Combined, these two criteria create a lot of lobbying and a 'run' on PI's with a high H-index (Observation notes, pre-clinical research group, September 2012).

In this frame of comparison, an increasingly competitive funding landscape forms the background for situations in which project proposals are being made comparable on the basis of how the PIs in the consortia score on the H-index. This ratio of published articles/number of citations homogenises, simplifies, and enables funding agencies to rank consortia and prioritise proposals by 'enlisting' PIs via their proven track record (as expressed in their H-index). Recognising the importance of the H-index encourages scientists to use it even if this is not officially required. One of our informants mentioned taking part in a 'grant proposal preparation class' at his institute. The institutional research policy advisor (and host of the workshop) advised participants to mention their H-index if they felt it could help them stand out in the ranking of research proposals and researchers during the prioritisation work done by review committees. These ways in which researchers and policy officers act strategically with performance indicators are not (yet) part of the official evaluation criteria. However, these actors play an active role in these evaluation systems. The scientific system is highly competitive. Therefore, it is in the interest of institutions and researchers if high-scoring individuals actively display their scores, thereby fuelling the further development of indicator-based research assessment (Wouters 2014).

Similarly, hospitals tend to focus their quality policies on those areas which are important for their score on rankings. For this purpose, hospitals benchmark themselves on underlying performance indicators, taking particular notice of hospitals in their direct environment. Programmes that focus both on registration work and quality improvement are set up especially in those areas where hospitals score relatively low. For instance, one of the hospitals we studied did rather poorly on the performance indicator for malnutrition. The quality manager was requested to investigate the causes of the low score. It appeared that the hospital failed in measuring the nutrition status of elderly patients at their fourth day of admission, as was required by the performance indicator. Subsequently, nutrition assistants were trained to conduct these measurements. From the interviews with healthcare professionals, it appeared that this reorganising of care goes against areas of care that are not represented in the rankings, or that are not made measurable. Similarly, as discussed above in the example of the pressure ulcer scores, ranking practices became embedded in the hospitals to stimulate professionals to do registration work.

Again, we see similar processes in universities and hospitals. In both institutions, strategic behaviour is induced through the reputation game of the ranking practices. Ranking practices direct focus and activities, even though – in the same 'moment' – they also elicit criticism. The organisations under study seemed increasingly embedded in responsive ranking practices. On a number of levels, the organisations and individuals within them defined themselves in terms of a ranking (for instance, when they tried to get a handle on more complex comparative mechanisms at play).

When comparing our findings, we had room (both intellectually and methodologically) to move back and forth between our joint discussions and our research sites. In developing this collective comparative space, the performativity of rankings became a much-debated topic. We ended up constructing similarities that related, for example, to an equal emphasis on 'good scores' and the policing of existing organisational and working routines to enhance these scores. Simultaneously, our focus on similarities also enacted and underscored differences. For instance, in the academic context we found that performance was increasingly related to individual performance (think about the H-index mentioned above). While IW and RB translated this outcome to the hospital setting – attempting (perhaps expecting) to discern a similar shift to individual performance in medical work – they did not find this result. Discussing our ethnographic moments, surprises, and expectations helped create new lenses to reconsider our data and research fields. In the end, transparency about individual performance seemed in conflict with medicine's emphasis on socialisation and moral protection of physician-colleagues (Bosk 2003 (1979); Wallenburg et al. 2013).

Coordinating Ranking Practices

On a strategic level, rankings seem to affect university and hospital policies in a number of ways (Marginson 2012; Rauhvargers 2011; 2013). These include the bringing in of new types of knowledge like reputation management and marketing; the realignment of administrative processes and the development of new types of research/care and accountability processes; the 'buying of CVs' to enhance measured performance; and the responsive ranking practices that our informants resorted to in order to make sense of more complex comparative strategies for the purpose of performance measurements. These and other feedback mechanisms co-define how researchers, healthcare professionals, and policymakers operationalise the notion of 'high quality'. Interestingly, these feedback mechanisms may result in strategic behaviour which potentially undermines the validity of the performance indicators that ranking practices are based on at large. This is not merely the result of top-down criteria that 'trickle down' to local research practices. Interactions from the bottom up between people involved at different levels within the organisation are equally relevant. Let us take a closer look at the fieldwork in the hospital sector.

The hospitals studied went through great changes in terms of the organisation of administrative processes. What is euphemistically called an 'uitvraag' (an information demand by an external party) sometimes involved many months of work for the quality and information departments in collecting information from different sources in the hospital. This administrative work entailed many 'investments in form' to bring the information together (Thévenot 1984), including the involvement of health professionals to collect and register indicator information and the standardisation of care processes to enable data collection. Apart from information guiding the treatment process, health professionals had to collect data on all kinds of scores necessary for performance indicators. Nurses, for example, had to do risk assessment for pressure ulcers, delirium, and malnourishment, and had to regularly check whether a patient was in pain. The hospitals we studied had all installed different methods to make sure registration of care was actually done. These included building indicators in the electronic patient record, disciplining professionals by publishing information on registration, and 'policing' professionals to make sure registration was actually done. However, as one of the doctors we interviewed indicated, such policing is sometimes hardly possible:

> The urologist argues that every time new measures come up 'the hospital board wants us to participate in that'. He goes on to say 'I just give the desired scores. Taking a biopt in one day is impossible, but I just indicate that we do it nonetheless. I don't spend more than five minutes on this. It is uncontrollable' (12 December 2012).

While hospital administrators and quality managers aim to standardise healthcare processes (and with that, the collection of data as much as possible), health professionals work around the system by enacting a form of 'pragmatic compliance'. They just 'tick a box', as the urologist above points out. In this way, he complies with the demands put on him through the rankings while not changing his work practices, as he is aware that not ticking the box might have more serious consequences, if only to be publicly displayed within the hospital to be a 'good' or 'bad' performing ward (as was the case with the pressure ulcer scores of nurses). This does not mean, however, that indicators are not taken seriously. The same urologist participated in several working groups both within the hospital, and in his medical association, developing performance indicators and related policies. A surgeon stressed the increasing importance of performance indicators developed by the medical professional associations:

> SURGEON: The Netherlands Association of Surgeons (Nederlandse Vereniging van Heelkunde [NVvH]) possesses a complication registry. For an honest registration it's crucial that this information is not made public [...] Two years ago, Hospital X [a neighbouring hospital] had many reoperations for colon surgery. A delegation of the NVvH visited the surgeons. This all went quite harmoniously, you know, they came to see what happened and how things could be improved.
> IW: Yet, I can imagine that such a visit says something; they aren't there for nothing.
> SURGEON: Of course, of course, they [the surgeons of hospital X] were fed up. They knew something was wrong. They had to act (2 November 2013).

The excerpts of both the surgeon and the urologist reveal medicine's ambivalence towards performance indicators and rankings. Physicians feel a certain resistance towards external monitoring, but at the same time are driven by an interest in legitimising and developing their professional work. This results in what Levay and Waks (2009) have pointed out as 'soft autonomy', which combines professional internalisation of originally non-professional auditing practices with maintaining professional control over evaluation criteria. However, whereas Levay and Waks (along with other scholars studying changing professionalism) have emphasised the medical profession's creative capabilities to capture external attempts to regulate their work (e.g. Waring 2007; Currie et al. 2012; Kuhlmann 2008), our research shows that despite the incorporation of performance indicators by the medical profession, they also act as a tin opener, elucidating the working routines of health professionals – making these visible, comparable, and negotiable.

We observed a similar dynamic in the university context. As part of the fieldwork at a cell biology laboratory, we were granted access to the yearly appraisal of one of the four group leaders with the head of the department. The meeting was held a couple of months after the institutional research assessment (held every six years) had taken place, and when the institute was in the middle of processing the results. The international committee performing the evaluation had followed procedures laid out in the Dutch 'Standard Evaluation Protocol' (SEP), and had used 'informed peer review' (see Colwell et al. 2012). This is a system in which peer review provides the overall framework for evaluation, but statistical data and citation indicators play a specific, often obligatory, role. Heads of departments are being held accountable on the basis of these assessments of their groups. Some managers use the numerical information to help make decisions about departmental research priorities, the use of lab space, and the distribution of other material and financial resources. In the yearly appraisal, the group leaders seemed well aware of these numerically driven decision-making processes. However, as seen below, Professor P's own presentation in the appraisal, for instance, was also saturated with other indicators (particularly the number of articles and the Journal Impact Factor):

> PROFESSOR (P): We have published nearly fifty articles, that means nearly one a week, and this is for the entire section; it is really unbelievable, two of them are really breakthrough papers. When I go somewhere [...] they have all read it; it attracts a lot of attention [...] I am currently working with [two Chinese postdocs] on a couple of very good papers. We will be able to send them to top [i.e. high impact factor] journals [...]
>
> HEAD OF THE DEPARTMENT (H): I know you're charmed with the Chinese, they score high, but they do leave afterwards.
>
> P: Yes, but they do not need much supervision; I see them briefly during the weekend.
>
> H: But there will be polarisation in your group if not everyone can live up to that level.
>
> P: Yes, but what do you want? We score 'very good', not 'excellent'.

[Here he refers to scores on the institutional evaluation]
H: You would have scored excellent if the past two years would have been taken into account [in the bibliometric analysis].
P: This did happen with other departments!
H: No, we stuck to that rule. If other departments were sloppy they were reproached for that [...] These numbers are slow; it takes a long time before you get above a '2'.
[Here, H points his finger at one of the indicators in the bibliometric report, the group's 'Mean Normalised Citation Score' (MNCS). The bibliometric analysis uses a relatively long citation window of five years and did not include the last two years. Calculation of the Journal Impact Factor is 'faster' because it is done on the basis of a two-year citation window.]
P: I am interested in excellence. If the assessment procedures do not match the work done, things will become difficult (Observation notes, 26 September 2013).

In the yearly appraisal, two indicators are drawn on to arrive at: 1) an 'implied' ranking of the professor's group compared to other groups in the department, and 2) a reputational ranking of the journals that the group targets as outlets for their articles. In the former case, it is striking how a complex assemblage of indicators that forms the basis of the institutional evaluation is simplified, and now only revolves around this one indicator (the MNCS). In the appraisal, two ranking practices come together: institutional (via the MNCS) and disciplinary (via the Journal Impact Factor). Again, the measures act as 'tin openers'. For instance, they enable the group leader to make a point about the other ranking game he is involved in (a comparative practice within molecular cell biology in which excellence is measured mainly through the impact factor). The professor celebrates the performance of his Chinese postdocs who have succeeded in publishing a *Nature, Cell or Science* (NCS) paper. The reputation of his group is defined in part through the reputational ranking of the journals its members publish in. A reputational ranking of journals makes perfect sense for the PI, because it also helps him make decisions about managing his group (e.g. through the amount of 'work' they have done in relation to their performance), or about how to 'rank' his employees in relation to where to allocate specific resources. Such ranking practices seem to form a routine part of peer review in his discipline. These processes take place on a global scale and are shaped in interactions between thousands of labs.

Institutional-level rankings are not that relevant in this process. As such, the excerpt above nicely reveals differences in 'accountability repertoires' (see Moreira 2005). That is, the indicators also enable the head of the department to caution the professor about his leadership style (which he draws in as a corollary of the reputational ranking of journals' dynamics and says is creating pressure in the PI's group). Accountability repertoires appear in different forms and pursue different goals. They are thus all considered valid and important. The actors involved need to make sense of these various co-existing repertoires, and attempt to find ways to combine them.

These different repertoires were also visible in the hospital context. Here, too, rankings and indicators not only operated through processes of self-control, but they were also opened up to new types of interactions (including with other actors), making negotiations on professional work possible. As one care manager noted,

> [a]nd the other thing is that we of course use [rankings and indicators] as a management tool to get through to medical specialists [...] [to get towards] particular improvement practices in the care process that have to be done. Step one, the ranking enters [the hospital]. In the following [...] [For example], cardiologists score badly. As a consequence I go and see the medical manager, or do sometimes even visit the whole group of specialists, and I tell them:
> 'Guys, this is really going badly here'.
> Then they would tell me: 'The numbers are not correct'.
> Then we first look at the numbers together which they delivered [...] And I tell them: 'This number was delivered, and you signed it. How come they are not correct nevertheless? What is the reason?'
> Then they say that the case mix is [...] different.[5]
> Then you check this out.

> Then you tell them: 'From the benchmark it seems that that is not the case' [i.e. incorrect case mix].
>
> Then you approach the core and say: 'Guys, you still score low, we took away variability, and now we have to discuss what we can do in our organisation, in our work process, in our medical policy, in our care process in order to make sure that there are better outcomes next time.'
>
> But then, nevertheless, the ranking is for me still an instrument in order to effect change. Rankings are not a goal in themselves (2 May 2013).

In their internal use, indicators, and the ranking practices they support, increase the power for executives because they open up the primary process of care or knowledge creation for strategic criteria. In other words, they serve as tactical means to enable managers to negotiate and shape performance improvement agendas with professionals and researchers. Managers thus act as the ones undertaking the comparative work. Although health care practitioners and scientists conduct comparative work as well, in the end the managers brought the collective comparative work together and were accountable to external regulators assessing their organisation (whether these were the health care inspectorate and health insurers in the hospital case, or the heads of department in the university case). This also encouraged practitioners to streamline work processes or reduce the number of medical complications (as in the excerpt above). Therefore, ranking may act as a 'tin opener', but it also induces a new coordinating role to managers.

Considering our own comparative work, we (unconsciously) enacted a third comparative strategy. Besides studying shared research moments and seeing our research projects through the lenses of the other, we also grappled with the heterogeneity of ranking practices and observed how these are coordinated in everyday organisational work. Much more than trying to learn from 'the other research project', here we brought our findings together and considered them as one pool of data. We searched for relevant lines in this data that taught us about how ranking practices are coordinated and how this 'coordination work' (Mol 2002) influences debates about accountability and evaluation of 'good practice'.

JUMP: ENACTING COMPARISONS

In this final part of our 'hop-skip-jump' approach, we discuss some elements of the 'production process' of the comparison between the hospital and university rankings we described above. By analysing how we approached the comparison and what it brought us, we aim to contribute to recent theoretical work on comparative methods in qualitative social science (see Niewöhner and Scheffer 2010). Above, we have 'practised comparison' by conceiving hospital and academic ranking practices through the lens of the other, and by subsequently searching for connections. These lenses helped us to understand the dominance of 'measurability' within the organisations we studied. We also described the heterogeneity of ranking practices and how actors have to work to align the different ways in which they are enlisted.

Comparison often entails 'commensuration' (see Espeland and Stevens 1998), and that was also the case in our own comparative practice. For example, although hospitals and universities are more like nodes in networks than 'organisations', in a confined sense (Clegg, Kornberger, and Rhodes 2005), we created a correspondence between them by approaching hospitals and universities as bounded entities. In doing so, we revealed some of the politics of tabulation and differentiation intrinsic to rankings, and zoomed in on their particular enactments in university and hospital contexts. One of the intellectual driving forces behind our comparison was that we were slightly dissatisfied with the crudeness of some recent analyses that point to the normalising and disciplining effects of rankings (see Power et al. 2009; Espeland and Sauder 2007). It was our ambition to come up with a more differentiated understanding of the workings of rankings. It is not enough to explain the popularity of ranking by pointing to an increasing drive for 'competition' in neo-liberal 'audit societies'. Rather, we found the importance of competition to be an emergent property of highly situated ranking practices. The main purpose of both of our ethnographically driven research designs was to render visible the enactment or daily work of 'doing' rankings in real organisational practices, from an in-depth, whole-organisation perspective. Among other things, our comparison showed that rankings tend to evoke ambivalences as a result of their 'decentredness'. That is, they are held together through their fluidity; ranking is an effective comparative technology precisely because it is responsive, flexible, and capable of engaging multiple worlds (see De Laet and Mol 2000).

The performativity of our ethnographic mode of comparison was also visible in how we enacted a classical comparison between professional and managerial work, often employed in the analysis of quantitative comparative techniques (Triantafillou 2007; Sauder and Espeland 2009). As analysts, we differentiated between the types of work connected to research and care on the one hand, and organising work on the other, by studying the interaction between the types of activities that we saw, for example, in the practice of 'pragmatic compliance'. However, we also noted that ranking became part of professional practices themselves, thus opening up new ways of interactions between the different types of work, which in a way transcended distinctions which were often made (also by us) between organisations, epistemic cultures, and work practices. For example, the observation of the meeting between the professor and his boss showed the intricate intertwinement between managerial and research work, where the question of who is comparing whom, or to what effect, is no longer obvious.

How did we involve ourselves in this comparative process? We sat together (a lot) to share fieldwork experiences in offices and conveniently located teashops; we engaged with the respective material from the two projects by exchanging draft texts, and sat down together again to discuss similarities and differences. Importantly, our comparison was shaped through a combined background in STS. We drew from a shared reservoir of sociological and anthropological literature on classification, governance, quantification, and accountability. Clearly, this shared background also shaped our own classifications and the categories we drew up in combining the empirical material. Our background in STS is, for instance, very visible in our description of the 'performativity of rankings' section (above). This particular classification was certainly influenced by a 'turn to performativity' in STS – a mode of analysis and description that has been used to counter representationalist world views (see Pickering 1995) by demonstrating how descriptions, theories, and models become involved in the constitution of research objects they set out to represent.

But our training in STS is not the only reason for wanting to problematise ranking practices. Our comparative analysis (and an input into our analysis) was certainly also driven by our own mixed reactions to being ranked. So, whereas in our academic environments our performance gets measured through our publications, we also share a commitment to engaged research (Wouters and Beaulieu 2006; Bal and Mastboom 2007) and try to contribute to discussions in the Netherlands on care and research systems by giving lectures, participating in public debates, and writing publications in Dutch that are less visible in ranking practices. In addition, we are implicated in ranking practices in a more direct sense. We relate to the fieldwork material as researchers do to their empirical 'data', but in the case of the university rankings there is also another relationship. SdR and PW work at the Centre for Science and Technology Studies (CWTS), a research institute that not only hosts researchers who critically examine the impact of evaluation on knowledge production, but that also produces bibliometric analyses, including the 'Leiden Ranking'. As such, the ethnographic work could have onto-political purposes in questioning how our colleagues practice bibliometrics, and how certain norms about knowledge production and 'excellence' are inscribed into citation databases and enlisted in rankings. The statistical experience of our colleagues rests on a great – yet positivistically inclined – sensitivity to category construction and classification. Questions of how 'users' are interpellated in bibliometric analyses, for instance, are not part of their acknowledged spectrum of analytic challenges. But like Stockelova (this volume), we find it unproductive to simply rebel against these prevailing frames of reference. Instead, we look for opportunities to carefully reinforce certain frames and challenge others. One opening we have is that there is an increasing need in the field for ethically responsible metrics, and for handles on how to generate productive feedback with 'users' about the 'misuse' of bibliometrics. We recently contributed to these discussions in an opinion piece for one of the leading information science journals (De Rijcke and Rushforth, forthcoming) at dedicated workshops and plenary sessions at scientometric conferences that we co-organised.[6] The great asset of being located at one of the leading scientometric centres is that both practices (the scientometric and the ethnographic) are forced to interrogate each other. We expect that this will lead to a better form of scientometrics (in terms of political as well as intellectual goals) and to a more informed ethnographic sensitivity.

IW and RB also work in a place heavily infused with benchmarking and cost-effectiveness research, and they collaborate in those kinds of projects. The original performance indicators of the Healthcare Inspectorate on which some of the rankings of hospitals are based were, for example, designed at the institute (Berg et al. 2005). Moreover, RB regularly sits on governmental committees discussing performance management systems in health care, and is involved to some extent in the ranking business. By being part of ranking practices in these diverse ways, and being attuned to STS types of analyses of quantification and commensuration, the projects we engaged in are in a way attempts to reflect on our own work and experiences. It made us aware of the pragmatic use of such comparative techniques on the one hand, and critically aware of their problematic nature on the other. This refrained us from becoming critical in a classical sociological sense of rankings, which – we like to think – has allowed us to do a more symmetrical analysis of them. However, as the above arguments on the consequences of our own analysis shows (i.e. bounding organisations and differentiating between managerial and professional work), such symmetry also came with a cost: in order to perform our symmetrical analysis, we had to engage in commensuration ourselves.

Our ambitions for this chapter are of course relative to the overlapping space we created between the findings of our individual projects.[7] By being explicit about our approaches, we wanted to 'thicken our ethnographic explication' (Niewöhner and Scheffer 2010: 10) by searching for concrete interactions in 'noncoherent practices' (Mol 2011) – both at the level of the ethnographic material, and at the level of our own cooperation. We worked out this overlapping space in an attempt to follow unfolding relations in the situations under study where rankings make differences – without arranging them into an ordered list.

ACKNOWLEDGEMENTS

The authors are greatly indebted to the insights and support of the participants in our fieldwork. We would also like to thank the other authors of this volume for their valuable interactions at the workshops in London. Finally, we express gratitude to the editors for their professional guidance; and to Madeleine Akrich, Thomas Franssen, Michael Guggenheim, and Alexander Rushforth for their useful feedback on earlier versions of this chapter.

NOTES

1 A third researcher, Julia Quartz (JQ), was later added to the team, but after we started working on this publication. See Quartz et al. (2013) for a full account of the hospital study.
2 The research was funded by the Netherlands Organisation for Health Research and Development (ZonMw).
3 There are international differences in the introduction of rankings and other comparative techniques; in the UK, hospital rankings were introduced in 1983, while in the US the first rankings appeared in the early 1990s. In the Netherlands, the first ranking was published in 2004 (see Pollitt et al. 2010 for a comparative analysis of Dutch and English hospital ranking systems).
4 http://www.cvon.eu/cvoncms/wp-content/uploads/2012/07/nhs_cvon_call2012.pdf [accessed 12 September 2012]
See p. 5. In this comparative framework, Prof D is expected to be highly competitive; his H-index was 91 at the time of applying for funding [E-mail from one of his postdocs, 17 September 2012, in which the postdoc used Google Scholar for the calculation of the H-index]. This is quite high in his own field (basic research). The number will certainly stand out when compared to more clinically oriented medical scientists in the funding scheme.
5 Case mix refers to the characteristics of patients treated on the ward in terms of age, sex, co-morbidities, and the like, which might affect outcomes of clinical work.
6 International workshop on 'Guidelines and Good Practices of Quantitative Assessments of Research,' held on 12 May 2014 at the Observatoire des Sciences et des Techniques in Paris (http://www.obs-ost.fr/fractivit%C3%A9s/workshop_international). Special session 'Quality standards for evaluation indicators: Any chance of a dream come true?' at the 19th international Conference on Science and Technology Indicators (STI) in Leiden, 6–8 September 2014 (http://sti2014.cwts.nl/Program).
7 We borrowed this sentence from Madeleine Akrich's review of an earlier version of this chapter.

BIBLIOGRAPHY

Akrich, M., and V. Rabeharisoa, 'Pulling Oneself Out of the Traps of Comparison: An Auto-ethnography of a European Project', this volume

Bal, R., and T. Zuiderent-Jerak, 'The Practice of Markets: Are we Drinking from the Same Glass?', *Health Economics, Policy and Law*, 6.1 (2011), 139–145

Bal, R., 'Organizing for Transparency: The Ranking of Dutch Hospital Care', Paper presented at the *Transatlantic Conference on Transparency Research*, Utrecht, 2012

Bal, R., and F. Mastboom, 'Engaging with Technologies in Practice: Travelling the Northwest Passage', *Science as Culture*, 16.3 (2007), 253–266

Berg, M., et al., 'Feasibility First: Developing Public Performance Indicators on Patient Safety and Clinical Effectiveness for Dutch Hospitals', *Health Policy*, 75.1 (2005), 59–73

Bosk, C. L., *Forgive and Remember: Managing Medical Failure*, 2nd edn (Chicago: University of Chicago Press, 2003)

Burrows, R., 'Living with the H-index? Metric Assemblages in the Contemporary Academy', *The Sociological Review*, 60.2 (2012), 355–372

Clegg, S. R., Kornberger, M. and C. Rhodes, 'Learning/Becoming/Organizing', *Organization*, 12.2 (2005), 147–167

Colwell, R., et al., 'Informing Research Choices: Indicators and Judgment', *Report of the Expert Panel on Science Performance and Research Funding* (Ottawa, 2012)

Currie, G., R. Dingwall, M. Kitchener, and J. Waring, 'Let's Dance: Organization Studies, Medical Sociology and Health Policy', *Social Science and Medicine*, 74.3 (2012), 273–280

Dahler-Larsen, P., *The Evaluation Society* (Stanford, CA: Stanford University Press, 2012)

de Rijcke, S., and A.D. Rushforth, 'To Intervene, or Not to Intervene, is that the Question? On the Role of Scientometrics in Research Evaluation', *Journal of the Association for Information Science and Technology*, forthcoming

Dixon-Woods, M., K. Yeung, and C. L. Bosk, 'Why is UK Medicine no Longer a Self-regulating Profession? The Role of Scandals involving "Bad-apple" Doctors', *Social Science and Medicine*, 73 (2011), 1452–1459

Espeland, W. N., and M. Sauder, 'Rankings and Reactivity: How Public Measures Recreate Social Worlds,' *American Journal of Sociology*, 113.1 (2007), 1–40

——'Commensuration as a Social process', *Annual Review of Sociology*, 24 (1998), 313–343

Felt, U., ed., 'Knowing and Living in Academic Research. Convergence and Heterogeneity in Research Cultures in the European Context', [Final report for the Institute of Sociology of the Academy of Sciences of the Czech Republic, Prague, 2009]

Freidson, E., *Professionalism: The Third Logic* (Cambridge and Oxford: Polity Press, 2001)

Groen, P., *Startdocument 'Systeemfalen'. Achtergrondmateriaal voor de ZonMW Invitational Conference 'Systeemfalen van het gezondheidsonderzoek'* [Research report, Den Haag: ZonMW, 2013]

Harrison, S., and R. McDonald, *The Politics of Health Care in Britain* (London: Sage, 2008)
Hazelkorn, E., *Rankings and the Reshaping of Higher Education: The Battle for World-class Excellence* (London: Palgrave Macmillan, 2011)
Hirsch, J., 'An Index to Quantify an Individual's Scientific Research Output', *PNAS*, 102.46 (2005), 16569–16572
Jacobs, R., M. Goddard, and P. C. Smith, 'How Robust are Hospital Rankings Based on Composite Performance Measures?', *Medical Care*, 43.12 (2005), 1177–84
Jerak-Zuiderent, S., and R. Bal, 'Locating the Worths of Performance Indicators: Performing Transparencies and Accountabilities in Health Care', in A. Rudinow Sætnan, H. Mork Lomell, and S. Hammer, eds., *By the Very Act of Accounting. The Mutual Construction of Statistics and Society* (London: Routledge, 2011), pp. 224–244
Kuhlmann, E., 'Governing Beyond Markets and Managerialism: Professions as Mediators', in E. Kuhlmann, and M. Saks, eds., *Rethinking Professional Governance: International Directions in Health Care* (Bristol: The Policy Press, 2008), pp. 45–60
Levay, C. and C. Waks, 'Professions and the Pursuit of Transparency in Healthcare: Two Cases of Soft Autonomy', *Organization Studies*, 30.5 (2009), 509–527
Mol, A., *The Body Multiple: Ontology in Medical Practice* (Durham, NC, and London: Duke University Press, 2002)
——'One, Two, Three. Cutting, Counting and Eating', *Common Knowledge*, 17.1 (2011), 111–116
Moreira, T., 'Diversity in Clinical Guidelines: The Role of Repertoires of Evaluation', *Social Science & Medicine*, 60.9 (2005), 1975–1985
Nettleton, S., R. Burrows, and I. Watt, 'Regulating Medical Bodies? The Consequences of the "Modernisation" of the NHS and the Disembodiment of Clinical Knowledge', *Sociology of Health and Illness*, 30.3 (2008), 333–348
Niewöhner, J. and T. Scheffer, 'Thickening Comparison: On the Multiple Facets of Comparability', in T. Scheffer, and J. Niewöhner, eds., *Thick Comparison. Reviving the Ethnographic Aspiration* (Leiden: Brill, 2010), pp. 1–15
Pollitt, C., et al., 'Performance Regimes in Health Care: Institutions, Critical Junctures and the Logic of Escalation in England and the Netherlands', *Evaluation*, 16.1 (2010), 13–29
Power, M, et al., 'Reputational Risk as a Logic of Organizing in Late Modernity', *Organization Studies*, 30.2/3 (2009), 301–324
Quartz, J., I. Wallenburg, and R. Bal, 'The Performativity of Rankings: On the Organizational Effects of Hospital League Tables', *Research report* (Rotterdam: iBMG, 2013)
Sauder, M., and W. N. Espeland, 'The Discipline of Rankings: Tight Coupling and Organizational Change', *American Sociological Review*, 74.1 (2009), 63–82
Scheffer, T., and J. Niewöhner, eds., *Thick Comparison. Reviving the Ethnographic Aspiration* (Leiden: Brill, 2010)
Shore, C., and S. Wright, 'Audit Culture and Anthropology: Neo-liberalism in British Higher Education', *The Journal of the Royal Anthropological Institute*, 5.4 (1999),

557–75

Slaughter, S., and L. L. Leslie, *Academic Capitalism: Politics, Policies, and the Entrepreneurial University* (Baltimore, MD: Johns Hopkins University Press, 1997)

Stöckelová, T., 'Frame Against the Grain: Asymmetries, Interference, and the Politics of EU Comparison', this volume

Strathern, M., 'Binary License', *Common Knowledge*, 17.1 (2011), 87–103

Stengers, I., 'Comparison as a Matter of Concern', *Common Knowledge*, 17.1 (2011), 48–63

Triantafillou, P., 'Benchmarking in the Public Sector: A Critical Conceptual Framework', *Public Administration*, 85.3 (2007), 829–846

Van Dishoeck, A. -M., et al., 'Random Variation and Rankability of Hospitals Using Outcome Indicators', *BMJ Quality and Safety*, 20 (2011), 869–874

Wallenburg, I., 'The Modern Doctor: Unravelling the Practices of Residency Training Reform', PhD Thesis, Free University, Amsterdam, 2012

Wallenburg, I, et al., 'Negotiating Authority: A Comparative Study of Reform in Medical Training Regimes', *Journal of Health Politics, Policy and Law*, 37.3 (2012), 439–576

Waring, J., 'Adaptive Regulation or Governmentality: Patient Safety and the Changing Regulation of Medicine', *Sociology of Health and Illness*, 29-2 (2007), 163–179

Wouters, P. F., and A. Beaulieu, 'Imagining E-science Beyond Computation', in C. Hine, ed., *New Infrastructures for Knowledge Production: Understanding E-science* (London: Information Science Publishing, 2006)

Wouters, P. F., 'The Citation from Culture to Infrastructure', in B. Cronin, and C. Sugimoto, eds., *Beyond Bibliometrics: Harnessing Multidimensional Indicators of Scholarly Performance* (Massachusetts: MIT Press, 2014)

10

STEVE JOBS, TERRORISTS, GENTLEMEN, AND PUNKS: TRACING STRANGE COMPARISONS OF BIOHACKERS

Morgan Meyer

INTRODUCTION

IN THIS PAPER, I WANT TO REFLECT AND SHED NEW LIGHT ON ONE OF MY current research topics: biohacking. While I have been researching biohacking for a few years now, to date I have not yet examined its comparative dimension. The themes I have investigated thus far revolve around the materiality, boundaries, and ethics of biohacking. However, so far I have not problematised or made visible the issue of comparison, despite the fact that comparisons abound in discussions about biohackers. This article is thus an opportunity to use a comparative optics to 'make new discoveries' (Yengoyan 2006) on a subject that I felt I already knew well.

Biohackers are people who hack and tinker with biology. On the one hand, the phenomenon of biohacking can be easily localised (both temporally and spatially). The movement emerged in 2007/2008 and has largely developed in large US and European cities. On the other hand, in order to understand and analyse the phenomenon, comparisons with a wide and heterogeneous set of figures are made by science journalists and practitioners alike. For example, biohackers are concurrently compared to the following: seventeenth-century gentlemen amateurs; terrorists (whom Western powers usually locate in the East); the punk movement that emerged in the 1970s and their do-it-yourself ethics; and Steve Jobs and the Homebrew Computer Club.

The term biohacking is used today to designate a wide array of practices including the hacking of expensive scientific equipment by building cheaper alternatives; producing biosensors to detect pollutants in food and in the environment; and genetically re-engineering yoghurt to alter its taste, make it fluorescent, or produce vitamin C. Biohacking mobilises and transforms both molecular biology techniques and the ethics of hacking/open source. As such, it can be seen as a recent phenomenon. Its emergence as a distinct and visible movement can be traced back to the past eight or nine years. In 2008, for instance, DIYbio (the first association dedicated to do-it-yourself biology) was created.[1] Two years later, the *Biopunk Manifesto* (2010) was written by Meredith Patterson, one of the leading figures in the biohacking movement. In addition, at the time of writing this paper, there are a number of associations, laboratories, wikis, websites, and so on, dedicated to biohacking.

The rise of the biohacker movement has caught the attention of journalists and academics alike. Academics have followed and analysed the movement since around 2008 (see Schmidt 2008a; Bennet et al. 2009; Ledford 2010), and two books dedicated to the subject have recently been published: *Biohackers: The Politics of Open Science* (2013), by science and technology studies (STS) scholar Alessandro Delfanti, and *Biopunk: DIY Scientists Hack the Software of Life* (2011), by science journalist Marcus Wohlsen. In one way or another, this body of work has examined the ethics, risks, potentials, and openness of the movement.

The geographical spread of biohacking – like its temporal emergence – can also be delineated. According to the main website in the field (DIYbio.org), there are currently eighty-five DIY biology laboratories in the world, of which twenty-eight are located in Europe, and thirty-five are in the US on either the east or west coast. There are now biohacker labs and biohackers in cities like New York, Boston, Paris, San Francisco, Manchester, Vienna, and in recent years, initiatives have developed in places like Japan, Indonesia, and Singapore. The political geography of biohacking (and consequently, the arguments developed in this paper) thus needs to be emphasised. The biohacker movement is developing in Western and Westernised countries; laboratories are usually located in urban or suburban settings; and English is the *lingua franca* for the majority of the websites, articles, mailing lists, discussions, and wikis devoted to biohacking.

This paper focuses on how, and to what, biohackers are compared. This is a challenging question, for as we will see below, biohackers are compared to rather unlikely bedfellows. Not only are plentiful comparisons being made, but they are also drawn between different cultures and times, and between different – sometimes opposing – values and ethics. Unlike the 'comparator' which needs to be actively assembled, fed, and calibrated in order to provide comparisons (Deville, Guggenheim, and Hrdličková 2013), in the case of biohackers, comparisons are 'already there' and they are omnipresent. The frequency and disparity of these comparisons are what caught my interest in comparison and what compelled me to write this chapter. Why are such comparisons mobilised and why are such unlikely figures put side by side? What kinds of effects do such comparisons afford? How should we analyse these comparisons?

It is not unusual for hackers and computer programmers to be compared. Computer hackers, for instance, have been compared to public watchdogs, whistle-blowers, elite corps of computer programmers, artists, vandals, and criminals (see Jordan and Taylor 1998), while recent hacker networks like the *Anonymous* group have been compared to industrial machine breakers, and to Luddites (Deseriis 2013). The Homebrew Computer Club (initially a group of 'hobbyists') eventually became a group of 'business entrepreneurs' (see Coleman 2012), and Steve Jobs is today being compared to people like Thomas Edison or Walt Disney.

Using biohacking as a case study, I will reflect upon and problematise comparison. The list of potential benefits of comparison is long, and it is worth mentioning a few, such as how they help to explore new, unanticipated routes; move beyond national frameworks by varying scales of analysis; and identify social patterns while highlighting the singularity of the cases studied (de Verdalle et al. 2012). The practices, methods, and problems of comparison have been discussed in a number of academic texts over the past decade or so. For instance, Richard Fox and Andre Gingrich (2002) have made an important contribution by revisiting and (re)theorising comparison. Arguing that comparison is a basic human activity that deserves academic scrutiny, they lay out a specific programme for comparative approaches. Differentiating between weak or implicit comparison, and strong and explicit comparison, Fox and Gingrich push especially for the latter and highlight their plural nature (2002: 20). The explicit focus on comparison has now become increasingly common, so that people talk of a 'comparative turn' in the social sciences (see Ward 2010). In this sense, comparison is actively engaged with, problematised, and theorised. This interest is visible beyond the Anglo-Saxon world as well. In France, for instance, two collections of essays on comparison have been published in 2012 alone: one is in the journal *Terrains et Travaux* (featuring on its cover an orange and an apple – a classic image that at once depicts sameness and difference, and is one of the chief challenges of comparison). The other is in an edited book called *Faire des Sciences Sociales: Comparer* (Remaud, Schaub, and Thireau 2012).

In this article, I want to draw on this body of work in several ways. First, I am interested in several authors' emphases on 'thick' and multidimensional comparisons. Ana Barro, Shirley Jordan, and Celia Roberts (1998) have argued that comparison should be explorative, thick, and multidimensional. Jörg Niewöhner and Thomas Scheffer – who also argue for a 'thick' comparison – further emphasise that comparisons are performative in that 'they connect what would otherwise remain unconnected, specify what would otherwise remain unspecified, and emphasise what would otherwise remain unrecognised' (2008: 281). In a related way, Joe Deville, Michael Guggenheim, and Zuzana Hrdličková (this volume) talk about approaches that actively 'provoke' comparisons, while Tim Choy (2011) examines what comparisons do.

Second, I do not want to 'solve' the issue of comparison, nor tell a coherent account of what biohackers are and what they are not. I am, rather, exploring the *problems* that biohackers and their identities entail. In this sense, I follow Adam Kuper (2002) who reminds us that we have to 'begin with a problem, a question, an intuition' (2002: 161). He further writes:

I remain convinced that methodological difficulties are the least of our problems [...] We lack questions rather than the means to answer them. What we need in order to revive the comparative enterprise is not new methods but new ideas, or perhaps simply fresh problems (Ibid. 162).

I hold that biohackers are possibly such a 'fresh problem' since their identity is somewhat ambiguous and unclear, and since the probable risks and innovative potential of their activities are currently being debated. Discussions about biohacking reveal that there are many uncertainties and that it seems difficult to put their identity into neat categories. The questions that seem to drive most biohacking comparisons – Who are they? How can we make sense of them? Are they to be feared or hailed? – seem to have no clear answer.

Third, I also draw on Donna Haraway's and Marilyn Strathern's ideas around 'partial connections' and positionality. In her discussion about situated knowledge, Haraway writes:

> [h]ere is the promise of objectivity: a scientific knower seeks the subject position, not of identity, but of objectivity, that is, partial connection. There is no way to 'be' simultaneously in all, or wholly in any, of the privileged (i.e. subjugated) positions (1988: 586).

She continues:

> I am arguing for politics and epistemologies of location, positioning, and situating, where partiality and not universality is the condition of being heard to make rational knowledge claims [...] Feminism loves another science: the sciences and politics of interpretation, translation, stuttering, and the partly understood (Ibid. 589).

In her book *Partial Connections* (1991), Strathern further draws on Haraway's work and uses the term 'partial' to say that 'for not only is there no totality, each part also defines a partisan position' (1991: 39). The trope of 'partial connections' can be – and already has been – engaged with in work on comparisons.

For instance, Endre Dányi, Lucy Suchman and Laura Watts (cited in Witmore 2009) have compared seemingly incompatible field sites (a renewable energy industry, the Hungarian Parliament, and a research centre in Silicon Valley) and noted that there can be a 'remarkable repetitiveness' when these sites are connected through specific themes (such as newness, centres/peripheries, place, and landscape). Others have talked about 'partial comparisons' (Jensen et al. 2011) as a way to think about multiplicities while still recognising that 'there exists no single, stable, underlying nature on which all actors have their perspectives' (Ibid. 15). In this paper, I want to use these ideas in order to avoid one pitfall: the depiction of biohackers as a coherent whole that is able to be summated according to the different parts and comparisons reported in this article. In other words, the comparisons made can only be 'partially connected'. I will thus refrain from taking an analytical view 'from above', one that is detached from what takes place 'on the ground'. Instead, I will follow the actors themselves and consider their comparisons and knowledge claims to be valid and legitimate. In the remainder of this paper, I look in turn at four comparisons of biohackers (Steve Jobs, punks, amateurs, and terrorists). I will think *with* biohackers about comparison, rather than think *about* biohackers' comparisons. In doing so, I not only seek to examine what comparisons do and produce, but I will also be reflexive and critical about my own previous research.

FOUR COMPARISONS OF BIOHACKERS
Comparison One: Steve Jobs and the Homebrew Computer Club

At the first meeting of the DIYbio group in Boston in 2008, the comparison between do-it-yourself biology and the Homebrew Computer Club had already been explicitly made. Jason Bobe (2008), one of the founders of the movement, asked: 'Can DIYbio.org be the Homebrew Computer Club of biology?' While the relation was posed as a question, it did not take long for practitioners to talk more boldly about 'promises' and 'potentials':

[T]he promise of [the] DIY Biology movement opens up biology to potentially create the next Silicon Valley. They are Steve Jobs and Bill Gates of the mid-1970's or the Mark Zuckerberg of early 2000's. Imagine just before the PC or social media explosions (OpenWetWare 2014).

DIY biology has been featured in a great number of articles in the news media, including *Le Monde* and *Libération* (France), the *Guardian* and *Sky News* (UK), *Die Zeit* (Germany), and the *New York Times* (US). A large number of these articles mention Steve Jobs along with biohacking. In a report about DIY biology on the BBC, we read, for instance, that

[t]he organiser [...] believes in the value of the amateur. He says the industrial revolutions brought about by steam and computing were driven by creative individuals – think Bill Gates and Steve Jobs in California in the 70s, toiling in garages, changing the world. The coming revolution will be biological and DIY will play a key role (Shukman 2012)

In a recent survey on DIY biology, one practitioner asked the following rhetorical question:

[w]hat if government had told Steve Jobs that he couldn't play around with microprocessors because they could be used for missile guidance systems? (DIYbio community survey 2013)

In my research on biohacking, I have come across such comparisons many times. However, until writing this article, I never really considered them as such. Despite their frequency and the fact that they were articulated by practitioners themselves, the comparisons somehow seemed to be filtered out by my own theoretical and methodological grid. Why? Perhaps it was due to their hypothetical nature and overtly optimistic tone and claims. Perhaps it was also because innovation in the ICT domain is not my research area. Perhaps it was a combination of both of these elements. This is the first lesson that I have learnt in writing this chapter: there are some comparisons I feel more comfortable with than others, and some I more readily engage with. This first lesson leads me to formulate some questions to keep in mind for my own future work: Why do I follow some threads and not others? Can I be more symmetrical in following a wider array of comparative tropes (if not all of them) which are visible in my empirical material? Or, conversely, should I be selective and only follow some comparisons?

The pertinence (or robustness) of a comparison between DIY biology and Steve Jobs could be dissected and criticised. Yet, with others (e.g. Schmit 2008b), I argue that this issue needs to be left aside here, for this would distract us from a key aspect of such a comparison: understanding what such a comparison does. Linking DIY biology to Steve Jobs produces a promise; it is a promissory comparison. It places a familiar success story side by side with a far less known story – a story-in-the-making. It offers a narrative of expansion – from a garage to a company, from a small group of individuals to a large corporation. And it offers a narrative of change, innovation, and revolution. Such a comparison, in other words, produces a folding of temporality (past, present and future), scale (local and global), and notoriety (unknown and famous).

Let me reformulate my question: What does this comparison *do to the identity of biohackers*? In order to find an answer, a quote from biologist Robert Carlson (2007) – one of the first persons to have talked about 'garage biology' – proves insightful. He wrote: '[w]hether at the hands of Michael Dell, Steve Jobs and Steve Wozniak, the Wright Brothers, Otto Lilienthal, William Boeing, or the yet-to-be-named transformative individuals working in biology, successful innovation requires wide access to both technology and a multitude of parts' (Carlson 2007: 116). Carlson offers, en passant, an interesting and intriguing category: 'the yet-to-be-named transformative individuals working in biology' (Ibid.). Programmer and venture capitalist Paul Graham (2012) made a somewhat similar statement:

> We know there's room for the next Steve Jobs. But there's almost certainly also room for the first <Your Name Here>.

Comparing biohackers to Steve Jobs does something very specific: it produces a category for biohackers – a category that is open and future-oriented. This first comparison demonstrates that biologists can help us in our sociological analyses. It therefore makes sense for scholars to 'follow the actors' on the ground, and to take their descriptions and discourses seriously and be open to the analyses they provide. My position here is not only that we need to follow the actors, but also that we need to 'follow the comparison' from where it is made.

Comparison Two: Punks

The next comparison I want to explore is the one between the biohacker movement and the punk movement. A first observation is that the terms 'biopunk' and 'biohacking' are sometimes both used to describe one and the same thing. For instance, in her *Biopunk Manifesto*, Patterson (2010) alternatively uses the terms biohackers and biopunks. She writes that '[w]e the biopunks are dedicated to putting the tools of scientific investigation into the hands of anyone who wants them' and that biopunks 'experiment' and 'deplore restrictions' on research. At the same time, she writes that biohackers are committed to involving themselves in the political world and that they aim at 'creating new scientists out of everyone we meet'. Science journalist Markus Wohlsen's book, *Biopunk: DIY Scientists Hack the Software of Life*, contains the term 'punk' in the title, but rather uses the terms 'DIY biology' and 'hacking' throughout the book. In both of these texts, the terms are used on equal grounds: biohackers are biopunks, biopunks are biohackers. Actual comparisons can be found in the texts of two STS scholars. Delgado, for instance, writes that

> [i]n a DIYbio context, the use of tinkering seems to point to unruly and punk combinations [...] In their punk, unruly, domestic, and unfinished character, DIYbio designs hail heterogeneity and precariousness (2013: 69–70).

Moreover, in a blog post, I reflected upon the parallels between punk music and biohacking:

> The infamous album Never Mind the Bollocks, Here's the Sex Pistols (1977) can actually offer us some food for thought for reflecting about biohackers and biopunks [...] Never Mind turned out to be a highly influential album, a milestone in punk and rock music. It changed music. Punks, nowadays, are a recognisable figure in terms of music, fashion, revolts, and anti-establishment attitude. Will biopunks bring about a similar cultural revolution in science and technology? Will biohackers change, and have a tangible influence on, scientific practice, scientific institutions, and technologies? (Meyer 2012).

Both Delgado's comparisons, and my own, are rather tentative. While we both highlight the comparability between biohacking and punk, we are rather cautious in doing so (things 'seem to point to', and questions, rather than assertions, are formulated). Compared to the comparison with Steve Jobs – which is promissory and produces a (future) category – this comparison seeks to do something else: it is an analytic comparison. It tries to compare qualities and characteristics between two movements and thereby holds that a comparison sheds interesting light on an issue. What we both missed in our texts, however, is that punk can also be conceived as a counterpart. DIYbio co-founder Bobe, for instance, argued for the need to be transparent, friendly, and open to dialogue, and stressed that 'we want to encourage people not to be punk' (Delfanti 2013: 127). In other words, Bobe highlights difference, contrast, and non-comparability.

A noteworthy episode here is a forum discussion titled 'Wikipedia clean up', that took place in September 2012 (DIYbio discussion forum 2012/13). The first post opening the discussion stated that three Wikipedia articles – the ones on biohacking, DIYbio, and biopunk – were 'awful', and asked whether anyone wanted to do 'clean-up duty'. During the discussion that followed, several issues were raised and various comments were made. On the one hand, it was suggested that the articles could be merged for they were seen as 'synonyms', as 'intertwingled', or as 'the same thing'(DIYbio discussion forum 2012/13). One author asked: 'How about a merging of the articles "biopunk" and "biohacking," with a redirect from biopunk to biohacking?' (Ibid.). On the other hand, the point was also repeatedly made that biohacking and biopunk are 'not interchangeable', 'should not be synonymous', and that '[s]uffixes [such as] "-hacking" and "-punk" can have significant effects on discourse' (Ibid.). In one post, the following proposal was made: 'Biopunk's article should discuss the fictional and real-world dimensions of offgrid/outlaw/antiestablishment biotechnology, Biohacking/DIYbio articles should concern themselves with activities, methods, individuals and events' (Ibid.). In the end, no merger was made – 'Anyway, I've taken down the "merge" tag for the biopunk article', the penultimate post announces – and Wikipedia still has an entry on biopunk at the time of writing this article.

What are we to do with equality, comparability, and difference – these three possible relationships between biohacking and (bio)punk? Perhaps a better question to ask first is: what are we *not* to do in our analysis? Trying to 'solve' the comparison (by either choosing one relationship or trying to summarise all three of them) would not do justice to empirical complexity. One might also want to say that it is 'ambiguous' or 'multiple' or 'contrasting'. But this would yield another problem – that of reducing three relationships by using one overarching qualification. What *not* to do, as Haraway pointed out, is to try 'to "be" simultaneously in all, or wholly in any, of the [...] positions' (1988: 589), or, as Strathern (1991) reminds us, to seek 'totality'.

So we know what *not* to do. But what (to ask the question again) are we to do analytically with these three relationships? What more can we say? The answer that I want to propose is that we need to 'leave it there'. This English expression perfectly catches what we need to do analytically. We must refrain from any analytical move that would 'bring us back' to a central, singular, or total position; comparative moves *do* need to end. Like the end of a debate that does not lead to a consensus, we must recognise and accept that each side cannot be reconciled. We need to leave it *there*: talking about punks leads us into different directions and places, and we have to stay in these places. We need to stay 'on the ground' with the actors' various comparisons, and try not to move to an analytical position 'from above' where we would say something different about these comparisons. I thus refrain here from trying to summarise or conclude the above comparison between biohacking and punk (and from trying to contain the preceding paragraphs in only a couple of words). I rather want to propose a more modest move. While the comparison between biohacking and punk cannot be summarised in terms of its content, it can nevertheless lead to an insight regarding our methods: we sometimes need to 'leave it there'.

Comparison Three: Gentleman Amateurs

The third comparison I turn to is the one between biohackers and amateurs. Let us start with anthropologist/STS scholar Chris Kelty, who writes in an article on 'outlaw science' and public participation that

> it helps to have a figure to work with in order to understand how our world is changing. Terms like 'the public' and 'mainstream science' mean very little to most people, but thinking with figures whose features bring out some aspects and hide others can be a much more revealing enterprise (2010:1).

The author goes on to argue that 'Victorian gentleman scientists' are one such figure. In a similar way, I write in a paper of mine that

> [i]n order to understand DIY biology historically, sociologically and technically, we need to briefly come back to [...] the place of amateurs in science (Meyer 2015: 143).

I also make this link in another article, arguing that there is a 'long tradition' of amateur involvement – and I take amateurs in natural history as an example (Ibid 2013: 119–20). So what do comparisons like this aim to do? In a nutshell, they provide a broader picture by historicising a specific phenomenon. This is one of the requirements of academic texts: that one must provide a 'bigger picture' and make reference to similar/comparable/related works.

Yet, despite the conventional nature of such comparisons in academic texts, what catches my eye here are expressions such as 'it helps to', 'we need to', and 'we might gain'. Both cited texts pose comparability as evident: while there is a claim for the legitimacy of a move between fields and times, the validity or partiality of this move is not problematised.

Other texts that have delved into the comparison between DIY biology and amateurs include a paper by historian of science Helen Curry (2013), and Sophia Roosth's PhD (2010) in STS. Curry argues that both 'share characteristics' and that 'parallels can be found' (2013: 539, 563). Her text stresses likeness and historical continuity, while discontinuities and differences are not highlighted. Roosth, on the other hand, argues for a strict difference between DIY biology and amateurs: 'Unlike Victorian gentlemen amateurs, biohackers do not pursue or promote science as a path to personal improvement or refinement, but as a pleasure and a kind of political speech' (2010: 112). She further argues that the difference lies in 'observation' as opposed to 'making new things, building, tinkering, modifying' (Ibid. 119). Further arguments about discontinuity (as well as continuity) can be found in practitioners' accounts. DIY biologist and informatics student Lisa Thalheim argues that

> [a]mateur biology, in particular, is much older than biohacking or DIYBio. It's a fairly different culture made up of fairly different people, and is rooted more in the Victorian idea of the 'gentleman scientist' rather than the 20th century's hacker culture. I also don't see flocks of amateur ornithologists and amateur entomologists scrambling to join up with the biohackers. Apart from the fact that amateur biology and biohacking have very different underpinnings – socially, historically, and culturally – I'd find it a little distasteful to unilaterally appropriate this culture (DIYbio discussion forum, 26 September 2012).

Other practitioners, when questioned about the role of the movement in the future of innovation, for instance, have said that DIY biology represents

> [a] return to the 'gentlemen scientists' of the 19th century (Ibid 2013);

> It creates freedom for innovators to work on their projects on their own time and try methods and techniques that may not be used by the established

industry. Science was perpetuated by amateur scientists [...] why can it not be continued by such? (Ibid 2013)

Moreover, Meredith Patterson, author of the *Biopunk Manifesto* (see above), argued:

> Western culture has a long and exciting tradition of talented amateurs contributing to the progress of science, and I hope people remember that we're following in the steps of people like John James Audubon [...] as well as Edward Jenner [...] and [Jenner] was an amateur just like we are (interview with Patterson, cited in Anderson 2009).

Practitioners do provide historical readings about their own movement. A closer look at the suggested links with the history of amateur science shows that two slightly different arguments are made: while words such as 'following', 'tradition', or 'continuing' point to historical *continuity* ('DIY history is full of citizen science', as one person put it [DIYbio discussion forum, 2014]), talking of a 'return' and of getting innovation 'back into our hands' rather narrates a present that *reconnects* with the past. Practitioners' self-definition and writing of history therefore needs to be considered in academic texts. Considering that academics (be they sociologists or historians of science) have the monopoly in making historical connections and disconnections, this would be at odds with the position (of symmetry) that I have chosen to adopt in this article. There is a similarity between the scholarly comparisons and the ones done by the practitioners cited in this section: both either argue that there are similarities and continuities between DIY biology and other amateur sciences, or that there are not – and both comparisons are 'historicising' ones.

Regarding my own research, I have come to realise that there is a discrepancy between the comparison I drew in my previous work (biohacking-amateurs) and the comparisons I had not made until now (all the others). Why was the comparison between biohacking and amateurs evident for me? Because I could thereby connect biohacking (which I have only recently started to follow since 2011) to the theme of amateur science, a theme I am much more familiar with and that I have been working on for more than ten years. Amateur science therefore represents my own 'comfort zone' (see Strathern 2002). Thus, unsurprisingly, I have privileged this comparison at the expense of other comparisons (with terrorists and Steve Jobs, for instance). My third comparison leads me to a personal insight: I need to 'get out more'... out of my own comfort zones.

Comparison Four: Terrorists

The fourth and final comparison that I want to discuss is the one between biohacking and terrorists. Both of these are not compared per se, but rather linked through a 'hypothetical comparison' (see Krause, this volume). Discussions frequently refer to terrorists when the potential risks and dangers of biohacking are examined. One of the writers for the journal *Nature* explains that the DIY biology movement 'has been alternately hyped and decried as the solution to society's ills or the nursery for a bioterrorist scourge' (Ledford 2010: 652).

In a paper about biosecurity, legal scholar Brian Gorman reports about the 'intentional threat from terrorists or criminals seeking to exploit the improved access to lethal biotechnology in garages or community based hacker spaces' (2011: 426). Moreover, an article titled 'Garage-lab Bugs: Spread of Bioscience increases Bioterrorism Risks' reports that '[r]apid advances in bioscience are raising alarms among terrorism experts that amateur scientists will soon be able to gin up deadly pathogens for nefarious uses' (Anonymous 2010).

The common line of reasoning is this one: biohacking opens up science and technology to non-professionals. Therefore, science can be used and misused by these non-scientists: if it falls into the wrong hands (such as terrorists), the consequences of this can be dramatic. The link with terrorists does one thing very clearly: it crystallises and epitomises the danger of biohacking. The figure of the terrorist is used to represent evilness and unpredictable danger in a clear-cut way. In contrast to the promissory comparison with Steve Jobs, the comparison with terrorists is about threat. But like the comparison with Steve Jobs – producing the 'yet-to-be-named' individual – it also produces a vague, nameless social identity: the label of 'bioterrorist'. The location of the figure of the terrorist (or, in a sense, its 'geography') is also interesting to be spelled out. The terrorist is a figure that occupies several places: it is articulated, above all, in the US and in Western countries; it is often used to refer to countries in the East; and unlike Steve Jobs' 'success story' that can be easily localised, terrorists are portrayed as diffuse and potentially 'everywhere'. Unlike Steve Jobs or Steve Wozniak (who are named and thus 'singled out'), for example, the bioterrorist is never named.

These bioterrorists are not like the 'gentleman' amateurs seen above. And, unlike the complex punk-hacker relationship (which consists of equality, comparability, and difference), the only relationship that is asserted is avoidance. Whether it comes from public authorities or biohackers themselves, the message is the same: biohackers should not be equated with terrorists.

DIY biologists argue, for example, that '[b]ioterrorism is not a DIYBIO issue' (Sassaman 2010); that '[b]oys will be boys; hackers will be hackers; and terrorists will be terrorists' (eightpennies 2010); and that 'nobody in the DIY community was interested in doing it – and if they were, then they were part of the bioterror community and not the DIYbio community' (EJay 2012). Not only do they argue that there is a strict separation, they also argue that it is an unlikely association:

> A terrorist doesn't need to go to the DIYbio community. They can just enrol in their local community college' (Patterson, quoted by Bryan Bishop, DIYbio discussion forum, 2008).
>
> The idea of a terrorist somehow synthesising the next superbug is sort of beyond 'kind of far-fetched'. I mean, say you were a terrorist – do you somehow acquire the incredible, field-leading technical know-how and facilities to actually custom-make an all-new superbug, or do you get a plane ticket to Africa and get some ebola, and then breathe on people' (Bacter, DIYbio discussion forum 2011).

We need to mention here one famous story that has been widely circulated among biohackers: that of Steve Kurtz's arrest. Kurtz is the founder of Critical Art Ensemble, as well as a university professor and artist who uses biotechnology in his artwork. One morning, in May 2004, he found his wife dead at home. He rang the police, who upon seeing his laboratory equipment and Petri dishes, called in the Joint Terrorism Task Force. The rest reads like a plot for a movie: the street was sealed off, agents in biohazard suits seized his equipment, and Kurtz was arrested and detained on suspicion of bioterrorism. It became quickly clear that his wife had died of natural causes, but it took four years for all of the charges against Kurtz to eventually be dropped. This story has been reported in biohacker circles and has become, in a sense, the opposite of a 'success story'; Kurtz's arrest and the charges against him represent a kind of worst-case scenario for any future relationship between biohackers and authorities like the FBI. As Ledford writes in her piece in *Nature*, 'Biohackers are wary. They recall what happened to Steve Kurtz' (2010: 651). In more recent years, the FBI has subsequently developed a more open and communicative attitude – presenting itself as the 'new FBI'. For instance, at the FBI DIYbio outreach conference (organised in June 2012), the FBI declared that it 'cares about' and wants to 'work with' DIY biology practitioners, and that it sees them as 'partners' in a 'positive relationship'.[2] While repeatedly arguing that safety and responsibility were its main concerns, the FBI stated that its objectives were to be able to distinguish between 'white hats' and 'black hats' and to make sure the DIY bio community protects itself from 'nefarious actors'.

The figure of the terrorist is used to draw a clear boundary between good and evil, and between security and danger. It maximises difference. Yet, while maximising difference it also qualifies a potential connection between hackers and terrorists: this is a connection to be watched, policed, and prevented – both by biohackers and by public authorities. In other words, the comparison between biohackers and terrorists is an 'antonymic' comparison that works through negativity and non-connection. Out of the four comparisons discussed in this chapter, it is the one that univocally states what biohackers *should not be*.

ON THE RELATIONSHIP BETWEEN SCHOLARS' AND PRACTITIONERS' COMPARISONS

Having discussed these four comparisons, I want to come back and reflect upon the approach that I took. So far I have followed how, and to what, actors compare themselves. In the social sciences, such an approach has been promoted by various schools of thought. Ethnomethodological work, for example, seeks to capture how people make sense of the(ir) world, while actor-network theorists insist that we need to 'follow the actors themselves'. I have been sympathetic to such approaches when I followed actors' comparisons and I have been symmetrical as to whether these comparisons are right or wrong, plausible or implausible, or made by practitioners, journalists, or scholars. As such, the relationship between scholars' and practitioners' comparisons does not, at first sight, seem to be an issue. If we talk of a 'relationship' between both, we thereby suppose that there is a distinction to be made between actors and those who follow and study them; but this is arguably the opposite of what following the actors means. Following the actors thus also implies treating their comparisons as such, and not as mere analogies (or resemblances) or metaphors; that is, comparisons that are not literally applicable – or 'undigested', as Krause (this volume) calls them. There is an empirical and semantic reason for this: in the extracts quoted above, the actors have extensively used the verb *be* (i.e. 'they are', 'will be', 'just like we are', 'is not', 'not to be') along with terms like 'the same thing'. Another reason is methodological: I consider that actors provide accurate and legitimate connections a priori through their comparisons, and I do not want to create an asymmetry by considering some comparisons as more 'symbolic', or less literal, or real, than others.

Without going into detail, we can list some of the benefits to an approach that follows the actors. First, it forces us to take practitioners seriously and to thoroughly examine their categories, their sense-making, and their knowledge claims. Second, it provides empirically-rich and grounded accounts of the worlds we study. Third, it helps us to move beyond predetermined frames and be open to potentially new and unexpected routes. Fourth, it prevents us from making normative judgements and from having to take sides.

But what if I had chosen *not* to follow actors so closely? What lies beyond the frame of this chapter? While a proper answer to these questions would require a paper on its own, it is worth providing a few clues. For instance, instead of using the bulky category of 'the yet-to-be-named transformative individuals working in biology', I might have crafted my own category in the section about Steve Jobs. Instead of abstaining to summarise and conclude the comparison between biohacking and punk (and 'leaving it there'), I might have taken arguments 'elsewhere'. Besides contending that there is a match between scholarly comparisons and practitioners concerning the similarities/differences between DIY biology and amateur sciences, I could have pointed to a discrepancy: that 'on the ground' both arguments are made but that scholars have only made one argument in their texts – and that they thus have not properly done their job. And finally, rather than presenting the comparison with terrorists as such, I could have 'contextualised' it by locating it much more in the US by arguing that it 'sells well' in media articles, and by arguing that practitioners might be naïve when dismissing it right away.

Since I have been symmetrical in my approach, I have not differentiated between arguments that were made in academic texts, internet forums, media reports, interviews, conferences, or blogs. The difference between sociology, history, journalism, and biohacking did not preoccupy me. I was also not concerned about the potential difference between the comparison with amateurs on the one hand (which can be 'traced back' and for which there should be 'evidence'), and the comparisons with terrorists or Steve Jobs which are more speculative and not based on 'evidence' (but rather involve guesswork), on the other hand. Those unsympathetic to my approach would argue that what is missing here is context, critical distance, 'hidden' motives, and the 'added value' of sociological work.

In response to such criticisms, I would like to defend my position in three ways. First, fully developing a more critical and distant analysis would arguably require a paper on its own. It seems unlikely that within one paper, two different perspectives can be fully tried out. If we follow Haraway (1988), it is not possible to occupy two frames, two approaches, or two positions simultaneously when making knowledge claims. Our analysis is therefore necessarily situated. Second, given my own methodological and theoretical preferences and choices, it would be very difficult for me to write from a position I have never occupied before – one that would be 'above' my material and provide a 'contextualisation', and one that would ignore that classical modes of contextualisation have routinely been criticised in STS and related disciplines (see Morita forthcoming). Third, 'following actors themselves' does not at all mean that sociological analysis and theorising thereby becomes impossible. Even though I have refrained from *judging* comparisons, I have still *characterised* them by calling them promissory, analytical, historicising, and antonymic. While I presented how people compare and to what they compare, I have also examined what these comparisons do in terms of identity. Rather than follow individual actors, I have followed how comparisons hold together different practices, places, and temporalities, and consider what these comparisons are supposed to produce, define or specify. And I not only listed four sets of comparisons, I also contrasted these comparisons amongst each other – something that is not done by the actors I study. In the empirical material presented we have seen comparisons being made, but these were not reflected upon and problematised in the way I have done in this paper. It therefore does make sense to talk about a *relationship* between scholarly and practitioners' comparisons. While I did closely follow various actors' comparisons, I also used new terms, provided additional comparisons, and juxtaposed various actors. While this paper is not substantially *different* from the empirical material of my case study, it nonetheless *adds* connections to this material.

CONCLUSION: THE BIOHACKER MULTIPLE

In this paper, I have discussed four sets of comparisons. These comparisons produce several outcomes. They render a new and unfamiliar identity more familiar, and thereby do 'identity-work'. They do so by offering spatial, cultural, and temporal genealogies and frames of reference. In addition, such heterogeneous comparisons provide a variety of interpretational registers which are sometimes related, but are often also dualistic and oppositional. This, then, renders the figure of biohackers as particularly intriguing, ambiguous, controversial, and discussable. In other words, such comparisons produce a 'hot' topic – one that is open in many ways to be flexibly interpreted, to be engaged with, to be questioned, to be contested, to be feared, or to be hailed. There are several reasons why biohacking has become such a 'hot' topic and why comparisons proliferate:

- it is a recent and emerging phenomenon;
- it provides good stories for media articles;
- it is a 'fresh problem', yet in need of established reference points (on 'reference groups' see Merton and Kitt 1950); and
- the identity of biohackers is multiple and uncertain, and the riskiness and innovativeness of their activities are up to debate.

Comparisons do at least two things: they do identity work, and they produce topicality. I would like to suggest that there is scope for further analyses of the performativity of comparisons. The following hypothesis can be made: while comparisons with amateurs and punks are potentially benign, comparisons with Steve Jobs are potentially lucrative, and the ones with terrorists are problematic. The threat of being linked to terrorists – and the ban, limitation, or policing of their activities – is perhaps the most performative comparison for biohackers. Further academic work could thus examine if the biohacker-terrorist comparison has had an impact on the establishment of the DIYbio code of ethics (first drafted in 2011), on the convening of meetings with the FBI (like the one in 2012), and/or on the writing of articles in response to negative portrayals in the media. Another topic could be to study how DIY biologists describe their activities as promissory and revolutionary – and compare them to known success stories in order to seek public funding or venture capital – and, at the same time, to find out whether funders 'buy' these promises.

While I discussed a seemingly single entity – biohackers – comparing them led me into many directions, spaces, and times. There is (at the end of these comparisons and in this conclusion) no 'unity' that can be constructed. Rather, these different comparisons co-exist (Mol 2011). Since these comparisons are multidimensional and refer to figures at varying scales and times, condensing them does not seem to be an analytical option. Thus, while comparisons should be 'thick', we need additional terms to help us to think about the co-existence of these comparisons. The move towards analysing multiple comparisons (e.g. in a conclusion), and trying to draw them together and produce coherent arguments, should arguably be the opposite of 'thick' – if by thick we mean concentrated or dense. Analyses and arguments about 'thick' comparisons should not condense and summarise, but rather they should do the opposite: they should spread out and 'leave it there'. They should acknowledge vague and open social identities, and diffuse and decentred geographies.

Rendering comparisons explicit and reflecting on my own work in terms of comparison has yielded some new insights for me. In this paper, I did push several comparisons much more than I did in the past. Although I encountered them in my research, comparisons with terrorists and Steve Jobs, for instance, had been totally absent in my writing. The comparison with punks was minimal. The only comparison I did consider seriously was the one with amateur science. My own comfort zone (the privileged position from where I draw my comparisons) has thus become manifest in writing this paper. One implication for my own future work is that I need to be more explicit and reflexive about my own frames, preferences, and silences when tracing some comparisons and not others.

I want to finish by stressing that scholars should openly and creatively engage with comparisons. Comparisons need to be empirically traced and embraced by the scholar/comparator. If the actors studied provide comparison (even seemingly anachronistic and unlikely ones), scholars should closely follow such practices of comparison themselves. They can and should follow what these comparisons do and provoke, without a priori assessing their appropriateness. The approach that I have adopted and defended here was to follow actors' comparisons and to be symmetrical. Yet this still allowed me to provide an analysis that characterised these comparisons, by reflecting upon, problematising, juxtaposing, and contrasting them. The act of comparison is therefore useful to 'stretch' scholars' analytical arguments and scholarly positions in creative ways. They 'make explicit' and raise productive questions about scholars' own comfort zones; about their relationship to both empirical material and theory, and about their concerns when embarking on unanticipated routes.

ACKNOWLEDGEMENTS

Two un-anonymous referees, Monika Krause and Tereza Stöckelová, have provided incisive comments on an earlier version of this paper. Thanks are also due to Manuel Tironi and Jennifer Robinson for their remarks.

NOTES

1 Do-it-yourself biologists are also alternatively called biohackers – I therefore use both terms throughout this paper.
2 Quotes taken from <http://diyhpl.us/wiki/transcripts/fbi-diybio-2012/intro.txt> [accessed 22 December 2014].

BIBLIOGRAPHY

Anderson, T., 'Darning Genes: Biology for the Homebody', *h+*, June (2009) <http://hplusmagazine.com/2009/06/15/darning-genes-biology-homebody> [accessed 29 January 2014]

Anonymous, 'Garage-lab Bugs: Spread of Bioscience increases Bioterrorism Risks', *Homeland Security News Wire*, August 2010 <http://www.homelandsecuritynewswire.com/garage-lab-bugs-spread-bioscience-increases-bioterrorism-risks> [accessed 29 January 2014]

Barro, A., S. Jordan, S., and C. Roberts, 'Cultural Practice in Everyday Life: The Language Learner as Ethnographer', in M. Byram, and M. Fleming, eds., *Foreign Language Learning in Intercultural Perspective* (Cambridge: Cambridge University Press, 1998), pp. 76–97

Bennett, G., N. Gilman, A. Stavrianakis, A., and P. Rabinow, 'From Synthetic Biology to Biohacking: Are we Prepared?', Nature Biotechnology, 27 (2009), 1109–1111

Bobe, J., 'Don't Phage Me, Bro', *DIYbio blog*, May (2008) <http://diybio.org/blog/page/8/> [accessed 1 February 2014]

Carlson, R., 'Laying the Foundations for a Bio-economy', *Systems and Synthetic Biology*, 1.3 (2007), 109–117

Choy, T., *Ecologies of Comparison: An Ethnography of Endangerment in Hong Kong* (Durham, NC: Duke University Press, 2011)

Coleman, G., *Coding Freedom: The Ethics and Aesthetics of Hacking* (Princeton, NJ: Princeton University Press, 2012)

Curry, H. A., 'From Garden Biotech to Garage Biotech: Amateur Experimental Biology in Historical Perspective', *The British Journal for the History of Science*, 1.27 (2013), 539–65

Delfanti, A., *Biohackers: The Politics of Open Science* (London: Pluto Press, 2013)
Delgado, A., 'DIYbio: Making Things and Making Futures', *Futures*, 48 (2013), 65–73
de Verdalle, L. et al., 'S'inscrire dans une démarche comparative', *Terrains & Travaux*, 2 (2012), 5–21
Deseriis, M., 'Is Anonymous a New Form of Luddism? A Comparative Analysis of Industrial Machine Breaking, Computer Hacking, and Related Rhetorical Strategies', *Radical History Review*, 117 (2013), 33–48.
Deville, J., M. Guggenheim, and Z. Hrdličková, 'Same, Same But Different: Provoking Relations, Assembling the Comparator', this volume
DIYbio community survey, Raw Survey Data Produced in the Scope of the Woodrow Wilson International Center for Scholars report, *Seven Myths & Realities about Do-It-Yourself Biology* (Washington, 2013) <http://www.synbioproject.org/library/publications/archive/diybio_survey_results/> [accessed 29 January 2014]
DIYbio discussion forum, (2008-date) <https://groups.google.com/forum/#!forum/diybio> [accessed 29 January 2014]
——'Wikipedia clean up', Google Groups discussion between 26 and 28 September 2012, and on 3 March 2013, (2012/3) <https://groups.google.com/forum/#!topic/diybio/xePfD_Gjt-8> [accessed 29 January 2014]
Fox, R. G., and A. Gingrich, 'Introduction', in A. Gingrich, and R. G. Fox, eds., *Anthropology, by Comparison* (London: Routledge, 2002), pp. 1–24
Gorman, B. J. 'Patent Office as Biosecurity Gatekeeper: Fostering Responsible Science and Building Public Trust in DIY Science', *John Marshall Review of Intellectual Property Law*, 10.3 (2010), 424–449
Haraway, D., 'Situated Knowledges: The Science Question in Feminism and the Privilege of Partial Perspective', *Feminist Studies*, 14.3 (1988), 575–599
Jensen, C. B., et al. 'Introduction: Contexts for a Comparative Relativism', *Common Knowledge*, 17.1 (2011), 1–12
Jordan, T., and P. Taylor, 'A Sociology of Hackers', *The Sociological Review*, 4.4 (1998), 757–780
Kelty, C., 'Outlaw, Hackers, Victorian Amateurs: Diagnosing Public Participation in the Life Sciences Today', *Journal of Science Communication*, 9.1 (2010), 1–8
Krause, M., 'Comparative Research: Beyond Linear-causal Explanation', this volume
Kuper, A., 'Comparison and Contextualization – Reflections on South Africa', in R. G. Fox and A. Gingrich, eds., *Anthropology, by Comparison* (London: Routledge, 2002), pp. 143–166
Ledford, H., 'Life Hackers', *Nature*, 467 (2010), 650–652
Merton, R. K., and A. Kitt, 'Contributions to the Theory of Reference Group Behavior', in R. K. Merton, and P. F. Lazarsfeld, eds., *Continuities in Social Research* (New York: The Free Press 1950), pp. 40–105
Meyer, M., 'Never Mind the Biologists, Here come the Biopunks!' [Blog post, *Genotype*, July 2012] <http://esrcgenomicsforum.blogspot.fr/2012/07/never-mind-

biologists-here-come.html>
——'Domesticating and Democratizing Science: A Geography of Do-it-yourself Biology', *Journal of Material Culture*, 18.2 (2013), 117–134
——'Amateurization and Re-materialization in Biology: Opening up Scientific Equipment' in M. Wienroth, and E. Rodrigues, eds., *Knowing New Biotechnologies: Social Aspects of Technological Convergence* (London: Routledge, 2015), pp. 142–157
Mol, A., 'One, Two, Three: Cutting, Counting, and Eating', *Common Knowledge*, 17.1 (2011), 111–116
Morita, A., 'The Ethnographic Machine: Experimenting with Context and Comparison in Strathernian Ethnography', *Science, Technology, & Human Values*, forthcoming
Niewöhner, J., and T. Scheffer, 'Introduction', *International Journal of Comparative Sociology*, 7 (2008), 273–285
OpenWetWare, 'CH391L/S13/DIY Synthetic Biology' <http://openwetware.org/wiki/CH391L/S13/DIY_SyntheticBiology> [accessed 1 February 2014]
Patterson, M. L., *A Biopunk Manifesto*, 2010, <http://maradydd.livejournal.com/496085.html> [accessed 22 December 2014]
Remaud, O., J. –F Schaub, and I. Thireau, eds., *Faire des sciences sociales: Comparer* (Paris: EHESS Editions, 2012)
Roosth, S., *Crafting Life: A Sensory Ethnography of Fabricated Biologies*, PhD thesis, Massachusetts Institute of Technology, 2010
Schmidt, M., 'Diffusion of Synthetic Biology: A Challenge to Biosafety', *Systems and Synthetic Biology*, 1.1/2 (2008a), 1–6
Schmidt, R., 'Gaining Insight from Incomparability: Exploratory Comparison in Studies of Social Practices', *Comparative Sociology*, 7.3 (2008b), 338–361
Shukman, D., 'Early Days in a DIY Biological Revolution', *BBC News*, 27 March 2012, <http://www.bbc.co.uk/news/science-environment-17511710> [accessed 1 February 2014]
Strathern, M., *Partial Connections* (Maryland: Savage, 1991)
——'Not Giving the Game Away', in A. Gingrich, and R. G. Fox, eds., *Anthropology, by Comparison* (London: Routledge, 2002), pp. xiii–xvii
Ward, K., 'Towards a Relational Comparative Approach to the Study of Cities', *Progress in Human Geography*, 34.4 (2010), 471–487
Witmore, C., 'Innovation, Future(s) Making and Archaeology', *Archeolog* [blog entry, posted on 1 June 2009] <http://traumwerk.stanford.edu/archaeolog/2009/06/innovation_futures_making_and.html> [accessed 29 January 2014]
Wohlsen, M., *Biopunk: DIY Scientists Hack the Software of Life* (New York: Current, 2011)
Yengoyan, A. A., ed., *Modes of Comparison: Theory & Practice* (Michigan: University of Michigan Press, 2006)

11
AFTERWORD: SPACES OF COMPARISON
Jennifer Robinson

SPACES

COMPARATIVE IMAGINATIONS ARE INTRINSICALLY SPATIAL – NOT IN THE sense that they necessarily deal with different physical spaces as such, although they might, but because the imagined spatiality of their functioning is an important stake in how they can be put to work. Thus, 'spatial' questions arise about how different entities can be delimited; how they might be assembled as so many 'cases'; how these might be imagined to relate to the concepts which both do the work of demarcating entities and which emerge from the comparative encounters. Moreover, the geographical reach of concepts is of issue, including how they might be put to work beyond the specific cases considered. Classically, for a comparative method, specific cases, whether territorially defined or not, are brought into some kind of relationship through shared conceptualisations of phenomena – to select from the papers in this collection this might be a social characteristic, such as a 'profession' like biohacking, or an action like networking amongst patient groups, or an object like building characteristics. They might also be brought together through an understanding of shared processes which work out differently in each case (like neoliberalised audits of health and academia, or care for the elderly in more or less privatised situations), or which empirically tie together specific cases (as with the networks amongst patient groups, or architects, or design principles common to different elements of the built environment).[1]

However cases are defined, any conceptualisation involves a reduction (or an abbreviation, to follow Lefebvre 2009) of the fullness of empirical reality. This is a somewhat pragmatic observation (a concept per thing would be a clumsy intellectual world), but also is productive of building shared understandings. We can think about this spatially, too, indexing a range of issues surrounding how we understand the relationship between concepts and cases, including seeing cases as singularities, specificities, concrete totalities, or involving various kinds of abstraction (concrete abstraction, universalisation, generalisation, concepts). Comparative imaginations thus involve thinking across difference, with a number of cases necessarily differently located in relation to each other and also potentially differently placed in relation to both wider processes and concepts. Moreover, there is a clear spatiality involved in thinking about what the entity of comparison might be, how it might be traced, defined, or bounded – the territorialisations, figurative or physical, that allow a phenomenon or entity to emerge for comparative reflection. We could also be drawn to consider the spatiality of the form of comparison itself: that is, to reflect on the ways in which ideas and insights might be explored through engagement across a number of specific instances. And also to consider the spatiality of comparison's analytical 'results': how these insights might turn out to indicate a poor fit with encounters with other related instances, or might be able to travel productively far beyond the instances or sites of their invention, or even to apply everywhere.

The essays in this collection expand our understanding of the spatialities of conceptualisation, differentiation, and territorialisation entrained in contemporary comparative imaginations. But – and this is to some extent to follow the invitation issued by Deville et al. to read both with and against the grain of the science studies approaches prevalent in the essays – they also invite us to revisit the spatiality of the comparative imagination itself, and to interrogate the processes of conceptualisation emergent in comparative practices, both those comparisons 'found' in the world and those invented in the service of academic practice.

The spatialities of comparisons thus embrace some core methodological conundrums in the social sciences, including how to manage the differentiation of phenomena resulting from diverse contexts; how to fold concerns with specificity and singularity into wider narratives and explanations; the geographical reach of insights and concepts (universalism, more limited generalisations, or simply the usefulness of concepts generated in one situation for others); the connections across space which implicate different social outcomes in a shared genesis; and not least in relation to this book, the material and imaginative alliances of people, objects, techniques, and practices implicated in the production of specific comparative practices (academic or not). This last one is important for this book as most authors share the critical insights of a post-representational (irreductionist) science and technology studies approach, and place comparison as one facet of emergent practices. This is a very generative way to approach comparison. It draws us to see comparability across different cases as an achievement of complex formations of objects, practitioners, and scholars – focusing on what is actually done and assembled through comparative practice – rather than a formal procedure which can be specified in advance as method. This proves to be a very productive way forward to address the now well-rehearsed critiques of the scientific approach to comparisons which provides a recipe for proceeding with the 'natural experiments' that comparisons can work with (for example Lijphardt 1971).

Thus, classically, comparison attempts to identify shared variables across 'cases' and to use these to assess the relative importance of different processes or phenomena in explaining differentiated outcomes. This has supported many concerns and debates about defining commensurable variables across different cases, assumptions of causality amongst 'variables', and how to demarcate a 'case'. And this is in addition to the endemic problems in social science research with small-N comparisons, endogeneity of variables (cases are interconnected) and multicausality (how to isolate the effect of different variables – see Lijphardt 1971 and Franzese 2007 for some discussion of these). Reaching into a different idiom of comparative practice, Monika Krause (this volume) focuses in on the 'case' and its conventionalisation within the framework of clinical trials which set different groups into a competition to ascertain which 'works', or wins.

Comparison, she suggests, becomes like the 'race track' – the conditions which are set in place to be able to draw some analytical conclusions. This emphasis on the ways in which scientists or observers create the conditions for the 'event' (the experiment) emerges out of the Science and Technology studies tradition. For example, Isabelle Stengers insists that the achievement of 'rapport' across different entities is singular, and 'has the character of an "event" rather than of a methodological enterprise' (2011:49–50). Staging the 'race' and inventing the 'race-track' in the clinical trial, then, would be exemplary of this. However, we cannot rush too quickly to displace the concern with method, or with what the 'scientist' considers to be a fair or good practice. As Stengers continues, there might be a desire to ascribe objectivity to 'experiments' which are thought to be produced naturally. For example, social comparativists are often reliant on the emergence in the world of variation which they can think with: experiments prepared by the ubiquity of differentiation in social outcomes. However, Stengers is also stringent in bringing the figure of the scientist back in to the production and use of these events. As she reminds readers, it is the 'possibility of a collective game to bind colleagues' (2011: 54), or a common concern, which establishes the analytical potential of the methodological event, and its scientific meaning.

PRACTICES

One way to take forward an interrogation and possible re-invention of comparative method, then, is to consider what scientists actually do in the name of comparison. So rather than rely on the quaint scientistic narratives which are retold in the interests of securing methodological certainty, or complicity, we might ask how meaning or method is part of the 'event' of producing commensurability. How in practice do comparativists authorise the narratives and findings which circulate in the name of that event? In urban studies, for example, I found that the work of forging comparability through trying to isolate variation in small-N samples led to the selection of relatively similar cities for comparison (so, in theory, fewer variables would be diverging across the cases). This seriously restricted the range of cities drawn on to inform wider interpretations of urban processes, as only most similar cities could be selected for comparison. But by following the actual practices of urban comparativists, it became clear that in fact what they found most productive for thinking with was the inevitable variety of outcomes to be found across different urban phenomena which, like most contexts or cases (territorially defined or not), are characterised by a rich and inexhaustible multiplicity of processes (Clark 1995; Kantor and Savitch 2005). The enormous restrictions associated with conventions requiring that most similar contexts be selected for comparison could easily be reconfigured to work with much more loosely defined 'shared features' (Robinson 2015).

The value of bringing into view the practices of making comparability has even more wide-ranging consequences in the analysis offered by Joe Deville, Michael Guggenheim, and Zuzana Hrdličková in this volume. For them, the comparator, the agency creating the 'event' of comparison, is 'an assemblage that undertakes comparative *work*', including the individuals, technologies, institutions, settings, and comparative practices of others. An open, often asymmetric and exploratory process of assembling the comparator emerges, as the authors 'bounce around' their cases, 'feeding the comparator'. Thus what comparativists and their socio-technical allies actually do matters – they make the comparator, they produce (in)commensurability, they compose the events to think with. Thus the spatialities of comparison – the definitions of the entities compared, the grounds for comparison, the potential for emergent conceptualisations – are not given in methods, or able to be defined a priori, but are generated in the practices of working across different cases.

As we follow the other authors in this book through their particular comparative experiments, the different elements of this comparator (science-fiction-like in its rumbling multiplicity, ubiquitous presence, its often ill-formation, unpredictability, and attendant emergent disturbances), are exposed and interrogated. The power relations and historicities of a number of the elements and events contributing to the monstrous '*rapport*' (Stengers 2011) being generated across entities and observations, across time and space, are teased out through reflections on a range of projects in which comparative experiments were important, or required by some or other element.

AFTERWORD

We read in a few of the papers in this book, including in the Deville et al. piece, of how supranational research institutions have been fabricating comparisons in their own image, requiring submissions for financial support to map onto the national imagination. Both the human agents of research and the empirical processes on which they are reflecting have been drawn in to the comparator in this way, pre-formed and at times highly ill-formed for the imagined task and shared conventions of the researchers. It could be we can read such examples of institutionally inventive framing of the comparator (Deville et al.; Akrich and Rabeharisoa; Stöckelová) as generative, giving rise to some happy accidents and opening up opportunities which were not there. Certainly, the questions which this process poses for European research practice are energising. Tereza Stöckelová reflects on her experiences of cross-national research projects funded by the EU and the Czech Republic as operating within the terms of the 'enactment [...] of the performative effects of the Eurobarometers', reinforcing the 'nation' as the point of reference, including in the institutional processes for navigating internal conflicts within the research team. Different national research styles caused disagreement about whether specific quantitative elements of a survey were essential and whether effective comparative insights seem to obstruct or even undermine the conventions of different researchers. But these sticking points are also generative. They recast the comparative exercise in a much looser form, suggesting an approach whereby different cases are simply useful for posing questions, interrogating categories, fine-tuning descriptions, and refining or disrupting concepts – all of which are some of the uses of comparative thinking which Krause so helpfully outlines. And they dislocate the nationally orchestrated conventions of research practice, perhaps raising questions about nationally dominant methods, whether these are quantitative or ethnographic. These might make for fractious meetings of project researchers, but the opportunity to stage and work through some of the deep tensions embedded in (always hierarchical and power-laden) research contexts by reference to external sources of authority may be welcomed by different constituencies within national research environments where, for example, strict quantitative research protocols might be undermining critical researchers.

However, this also brings into the frame the globalised power relations of knowledge production, which Stöckelová (this volume) exposes through her discussion of the Anglocentric review processes shaping publication in 'international' English language outlets (Akrich and Rabeharisoa also discuss how the conventions of an outdated scientific comparative practice weigh heavily on efforts to publish research). This skews the reference points within the national-performative research teams, and limits the counter-hegemonic potential of such collaborative projects. The bureaucratic-national-performative comparisons fostered by the EU and by national research funders may have some potential to bring different research practices into a productive confrontation, challenging hegemonic research cultures. But this seems to be vastly outweighed by the outdated territorial imagination which bears down on the need to reinvent comparative imaginations to match the much messier and diverse spatialities of phenomena being researched.

Here the thoughtful paper by Madeleine Akrich and Vololona Rabeharisoa is helpful, as they explain how in their EU-funded project they moved from the institutionally over-determined expectation that national context would both matter and explain the variations they might observe, to building a comparative imagination resonant with the transnational interconnections amongst the case studies, mutually shaped by shared circuits of knowledge. Abandoning the national framework, then, the teams worked together to generate common questions for approaching the different territorially distended cases (see Peck and Theodore 2012). 'Making comparators' (in a retrospective application of Deville et al.'s useful analytic), they also arrived at a position where each case was treated 'in its singularity'. Thus most helpfully for assessing the spatialities of the comparative imagination, they explain that bringing the different cases together in their shared analytical discussions 'did not consist of extracting a few dimensions out of the singularity of each case, but rather thickening its singularity in light of the other cases' (Akrich and Rabeharisoa, this volume).

Thus, rather than seeking 'abstraction' or hoping to raise observations to 'generalisations', they imagine a quite different spatiality to the comparative imagination – one in the service of singularisation – to understand each case better. They also highlight the potential diversity of geographies of cases themselves, seeking to think more fully about the 'common practices' of the different territorially extended patient and activist networks which they were analysing.

This example of comparison thus brings out two key spatialities at stake in rethinking how comparative imaginations might be practically put to work in contemporary social analysis. On the one hand, we are confronted with the meaning of the case – what its status is in relation to 1) other cases, and 2) the concepts and theoretical insights which inform analysis of the topic. On the other hand, we are confronted with the poverty of predetermined territorialisations as the basis for comparative reflection. National entities are not necessarily the relevant spatial 'container' for comparisons; once the constraints of the national-scale comparison imposed by the funding institutions had been sidestepped, the networks and their transnational interactions provided a distinct starting point for reflection. This is a salient reminder that determining the comparative entity is always both conceptually and empirically contextual: there is no pre-given spatiality to entities. Supposedly territorial entities for comparison (such as nations, cities, neighbourhoods), have no a priori salience. These are always socio-spatial configurations, such as 'local administrations', or 'transnational networks': cities as such, or national territories as such, are not often useful bases for comparison. But the extraordinary social complexity and multiplicity which we so readily associate with such territorially defined entities is also a relevant concern even for tightly targeted conceptual entities: a professional biohacker, for example, has a fundamental indeterminacy, a concrete multiplicity, as evident in the variety of relevant comparators which open out from this practice (Meyer, this volume).

Alice Santiago Faria's neat essay on how she came to think across two buildings, in different contexts and time periods, is instructive in considering the spatiality and nature of the entities which might be drawn on to develop comparative insights. Her architectural practice grabs our attention with a number of comparative moves in the history of that field: the seemingly ahistorical architectural conventions from the nineteenth century which compare purely the forms of similar buildings in different contexts; or those conventions which, perhaps strangely to the sociological imagination, lift the elements of buildings out of their structural and contextual setting to compare bits and pieces, like walls, roofs, openings; the formalist twentieth-century art critique driven by categories; and, taking a cue from Giedion, a major thinker of the modernist period in architecture, the possibility to displace the contextualist and historicist analysis which ties buildings to places and times emerges through the analytical importance of attending to the interweaving of places and times to forge a critical historical understanding of architecture. Resonating with Walter Benjamin's analytical 'constellations', referencing the multiplicity of possible historical analyses emergent in the present, but stretching across different times and places to generate the resources to understand the 'now' (Benjamin 1999; Robinson 2013), Giedion provides an inspiration for Faria to think across two quite different buildings, a train station in British colonial Bombay and a cathedral in Portuguese colonial Goa. Her final comparison is quite historically inflected but finds inspiration in the range of comparative traditions in architecture to bring the two buildings into comparison through understanding their design, architects, function, and form. What started out for her as an impossible comparison yielded rich insights across the two cases.

This bears some similarity to the 'tinkered' comparison of Peter Lutz, who finds himself approaching his two divergent case studies through the sceptical lens of scholars pronouncing the impossibility of comparing US and Swedish health care systems, but finds inspiration in the idea of the 'mediating passages' of his own back and forth across the two contexts (as well as some empirical connections between the two cases) and suggests that what is at stake is whether these journeys 'produce [...] noteworthy scientific knowledge towards some purpose'. This may seem a modest ambition, but I want to dwell on this for the remainder of this short commentary as this strikes me as an important determinant of the point of undertaking comparative experiments. We can reconnect with Isabelle Stengers' insistence that scientific insights rely on the practices, conventions, and expectations of the community of scholars generating them.

CONCEPTS

It is an exciting feature of this collection that the researcher and his/her methodological conventions are displaced from attention in favour of the dynamic productivity of the field of comparative practice in which s/he is implicated and embedded. The last papers from this book which I want to talk about put this decentring to work in the service of rethinking the comparative method itself. Together they realise some excellent insights by taking as their starting point actually existing comparisons: comparisons that are made not by scholars in the interests of generating analytical or conceptual insights, or deepening their understanding of a situation, but 'found' comparisons, in the field. Morgan Meyer explores the comparisons made in public and specialist debates concerning the identity and social meaning of 'biohackers', and Christopher Gad and Casper Bruun Jensen are concerned with the 'indigenous' comparisons being made on the bridge of a Danish fishery inspection vessel. Each paper finds fascinating ways to think productively with these comparisons, informing their own academic analyses. And both comment on the open-ended nature of the interaction amongst their own comparative reflections and those they encountered in the field. This too is a product of the rich STS insights which place researchers in the 'midst of things', part of emergent practices, as Gad and Jensen observe, defying any clear distinctions, then, between description and conceptualisation, informant and researcher, human and technology. 'Tracing comparisons ethnographically', or tracing the empirically existing lateral connections between cases, opens up cases to perhaps unpredictable sources of reflection and insight (they cite the interesting work of Maurer (2005), linking Islamic banking and alternative currencies). They suggest a 'dynamic interplay between our intellectual preoccupations *and* what we encountered on the *West Coast*'. Thus, numerous comparisons in practice draw analysts to proliferate insights, to pursue lateral connections. In their view, there is no need then to specify 'a new comparative agenda *tout court*'; this, they suggest, is delimiting and uninteresting.

However, I return here to Stenger's figure of the intellectual community of practice, generating, debating, and contesting what makes for valid knowledge or results, and I would like to stretch this point as a possible counterweight to this last claim from Gad and Jensen and suggest rather that that we do need to reflect more thoroughly on the specific generativity of comparative imaginations and tactics for academic analysis. Deville et al. in the Introduction to this volume direct us to the need for a critical reflection on these 'found' comparisons. The point would be that critical reflections on found comparisons, and the assumptions which underpin them, might or might not reveal them to be useful. For it is the case that found comparisons both generate comparability and profoundly close it off. There are political questions, too. Why should any particular comparative practice or insight be one which receives attention and encouragement from those agendas and concerns which inform scholarly debate? And, perhaps more directly, how exactly can 'lateral comparisons' which draw cases together because they are part of the same field of practice and suggest some scholarly potential in thinking them together, be generative of insights? What might be some possible dissonances or contradictions here with the projects of critical and scholarly research?

In urban studies, on the one hand, it is clear that as cities are profoundly transnationally interconnected they offer great opportunities to generate comparative analyses through the astonishing array of practical and emergent comparisons and connections amongst cities which are characteristic of global urban policy, design, investment, and many other fields of urban practice. However, in terms of using 'found comparisons', Nick Clarke (2012), for example, observes the deep political power relations which frame various actually existing transnational comparisons. He observes that 'northern' practitioners in transnational north-south policy networks were very dismissive of the possibility of learning from 'southern' cities, or those outside their region. This comparison in practice, then, draws on and reinforces the very spatial imagination which critical urban studies feels the need to contest. Many transnational knowledge networks generating practical comparisons insert geopolitical power relations in the place of useful analytical constellations (whether these are enacted across the EU, the G8, or the growing BRICS networks, for example), and others generally create politically powerful effects – the example of ranking and competitive comparisons in practice outlined by Sarah de Rijcke et al. in this volume is pertinent here. In urban studies, where the postcolonial imperative to enrich wider conceptualisations of the urban through insights drawn from the experiences of any city, found comparisons can be very disabling insofar as they authorise established conventions normatively valuing some cities over others. Of course we have the potential to identify these power relations and then use analytical resources to identify them at work within scholarly discussions, and elaborate our critiques accordingly. And it is certainly possible to trace an alternative, more generous account of the prolific policy interconnections across many different geopolitical divisions which can frame a dynamic reconfiguration of the conceptual landscape of the urban (McCann and Ward 2011; Robinson 2011; Roy and Ong 2011). But there is no reason why found comparisons will be interesting or generative for any particular intellectual or political project.

More generally, while appreciating the generative potential of building understandings of comparison by attending to comparative practices, I suspect there is an important continuing place for more epistemological or critical reflections. The insightful results reported from irreductionist approaches which place scholarly enquiry in the midst of practices-researchers-things-technologies might be complemented by equally productive possibilities in the critical conversations which scholars can have about what kinds of comparative imaginations and tactics might be put to work productively, as method and procedure, to address the conundrums of our intellectual and practical labours today. Thus, with Krause (this volume), I would want to ask more directly what use comparative reflections could have for building the insights which scholars might wish to debate, contest, and validate? And I would also like to probe the specific challenges of building conceptualisations across difference. An inflection point for me in this is Gilles Deleuze's *Difference and Repetition*, which is an extraordinary statement about the potential for thinking with 'difference' to aid our understanding of processes of conceptualisation – and comparison. George Steinmetz (2004) cites Peter Osborne as noting that 'strictly speaking the incomparable is the unthinkable' (p. 390). The question Deleuze poses is 'how do we come to know something? How do the phenomena we encounter come to be known and understood by us'? Far from being a call to abdicate from the processes of concept formation (Grossberg 2014), Deleuze brings the resources of Western philosophy to reformulate how this can be thought in a post-Kantian, post-representational world. In my reading, he offers quite some inspiration for a reconfigured comparativist imagination (Robinson 2016).

Thus, to encourage a more geographically wide-ranging inspiration for the analysis of the urban it has been very helpful to mobilise a comparative imagination but also essential to directly address and seek to reconfigure the core assumptions of the form of comparative imagination we have inherited in this field (Robinson 2011; 2014). Here is where I find much common ground with the motivations for a tactical shift to focus on comparative practices which have been put forward by authors in the current volume. Specifically, I feel it is necessary to move beyond the common architecture of explanation which opposes wider systemic processes with their contextualised and hybridised outcomes. Even in its postcolonial idiom (for example, Chakrabarty's (2000) ideas of Capital 1 and Capital 2) this imagination, which preserves the idea that processes (such as global capitalism) derived in analysis can be identified locally in a hybrid, differentiated form, generates a view of many places as residual to theorisation, marking only the hybridisation of processes derived (and already conceptualised) from elsewhere. This both retains the centrality of conceptualisations informed by only some contexts, and reduces the study of different places to a form of 'defanged empiricism', unable to transform understandings of these wider processes and leaving conceptualisations relatively intact (see Chaudhary 2012; Connell 2007). Providing a foundation for a comparative imagination which would feel free to draw on any city in elaborating the conceptualisation of urbanisation would benefit from reimagining this relationship between cases and concepts.

Thus the key comparative ambition to *explain outcomes* can benefit from reframing the meaning of the 'case' in comparative analysis as not simply an example (perhaps hybridised) of apparently wider overarching processes (Jacobs 2012), but as specific outcomes (singularities) which open opportunities to conceptualise the manifold dynamics constituting the urban. In this framing, both Walter Benjamin in his emphasis on the infinity of possible interpretations of any given moment in history – constellations of the 'now' (Robinson 2013) – and Deleuze can inspire us to rethink the spatiality of comparison. In a Deleuzian idiom, we might consider that the urban manifold in its many expressions 'makes itself known to us', as AbdouMaliq Simone (2011) puts it. This generates new problems for us to reflect on, prompting processes of

AFTERWORD

conceptualisation. In the case of thinking cities (in a world of cities), we are very quickly drawn to bring the experiences and conceptualisations of experiences in other cities to bear on any specific problem we are confronted with. Whether tracing the shared connections that are associated with the empirical emergence of different urban outcomes, or composing analytical proximities across different cases in the idiom of thinking with elsewhere, conceptualisation of any given urban outcome is placed in relation to the wider urban world. In this imagination, which is not to prejudice the specific methodologies for exploration, conceptualisation is a dynamic and generative process, shaped as much by the rumbling intensities of the material world as by our fragile and often incoherent efforts to understand, subject to rules of experimentation and revisability, embedded in wider conversations, but with the potential to start conceptualisation anywhere, with any singularity (Deleuze and Guattari 1994).

Much is at stake for urbanists in reconfiguring the comparative imagination. Not only is there an urgent need to enable any urban outcome or process to inform theorisation, but such a postcolonial move also requires both new spatialities of method and new cultures of practice. Thus, the politics of how comparative imaginations are imagined and practised can be intense. In the face of calls for new theories and new subjects of theorisation for a globalised and postcolonial urban world, some thinkers seek to close down experimentation, reassert the parochial universals of extant theorisation, and dismiss new initiatives without due critical engagement. Even more troubling, the very uneven institutional organisation of global knowledge means that scholars are very differentially resourced in the emerging conversations about urban experiences, making their transformation precarious. A vital and urgent consequence of any comparative imagination, then, is that the mode and style of urban theorisation itself is transformed from an authoritative universalising voice emanating from some putative centre of urban scholarship to a celebration of the conversations opened up amongst the many subjects of urban theoretical endeavour in cities around the world, valorising more provisional, modest, and revisable claims about the nature of the urban. In my own practice, the spatialities of conceptualisation and comparison require direct and ardent contestation and reconstruction. This volume makes an outstanding contribution to that project, and will journey with me, and I hope many others, through their comparative experimentations.

NOTES

1 This paragraph and the following ones draw on Robinson (2014, pp. 66–68).

BIBLIOGRAPHY

Benjamin, W., *The Arcades Project* (Cambridge, MA: Harvard University Press, 1999)
Chakrabarty, D., *Provincialising Europe* (London: Routledge, 2000)
Chaudhary, Z. R., 'Subjects in Difference: Walter Benjamin, Frantz Fanon, and Postcolonial Theory', *Differences*, 23.1 (2012), 151–183
Clarke, N., 'Actually Existing Comparative Urbanism: Limitation and Cosmopolitanism in North-South Interurban Partnerships', *Urban Geography*, 33.6 (2012), 796–815
Connell, R., *Southern Theory: The Global Dynamics of Knowledge in Social Science* (Cambridge: Polity Press, 2007)
Deleuze, G., *Difference and Repetition* (New York: Columbia University Press, 1994)
Grossberg, L., 'Cultural Studies and Deleuze-Guattari, Part 1', *Cultural Studies*, 28.1 (2014), 1–28
Jacobs, J., 'Commentary: Comparing Comparative Urbanisms', *Urban Geography*, 33.6 (2012), 904–14
Lefebvre, H., *Dialectical Materialism* (Minneapolis: University of Minnesota Press, 2009)
Lijphart, A., 'Comparative Politics and the Comparative Method', *The American Political Science Review*, LXV (1971), 682–693
Franzese, R., 'Multi-Causality, Context-Conditionality, and Endogeneity', in C. Boix, and S. Stokes, eds., *Oxford Handbook of Comparative Politics* (Oxford: Oxford University Press, 2007), pp. 27–72
Kantor, P., and H. V. Savitch, 'How to Study Comparative Urban Development Politics: A Research Note', *International Journal of Urban and Regional Research*, 29.1 (2005), 135–151
Maurer, B., *Mutual Life, Limited: Islamic Banking, Alternative Currencies, Lateral Reason* (Princeton, NJ: Princeton University Press, 2005)
McCann, E., and K. Ward, eds., *Mobile Urbanism: Cities and Policymaking in the Global Age* (Minneapolis: University of Minnesota Press, 2011)
Peck, J., and N. Theodore, 'Follow the Policy: A Distended Case Approach', *Environment and Planning A*, 44 (2012), 21–30

Robinson, J., 'Cities in a World of Cities: The Comparative Gesture', *International Journal of Urban and Regional Research*, 35 (2011), 1–23

—— 'The Urban Now: Theorising Cities Beyond the New', *European Journal of Cultural Studies*, 16.6 (2013), 659–677

—— 'New Geographies of Theorising the Urban: Putting Comparison to Work for Global Urban Studies', in S. Parnell, and S. Oldfield, eds., *Handbook for Cities of the Global South* (London: Routledge, 2014), pp. 57–70

—— 'Comparative Urbanism: New Geographies and Cultures of Theorising the Urban', *Internal Journal of Urban and Regional Research* (2015)

—— 'Thinking Cities through Elsewhere: Comparative Tactics for a More Global Urban Studies', *Progress in Human Geography* (2016, forthcoming)

Roy, A., and A. Ong, eds., Worlding Cities: Asian Experiments and the Art of Being Global (Oxford: Wiley-Blackwells, 2011)

Simone, A., 'The Surfacing of Urban Life', *City*, 15.3.4 (2011), 355–364

Steinmetz, G., 'Odious Comparison. Incommensurability, the Case Study and Small Ns in Sociology', *Sociological Theory*, 22.3 (2004), 371–400

Stengers, I., 'Comparison as a Matter of Concern', *Common Knowledge*, 17.1 (2011), 48–

MATTERING PRESS TITLES

On Curiosity
The Art of Market Seduction

FRANCK COCHOY

Practising Comparison
Logics, Relations, Collaborations

EDITED BY
JOE DEVILLE, MICHAEL GUGGENHEIM AND ZUZANA HRDLIČKOVÁ

Modes of Knowing
Resources from the Baroque

EDITED BY
JOHN LAW AND EVELYN RUPPERT

Imagining Classrooms
Stories of Children, Teaching, and Ethnography

VICKI MACKNIGHT

Lightning Source UK Ltd.
Milton Keynes UK
UKOW02f0633260816

281463UK00002B/62/P